DIVIDED BY A COMMON HERITAGE:

THE CHRISTIAN REFORMED CHURCH
AND THE
REFORMED CHURCH IN AMERICA
AT THE BEGINNING OF THE
NEW MILLENNIUM

THE HISTORICAL SERIES OF THE REFORMED CHURCH IN AMERICA

NO. 54

DIVIDED BY A COMMON HERITAGE

The Christian Reformed Church
and the
Reformed Church in America
at the Beginning of the
New Millennium

Corwin Smidt
Donald Luidens
James Penning
Roger Nemeth

WILLIAM B. EERDMANS PUBLISHING COMPANY
Grand Rapids, MI / Cambridge, U. K.

Wm. B. Eerdmans Publishing Co.
255 Jefferson Ave. S. E., Grand Rapids, Michigan 49503/
P.O. Box 163, Cambridge, CB3 9PU U.K.
www.eerdmans.com

Printed in the United States of America

The Historical Series of the Reformed Church in America

The series was inaugurated in 1968 by the General Synod of the Reformed Church in America acting through the Commission on History to communicate the church's heritage and collective memory and to reflect on our identity and mission, encouraging historical scholarship which informs both church and academy.

General Editor,
     The Rev. Donald J. Bruggink, Ph.D, D.D.
     Western Theological Seminary
     Van Raalte Institute, Hope College

     Laurie Baron, copy editor
     Russell L. Gasero, production editor

Commission on History
     James Hart Brumm, M.Div., Blooming Grove, New York
     Lynn Japinga, Ph.D., Hope College, Holland, Michigan
     Mary L. Kansfield, M.A., New Brunswick, New Jersey
     Hartmut Kramer-Mills, M.Div., Ph.D, New Brunswick, New Jersey
     Jeffrey Tyler, Ph.D., Hope College, Holland, Michigan
     Lori Witt, Ph.D., Central College, Pella, Iowa

Contents

Tables

Acknowledgments

After thirty years of studying the Reformed and Christian Reformed churches, we are indebted to many. At one stage or another, our research has been supported by both denominations, which have drawn on our findings for programs and planning. We are grateful for their frequent support, often in the face of hard findings and conclusions.

We are professors at Calvin College and Hope College: Corwin Smidt and James Penning in Calvin's Department of Political Science, and Donald Luidens and Roger Nemeth in the Department of Sociology at Hope. In these capacities we have benefited greatly from institutional support in the form of research assistance as well as of colleague and student involvement. Throughout the years, more than two dozen students have had a hand in the tedium of stamping and stuffing envelopes as well as coding, entering, and analyzing reams of data. For our home institutions and for all the colleagues and students who have had a share in our research, we are most thankful.

Major funding for one or another phase of this research has come from several sources. The Lilly Endowment has been particularly generous, helping fund the national surveys of Reformed Church laity and clergy reported in the following discussion. The Knight Foundation, through faculty development grants to Hope College; the Calvin Center for Christian Scholarship at Calvin College; and the Foundation of the Christian Reformed Church in North America, R. Jack and Rosemary DeVos, directors, have also provided important funding for the research that appears here. We express our appreciation to each of these entities, as well as to the Historical Series of the Reformed Church in America for publishing this volume.

Finally, we are each indebted to our wives for the years of support and encouragement we have received from them. Each is an heiress of the "common heritage" of which we write, each has a vested interest in the lives of these denominations: Peg McNamara Luidens, as a daughter of Peter Stuyvesant's original church in Jersey City; Kathy Cupery Nemeth, as the daughter of a Reformed Church pastor who served throughout the Midwest; Marilyn Huisjen Smidt, as a daughter of the First Reformed Church in Fremont, Michigan; and Marge Scholten Penning, as a daughter of the Millwood Christian Reformed Church in Kalamazoo, Michigan. To each of them we dedicate this volume, our "life's work" of research and reflection on these denominations that we love.

CHAPTER 1

Divided by a Common Heritage

Like other human associations, religious groups tend to produce distinctive cultures. This is true even when religious groups have much in common, such as a similar theology and a unique ethnic heritage. When theology and ethnicity are closely tied, religious groups have a powerful potential to shape members' worldviews—including their perspectives on beliefs, work and vocation, and politics—and to forge distinctive social boundaries. In order for these distinctive religious cultures to survive, the particular values, practices, and endeavors of these groups must retain their vitality among the members and be passed on to future generations. When this does not occur, the distinctive nature of the religious group is likely to dissipate, with its particular attitudes and practices being either largely abandoned or heavily modified by the broader cultural context.

The Christian Reformed Church in North American (CRC) and the Reformed Church in America (RCA) are two denominations that are closely related in their theological and ethnic heritages. Although they have existed as separate entities for a century and a half, they continue to exhibit important similarities. Most significantly, both remain clearly Reformed in their theology and primarily Dutch in their ethnic base. Both employ a "Presbyterian" ecclesiastical structure, are relatively small in numerical size, and are located primarily in overlapping geographical sections of North America. Moreover, both denominations are undergoing major transitions; they are increasingly

1

challenged by forces that threaten to erode their religious distinctiveness and, perhaps, endanger their very existence as separate denominations.

In light of these challenges, the General Synods of both the CRC and the RCA passed overtures in 2002 encouraging greater programmatic cooperation between the two denominations. Although this was not the first such discussion of greater cooperation, these actions reflect a growing recognition that what divides the two religious bodies may be less crucial than what unites them. Indeed, much of the discussion that accompanied these overtures dealt with the possibility of a future merger between the two denominations.

The bases for these actions have much to do with the trends and challenges confronting both denominations. Among the factors moving the two Reformed bodies closer together are declining and aging memberships, the lack of significant geographical expansion beyond their historic denominational pockets, and an inability to make substantial inroads among minority ethnic groups in the United States and Canada.

There are undoubtedly other theological and cultural factors at work as well. The primary purpose of this book is to provide an examination of the religious life of the Christian Reformed and Reformed churches at the turn of the millennium and to assess the changes that have been evident in both bodies over the past twenty-five years that may inform the discussion of greater partnership. We will examine the theological perspectives of each denomination's clergy and parishioners, the religious commitments of each group's members, and the nature and levels of civic and political engagement by the clergy and laity in both churches. In addition, we will examine the nature of congregational life in the two denominations as well as some of the major issues that have confronted, or continue to confront, the internal lives of both religious bodies.

Though this volume is an academic study, it is written in such a way as to make it accessible to lay members of the two denominations. And while this work has broader scholarly significance, it is intended to be scholarship that may educate and aid members of the two church bodies at the turn of the millennium. The authors are social scientists; accordingly, we seek to provide a careful, balanced, and honest assessment of the two denominations. Yet, we are not writing as disinterested parties. Two of the authors (Donald Luidens and Roger Nemeth) teach sociology at Hope College and are members of the

Reformed Church in America. The other two writers (James Penning and Corwin Smidt) teach political science at Calvin College and are members of the Christian Reformed Church. Don Luidens is a life-long member of the RCA, while James Penning has been a member of the CRC all of his life. Two of the authors have had seminary training: Donald Luidens, the son of RCA missionaries to the Middle East, is a graduate of Princeton Theology Seminary, while Corwin Smidt, the son of a pastor in the RCA, attended New Brunswick Theological Seminary.

Thus, this book is written by Christian scholars, members of the two denominations, who have a love and appreciation for both the CRC and RCA. We do not seek to disparage either body; rather, we seek to build up Christ's church as it is manifested in the two denominations under study. It is our hope that this volume will not only serve to provide an important benchmark for the religious life of both bodies, but that it will enable members of each denomination to understand the other better, to recognize their similarities and differences, and to be better equipped to address the challenges they face today.

Secularization

The modern world poses formidable challenges to contemporary denominations such as the CRC and RCA. While these challenges are not limited to the forces of secularization, certainly much has been made of its effects on contemporary religious life. Moreover, the Reformed faith generally encourages engagement in, as opposed to withdrawal from, the cultural context within which the church is located. Such engagement naturally raises questions about the extent to which church members are shaping culture or are being formed by the culture of which they are a part. While there is some dispute regarding the extent to which the church has actually been influenced by the broader secular culture, a recent survey revealed considerable concern among Christian Reformed ministers over the perceived secularization in the religious life of denominational members (Penning and Smidt 1997).

Few concepts have occupied a more central position in the modern social scientific study of religion than has secularization—the idea that religion is simply a vestige of premodern cultures, destined to decline in importance and ultimately disappear altogether in an age of science and reason (Hadden 1989, 3). While a detailed discussion and critique of the theory moves well beyond the focus of this chapter, it may be helpful for our present purposes to briefly outline some of the major contentions of, and problems with, secularization theory.[1]

Secularization Theory

Secularization theory is actually rooted in the broader theory of modernization. Modernization theory posits that modern societies stand in stark contrast to traditional societies, and that these differences affect all aspects of life. Further, the theory contends that traditional societies are characterized by considerable simplicity. Their economies are primarily agrarian; they exhibit little variety in occupations and community structures; and they depend on low levels of technological development. In traditional societies, social relationships are primarily personal and intimate in nature; the people are relatively homogeneous in their make-up, and their social solidarity comes from similarities in worldview and role expectations. Most significantly, all aspects of social life in such premodern societies are understood to be woven together by "deeply rooted traditional modes of thought and behavior that are, almost without exception, religious or sacred in nature" (Hunter 1983, 5).

In contrast, modern societies are urban and have economies which are characterized by relatively varied occupational and social structures and depend on considerable technological sophistication. The cultures of modern societies exhibit high levels of cultural pluralism, which is mandated and reinforced by frequent interaction among people of diverse backgrounds and value systems. With their awareness of such different perspectives in their midst, members of modern societies are supposedly more likely than members of earlier societies to possess worldviews that are skeptical of traditional values—including religious ones. The social cohesion of modern societies is thought to be achieved less through moral consensus within society than through the interdependence engendered by formal structures and institutional networks.

The basic premise of secularization theory is that "modernization necessarily leads to a decline of religion, both in society and in the minds of individuals" (Berger 1996/97, 3). Scholars have typically viewed modernization as a process that quenches sources of religious feeling and undermines religious authority and beliefs. While many

---

[1]   For a more thorough discussion and critique of the theory of secularization, see Penning and Smidt (2002), chapter 2.

contemporary elements could affect religious life, certain features of modernization have been viewed as exerting especially deleterious effects on the sustainability of religious worldviews. One such element is the growth in the prestige and authority of science because, for many modern people, "trust in science is held to be antithetical to religious faith" (Douglas 1982, 8). Since core elements of religion are viewed as encompassing "myth, magic, tradition, and authority," science is seen as "essentially undermining the credibility of a religious orientation," thereby making religious belief and commitment "much more tenuous for the man on the street" (Hunter 1983, 12).

Another aspect of modernization that supposedly has important negative ramifications for religion is cultural pluralism. In traditional societies, religious people generally posited their own perspective as presenting the true and comprehensive understanding of reality. In order to sustain that claim, they created social systems composed of like-minded folk and distanced themselves from those with conflicting perspectives.

Spreading urbanization, increasing geographical mobility, and expanding media of mass communication served to create a pluralistic modern society made up of a growing number of diverse groups that exhibit relatively distinct cultural traditions. All of these processes expose people in modern societies to variant worldviews, and as a result, "discrepant if not antagonistic perspectives on reality" collide (Hunter 1983, 13). The presence of a plurality of perspectives claiming to be true undermines the social cohesion generally thought to be needed to sustain religious worldviews. In such an environment, a single, unified worldview becomes precarious, if not impossible.

Thus, according to classical secularization theory, modernization inevitably erodes religious commitment as industrialization, urbanization, rising educational levels, the spread of scientific values, and technological development combine to challenge traditional religious perspectives. These interrelated developments linked to modernity supposedly render religious perspectives largely implausible or irrelevant for people living within modern societies, leaving religious values and institutions to occupy, at best, marginal roles in social life.

Two options of response seem available to religious communities facing the corrosive effects of pluralism inherent in modernity. One route is accommodation. Religious institutions can adapt to the situation, play the pluralistic game of religious free enterprise, and come to terms as best they can with modernity's challenge by modifying their "product" in accordance with "consumer demands." The inherent danger to this approach, as highlighted by James Davidson Hunter, is that churches must "modif[y] the content and style of their beliefs" (Hunter 1983, 16). To engage in such cognitive bargaining with modernity places believers in a tenuous position, with one belief after another being confronted by modernity's definitions of reality, until, in the end, they lose their distinctiveness, their identity, and even their basis for existence (Dekker, Luidens, and Rice 1997, 3).

A second option open to religious believers is resistance. Rather than accommodate to modernity, believers may entrench themselves behind whatever socioreligious structures they can maintain or construct, continue to profess the old religious beliefs, and act, as much as possible, as if nothing has changed (Berger 1967, 152). One risk of this strategy, of course, is social marginalization. Moreover, the ability of religious groups to maintain cultural isolation is likely to be quite limited: "the walls around it (the subculture) must be very thick indeed if the cognitive contamination of pluralism is to be kept out" (Berger 1992, 43-44). Moreover, this insulation can make the group's beliefs and actions irrelevant to the modern context.

Religious groups, then, apparently find themselves in a no-win situation. Neither accommodation nor resistance appears to be a workable approach to the challenges of modernization. As a result, secularization theory suggests, these groups find themselves unable to cope adequately with changing times and, eventually, abandon their religious commitments and structures altogether.

Critique of Secularization Theory

Despite this bleak assessment, all is not necessarily lost for contemporary communities of faith. There has been considerable critique regarding the theory, the conceptualization, and the reality of secularization. First, the concept of secularization has been defined in such an amorphous fashion that it can basically mean whatever a given researcher wants it to mean (Dobbeleare, 1981 and 1984).[2] Among analysts, the term "secularization" has been used to represent different kinds of phenomena that have marginal relationships to each other: it has been used to describe (1) a decline in religious involvement and beliefs, (2) the adaptation of religion to modernization, and (3) the

---

[2]   In fact, some scholars (e.g., Martin 1965) have gone so far as to advocate the abandonment of the concept.

restriction of the range of influence of religion within public life (Dekker 1993). These different dimensions of secularization correspond closely with different levels of analysis. The first dimension incorporates the *individual* level of analysis; the second reflects an *organizational or institutional* level of analysis; and the third represents the *societal* level of analysis.

While secularization can transpire at all three levels (i.e., the individual, institutional, and societal), it may simply occur within one particular domain alone, and it may also manifest itself in different ways within a particular domain. For example, at the individual level, secularization could occur as (a) the erosion of one's religious beliefs, (b) the selection of one's religious affiliation on a utilitarian basis (e.g., in terms of enhancing one's business opportunities), or (c) the decline of the relevance of religion for other areas of one's life. Failure to specify either the particular locus of secularization (i.e., individual, organizational, or societal) or the defining qualities of secularization within a particular domain can lead to confusion in research.

Secularization theory can also be challenged analytically. Too often in the writings of scholars who advance the theory, form is confused with substance, resulting in any religious change being viewed as secularization. The simple dichotomous model posited above—namely, that there are only two responses to secularization available to religious communities, either accommodation or resistance—leads to this confusion, as any change, from traditional viewpoints or practices must be viewed, within such a framework, as evidence of some level of accommodation.

There is, however, at least one other option available to religious communities confronting the challenges of modernity—that of adaptation. This approach has been evident in the Reformed tradition when it insists on being "always reformed and always reforming." The assumption underlying this Reformed position, at least in theory, is that religious traditions can be reinterpreted in light of social changes without necessarily compromising their truth, denying their historical claims, or undermining their principles.

Secularization theory can also be challenged empirically. In fact, Hadden (1987, 588) has contended that "secularization theory has not been subjected to systematic scrutiny because it is a *doctrine* more than it is a theory." All too often, one's approach to secularization simply reflects personal ideological perspectives and values (whether religious or secular in nature). Thus, as Finke (1992, 145) has argued, debate over the theory of secularization has, perhaps more than for any other theoretical issue, "fallen prey to subjective beliefs, personal experiences, and historic nostalgia."

The presumed incompatibility of scientific rationality and religious beliefs posited in secularization theory can also be exaggerated. The situation may be much more complicated than the simple formula that the scientific worldview comes to dominate and replace the religious worldview. First, even if one's scientific beliefs were to conflict with one's religious positions, it is not inevitable that such cognitive dissonance would result in individuals seeking compatibility of their beliefs across both domains; humans are fully capable of holding and expressing contradictory beliefs by compartmentalizing their thinking (Corbett 1991, 25-26, 141-145).[3] Second, while science may at times challenge and perhaps even undermine certain claims of religion, "it cannot provide the primary satisfactions that have long been the *raison d'etre* of religions" (Stark and Bainbridge 1986, 431). Finally, to the extent that religion entails a subjective sense of awe and mystery, it is very possible that the more science reveals about the universe, the "more awe-inspiring (and so presumably sympathetic to religion) the universe appears" (Douglas 1982, 9).

Contemporary Challenges to Denominational Vitality

While it is unclear how much of a threat secularization is to contemporary denominations, few social analysts would dispute that powerful social forces exist to challenge the vitality of denominational life today. Generally speaking, religious groups embody human efforts to institutionalize particular theological movements and patterns of religious life. Denominational organizational structures are formed to provide order, facilitate communication, and expedite ministry. In addition, denominations usually promote particular boundaries of social and cultural behavior, while providing their members with particular religious identities. In this light, it is important to recognize that denominations such as the CRC and RCA are historical entities

---

[3]   For example, voters frequently hold conservative positions on some public issues, while expressing liberal perspectives on others, and relatively few voters can be classified as possessing consistent ideological beliefs. In a similar fashion, individuals may well draw upon facets of different symbolic systems of thought so that they can "cope with broad questions of meaning and purpose" (Wuthnow 1992, 24).

and are, at least in part, human creations. They have not always been present in the life of the Christian church but emerged at particular points in human history.

The Reformation provided an alternative to the Roman Catholic Church as the structure by which the church was united within one religious body. Denominational structures emerged as a means to find a workable consensus in the midst of the dissent and differentiation that occurred in the wake of the Reformation (Wentz 1999, 29). Most denominations have, over the course of time, come to view their own particular entity to be both a legitimate and a self-sufficient representation of "Christ's church." At the same time, they have not necessarily seen themselves to be the only legitimate representation of the church. Thus, most denominations, within limits, are willing to concede the authenticity of other denominations, even as they claim the primacy of their own.

Certainly, over the past several decades, there have been a number of important social and cultural changes within North American life that have important ramifications for the vitality of denominational life. The period from the end of World War II into the early 1950s was one of relative stability, if not growth, in American religious life. However, by the late 1960s and early 1970s, important changes were taking place in nearly every major religious institution (Root and McKinney 1987, 11-39). These changes have affected all denominations, as the theological, ritual, and social practices that have served to sustain distinct religious traditions and denominational life are now being eroded. Whether one points to "secularization," the increased geographic mobility of all Americans, or the dramatic rise in levels of education, the cultural and social bases on which many denominations were built have all but disappeared. Moreover, the isolated ethnic enclaves that served to sustain many denominations have seen their boundaries become relatively porous, if not disappear altogether. All of these changes make it increasingly difficult for denominations to sustain themselves in the ways they have in the past.

Individualism

Denominational life has been influenced by the individualistic, subjective, and anti-institutional spirit of contemporary American life. Given these particular cultural values, religious faith today is coming to be shaped more by the personal preferences and values of the believers themselves and less by the social and ethnic characteristics of religious groups that served to sculpt denominational life in the past.

While these changes are not likely to lead to the disappearance of religion or to the full demise of denominational life, they certainly will serve to redefine its nature. Religious faith will be shaped less by the social characteristics of groups of Americans and more by their personal preferences and values. Even now we are seeing a shift from "the religious" to "the spiritual," as many Americans willingly define themselves as spiritual while rejecting ties to "organized religion." And, it is likely that such an emphasis on spirituality will continue to gain cultural currency over the next several decades, while many denominations may experience, at the same time, a continued decline in attendance.

With this severance of individual spirituality from institutional religion and its collective authority, believers will increasingly exhibit personal autonomy, as individuals become more and more idiosyncratic and eclectic in forging their religious faith. Spiritual people will increasingly feel free to select the particular components of faith and practice to which they subscribe, combining fundamental beliefs from one religious tradition with elements of other culturally available religious perspectives. As congregants become more reluctant to accept religious teachings simply on the basis of the authority of outside sources, churches will increasingly lose their ability to define what constitutes *the* religious good for members.

Associated with such increasing individualism, a greater emphasis is likely to be placed on religious tastes than on religious heritage. As churches seek to attract and hold "spiritual people" as part of their particular congregations, the distinctive emphases of denominational theological traditions will become a quaint historical legacy rather than a foundation of congregational life. Certainly, there will continue to be members who favor a distinctive and consistent theological emphasis reflecting a particular religious tradition; nevertheless, congregations will increasingly engage in niche marketing to attract distinctive types of parishioners to join their particular fellowships.

Demographic Changes

In addition to cultural changes, various demographic transformations are already shaping and molding denominational and congregational life in significant ways. Declining birth rates are affecting the vitality of many congregations, as denominational growth is no longer linked to large family size, the pattern that long prevailed in most denominations in the United States—particularly ethnically based churches like the RCA and CRC. Moreover, declining birth rates lead to an eroding economic work force with a resulting increased demand for employees to extend their traditional working hours. This demand has had a significant impact on churches' ability to draw on the outreach volunteers which traditionally undergirded the vitality of congregational life.

Coupled with such lower birth rates has been an increase in life expectancy. Over the last century, the average age of populations in developed countries has risen dramatically. Churches have been challenged to address the spiritual and physical needs of an aging membership while still engaging young members. This has been further complicated by the distinctly different forms of worship preferred by the younger and older constituencies within the church. Many senior members have been the strongest supporters, financially and actively, of local congregations, yet they are finding that "their" styles of traditional worship are being transformed by newcomers. These divisions between those favoring more traditional forms of ministry and those promoting more contemporary forms of worship and ministry, divisions which are often age related, will likely sharpen both within and across congregations.

The Distinctive Nature of the CRC and RCA

Other challenges confronting the CRC and RCA are somewhat more distinctive to them. Since neither denomination's polity is congregational in nature, both the CRC and RCA are struggling with the antidenominational spirit of our day that erodes loyalty to each body. A spirit of congregational independence is increasingly common in both the CRC and RCA, reflected in a broad decline in giving to denominational programs and agencies. On a congregational level, it is evidenced by the decision by individual parishes to eliminate the denomination's name from their letterhead and identification signs in favor of such generic names as "Community Church" or "Neighborhood Fellowship."

In addition, the theological positions of both denominations within the current spectrum of American Protestantism create a distinctive challenge for both the CRC and the RCA. The level of theological orthodoxy expressed by RCA and CRC clergy as a whole places them in the middle of the spectrum of contemporary American

Protestantism (Guth et al. 1997; Smidt 2004). While this central positioning may have certain advantages,[4] it poses other challenges to denominational vitality, since groups that fall at the extremes tend to have more distinct religious identities. To the extent that unique religious identities undergird and sustain religious vitality, then those churches and denominations in the "middle" may have more difficulty over time maintaining their religious identity and vitality than those at the extreme edges of the continuum.

Opportunities

With religious life less supported and reinforced by other institutions of society and more a matter of individual choice, how might new churches be planted, sustained, and grown? How can older churches thrive in such a context? The answers given by scholars and church development experts have usually related to "meeting people's needs," developing distinctive identities and ministries, and "niche marketing." In their haste to meet prevailing "market demands," the supply of religious products is often packaged in a relatively uniform fashion, so that "one size fits all." With conformity in religious packaging, there is little choice in religious life, and any decline of religious belief, affiliation, or practice might simply be a function of limited "consumer options." Therefore, in order to enliven existing and new churches, "supply" may simply need to be brought into better conformity with "demand." This may be accomplished with a wider variety of congregations that promote different mission tasks, different worship styles, different theological emphases, and different programs to allow increased choice and greater religious involvement among the members of a community or society.

Associated with this shift in focus from a "demand" to a "supply" side is a sharpening of congregational identity and distinctiveness. Many churches have been encouraged over the past decades to develop unique mission statements and form distinct ministries; others focus on forging a sense of community. Some may choose to emphasize social justice, while others may focus on evangelism. Still other congregations focus on worship, emphasizing either a more liturgical or a more contemporary style.

---

[4]   For example, falling in the middle of the theological spectrum may well enhance the ability of the two denominations to serve as a bridge between evangelical and mainline Protestant traditions

Such individualism and voluntarism could as easily serve as the basis for religious revitalization as for the undermining of religion. The very ease with which people are able to shift from one religious affiliation to another can lead eventually to a greater moral and value consensus within specific religious bodies (Roof and McKinney 1987, 69-70). Indeed, it would appear that switching between denominations is today less reflective of upward (or downward) social mobility as was true in the past. Instead, such changes are motivated more by considerations of moral culture than socioeconomic status (Roof and McKinney 1987, 218-222; Hadaway and Marler 1993, 111). Churchgoers who share a common faith outlook or worship style may cluster around particular religious bodies identified with those moral values and ministry efforts of which they approve. Thus, while religious affiliation in contemporary America may be much less "tribal" in nature than was previously the case, the reforming of congregations on the basis of common beliefs and styles may reflect "the freedom of Americans to choose with whom they will congregate in service to their most basic values" (Warner 1993, 1077). Conceivably, therefore, religious groups could forge clearer social and religious identities as they become more homogenous in nature.

The Present Study

Over the past several decades, while limited studies have been undertaken, there has been little systematic analysis done of either the CRC or the RCA that could provide a clear understanding of "who we are" and where we've been," which is necessary for effective planning and programming. For the most part, efforts to examine either the CRC or the RCA have focused on highly visible episodes in the histories of the two denominations, and, while useful, these studies cannot provide us with the broader perspectives on the churches that are needed today. For example, various brief articles have appeared in the denominational magazines, the *Banner*, the *Church Herald*, and the *Reformed Review*, based on occasional surveys of RCA and CRC congregants and clergy. Fuller papers have been presented at professional conferences or published in scholarly journals (such as the *Review of Religious Research*, the *Journal for the Scientific Study of Religion*, and the *Sociology of Religion*). Nevertheless, these narrowly focused reports have never been drawn together in a systematic fashion and are, therefore, insufficient to provide the broader understanding of the two denominations that is needed today.

Over the past two decades,[5] the authors of this volume have been able to collect considerable data on the two denominations. It is our hope that, when compiled and analyzed in a systematic fashion, these data can provide a more comprehensive portrait of the two Reformed communities. This volume seeks to accomplish that purpose by providing both a snapshot of the contemporary scene and a moving picture of denominational life over time. While its major focus is on the clergy, laity, and congregational life within both denominations at the turn of the millennium, it also assesses the nature and level of change experienced by both denominations over the past quarter century.

Several sources of data inform this comparative denominational study. First, a number of random surveys of RCA parishioners have been conducted over the past twenty-five years by Don Luidens and Roger Nemeth—specifically in 1976, 1986, 1991, and again in 1999. These studies examined the theological beliefs, institutional and personal practices, and structural loyalties of RCA churchgoers.

Similarly, several random surveys of CRC parishioners were conducted by church agencies over the past fifteen years—in 1987, 1992, and 1997. However, these denominationally sponsored surveys of CRC parishioners had a slightly different focus from the RCA studies: they were focused primarily on an assessment of the agencies themselves. Their purpose was not to ascertain church members' theological beliefs, religious loyalties, or devotional practices (although there were a few such questions contained in each survey). As a result, very little data exist that reveal the nature of, and the extent to which, particular doctrinal beliefs and religious practices were evident among CRC congregants thirty, or even fifteen, years ago. Because these agency surveys of CRC members do not provide much insight about their religious character, we are left with subjective perceptions of such change.

Some sort of "benchmark" data were needed to mark religious change among CRC parishioners by which to ascertain whether certain religious beliefs (such as belief in Christ's physical resurrection from the dead) or particular religious practices (such as reading one's Bible on a daily basis) are more or less common in comparison with the RCA. Therefore, in the spring of 2000, Corwin Smidt and James Penning conducted a survey of CRC parishioners that focused specifically on

---

[5]   See Appendix for technical details related to each survey.

religious beliefs, behaviors, and identities, providing data that closely paralleled the RCA's 1999 study.

While studies of parishioners are not always available for both the RCA and CRC church members, a number of contemporaneous surveys of CRC and RCA clergy have been conducted over the past several decades. The primary descriptions of CRC and RCA ministers in this volume are drawn from data collected in identical random surveys conducted of clergy from the two denominations in 1989, 1997, and 2001. These results are augmented by four studies of RCA clergy conducted in conjunction with the surveys of RCA parishioners.

Finally, this volume uses data related to congregational life in both denominations as gathered through the coordinated Faith Communities Today (FACTS) research project. This endeavor gathered the responses of knowledgeable individuals ("key informants"), usually clergy, in 14,301 congregations from forty-one diverse religious traditions—from Methodist to Mormon and Muslim; from Baptist to Bahai; from Presbyterian to Catholic and Jewish. In the CRC and RCA component of the study, surveys were sent to every congregation located in the United States. These questionnaires contained items related to the congregation's emphasis on ministry, the nature of its worship services, as well as the characteristics of the congregation's regularly participating adults. In the end, responses were received from a total of 399 RCA congregations and 514 CRC congregations in the United States; an additional 171 surveys were returned from CRC Canadian churches. Using these clergy, laity, and congregational data allow us to assess similarities and differences in congregations across the two denominations, investigate how CRC and RCA ministers and parishioners are alike and dissimilar, and compare clergy and laity within each denomination.

Outline of the Book

Chapter 2 narrates a brief history and social description of the two denominations. It does *not* provide a critical assessment of previous historical works on the two denominations; rather, it simply invites the reader into the "Reformed" world with a sweeping narrative of the histories of the two denominations as a means to give some context for the analysis that will follow. In addition, the chapter presents a brief snapshot of the two denominations in terms of the geographical distribution and social characteristics of their members at the turn of the millennium.

Chapter 3 analyzes the theological views of Christian Reformed and Reformed clergy and parishioners. First, the theological views of CRC and RCA clergy at the turn of the millennium are compared and contrasted, then the theological views of CRC and RCA laity. The relative congruity between the theological stances of clergy and parishioners within each denomination are then analyzed, suggesting areas of consonance and dissonance. The chapter concludes with an examination of the relative levels of change and stability in theological viewpoints among clergy and laity of the Reformed and Christian Reformed churches.

The focus of chapter 4 is on the nature and content of religious commitments among members and clergy of both denominations. These commitments are examined in terms of religious practices (e.g., church attendance and devotional life) as well as in terms of commitment to the historic confessions of Christian faith generally (e.g., the Apostles Creed) as well as to the confessions that are more specifically tied to the two denominations (namely, the Heidelberg Catechism, the Canons of Dort, and the Belgic Confession). The chapter compares and contrasts the religious practices and levels of commitment reported by laity and clergy from both denominations. In addition, it examines trends over time and makes comparisons of Reformed congregations with those religious practices and commitments exhibited by members of other Protestant communions. Finally, the chapter examines possible factors that may be responsible for any differences in religious practices that are found between the two denominations.

Chapter 5 examines the social and political engagement of parishioners and clergy within the two denominations, focusing on several key topics. First, the chapter addresses what serve as the primary political beliefs, identifications, and practices of CRC and RCA clergy and laity. Second, the chapter analyzes whether such beliefs, identifications, and practices have changed significantly over time. Finally, the chapter investigates what, if any, important inter- or intradenominational differences are apparent from the data.

Chapter 6 analyzes congregational life within the CRC and RCA today. Drawing from the data collected through the FACTS research project, the chapter analyzes the characteristics of Reformed congregations, first of all, in terms of their size and location. Then attention shifts to the reported emphases found in the worship services of such congregations, the types of programs such congregations offer, and the level of member participation within congregation life. Finally, the chapter examines the level and bases of conflict within Reformed congregational life today.

Chapter 7 addresses several important contemporary issues within the church that have generated heated debate as well as serious rifts within both the CRC and RCA. The issues involve the ordination of women within the church, the place of homosexuals within the church, and the rights of homosexuals within society today. The chapter closes with an examination of the perceptions of CRC and RCA clergy regarding the most important priorities of the church today.

The final chapter highlights the major findings of the volume and discusses their implications for the two denominations. The chapter reviews the major challenges confronting the two denominations, and it discusses several different future scenarios for these two denominations as the opportunities, costs, and consequences associated with staying the course, merging for survival, or merging for "purity" are assessed.

CHAPTER 2

'The Church's One Foundation'?
A Brief History of the CRC and RCA

The Christian Reformed Church and the Reformed Church in America share many common attributes that make it difficult for those living outside the two denominations to discern what, if anything, serves to divide them. Southern Baptists from Alabama or Lutherans from Minnesota may struggle to comprehend just what constitutes the important differences between the two denominations. For outsiders, any such differences may seem rather petty or inconsequential, especially when compared to the numerous similarities they share.

In fact, there are many reasons why one might expect that the CRC and the RCA would be a single denomination, particularly given the cultural and religious diversity found within both American and Canadian society. Theologically, the two groups share a common heritage. Both are confessional churches that subscribe to the same three confessions of faith.[1] Their ecclesiastical and liturgical practices are similar. Ethnically, they share a common Dutch heritage,[2] while

---

[1] The three documents are the Belgic Confession (1561), the Heidelberg Catechism (1563), and the Canons of the Synod of Dort (1618-1619). These creeds, penned during the late 1500s and early 1600s in Germany and the Netherlands, serve as the constituting documents of Dutch Reformed communities in the Netherlands and throughout the Dutch diaspora.

[2] However, the two denominations drew predominantly on different waves of Dutch immigration.

19

geographically both are largely concentrated in the same regions of the U.S. and Canada.[3]

Yet there have been, and continue to be, important differences between the two denominations. In part, the divisions result from the fact that the religious activities of their respective members are channeled in different organizational directions. Each body supports a panoply of denominationally sponsored programs and agencies—from missionaries to seminaries, from religious periodicals to clergy pension plans. Moreover, in many small towns and rural communities in which their churches are located, congregations of the two denominations may often be next door neighbors, even when they constitute the only two such houses of worship in the community. As a result, members of each church interact primarily within, rather than across, their respective denominational bodies. Different patterns of religious involvement on Sunday mornings are reinforced by other patterns of social interaction during the rest of the week, whether that interaction include church committee meetings, Bible studies, or church softball. Given that the CRC and RCA have experienced nearly a century and a half of separate denominational existence, their members have developed different institutional loyalties as well, serving to divide members of the two denominations further.

Differences between the two denominations are not, however, simply a function of these particular sociological factors. Important historical reasons caused the CRC to be formed as a denomination apart from the RCA. These past bases for separation continue to shape and color some of the important contrasting characteristics of the two denominations today.

Certainly most Christians seeking to be faithful disciples of Jesus Christ have come to recognize the necessity of establishing a balance between contrasting, often conflicting, demands of their faith. We are to seek justice, yet love mercy; we are called to separate ourselves from evil ways, yet instructed to "go into all the world." In their effort to be faithful servants, the leaders and members of both denominations have sought to remain true to their visions of the Christian faith and its Reformed expression. But, in doing so, each denomination has tended to emphasize different sides of particular "tensions" within the

---

[3]   Both denominations have sizable constituencies in New York and New Jersey and throughout the entire Midwest (with large majorities in Michigan and Iowa) and in southwestern Ontario, as well as significant numbers in pockets along the west coasts of the United States and Canada.

faith tradition. While the CRC has historically placed greater emphasis on doctrinal purity, the RCA has been more focused on sustaining church unity. The CRC has placed importance on fidelity to theological standards, while the RCA has tended to affirm personal piety and evangelism as hallmarks of members' Christian faith. Certainly, it must be recognized that these distinctions between the two denominations are relative, rather than absolute, in nature. But such differences emanate from the varied historical experiences that undergird each denomination.

This chapter examines the historic bases of the division between the CRC and the RCA and how these experiences continue to affect the ways in which the two denominations relate to contemporary life. Some of the principal differences that were evident between the two denominations at the end of World War II continue to be present today; other distinctions are far less evident now than they were a half-century ago. Yet, both denominations are experiencing intra- and intergenerational change that, in the end, may result in reducing current differences between the two. It remains to be seen, however, whether such differences will narrow sufficiently to foster any merger between the two.

The Reformed Church in America Prior to 1857

The Reformed Church in America holds the distinction of being the oldest denomination with a continuous ministry within the United States. While the Dutch who initially settled in "New Amsterdam" in 1609 came to the new world for economic reasons, they brought with them their Reformed faith. In 1628, only a decade after the Canons of Dort[4] had been issued, the first congregation of what came to be known

---

[4]   In 1618, "The Great Synod of Dordrecht" was convened in an attempt to resolve a raging controversy over the issue of predestination. Those opposed to the orthodox view that God alone effects salvation argued that humans cooperate with God in the process of salvation. Advocates of this view were sometimes known as "Arminians," after their most prominent leader, Jacobus Arminius. On April 24, 1619, after nearly five months of exhausting debate, the synod at last reached a unanimous decision condemning the Arminian position and proclaimed five doctrinal rules affirming orthodox teaching on predestination (Brouwer 1977). These five rules are now known as the "Canons of Dort" and are usually taught to Reformed Church youth in the acrostic of TULIP, with the initials standing for: Total depravity, Unconditional election, Limited atonement,

as the Reformed Church in America was begun in what is now New York City.

The Reformed Church existed as the established faith in New Amsterdam until 1664, when the English took control of the area from the Dutch. This shift to English control had several important ramifications for the Dutch church, despite the fact that under British rule members of the Dutch Reformed Church were permitted to worship freely. First, the church no longer received any financial support from the state. But, secondly, and more importantly, Dutch immigration virtually ceased. These changes moved an old theological issue to center stage, an issue that had been regarded as having been largely "solved." Specifically, this issue relates to whether the nature of the church is that of a separated community who have renounced the world or whether it is a body that embraces and includes all members of the civil community under its discipline. The Anabaptists had taught the former concept, Zwingli and Calvin the latter concept. Now under English rule, the Dutch had to choose whether "to live apart from the mainstream of culture or to become a part of it" (Hageman 1985, 100).

Under their current circumstances, the Dutch in America chose to follow the Anabaptists along the path of a separated community, as to be part of the mainstream of culture meant that they would eventually lose their ethnic heritage and become English. Thus, those who worshiped in Reformed congregations during the colonial era did so more "from loyalty to the ethnic community...than from theological motives" (Beardslee 1986, 9). However, despite the loss of financial support from the state, the determination of the Dutch people kept the church alive. During this same period of time, ecclesiastical relations with Amsterdam continued. Thus, by the time that the Dutch Reformed Church was chartered under English rule (1696), it exhibited little, if any, sign of "Americanization." By then, English had become the dominant language of the colonies, yet the Dutch language continued to be "the language of the home and church of the Dutch people in America" (Bruins 1985, 177). Moreover, the Dutch church continued to maintain its distinctiveness in the midst of other Calvinist communities, such as the Scottish Presbyterians and the New England Congregationalists.

Irresistible grace, and Perseverance of the saints. The Canons of Dort have been the source of periodic debate and contention within the Reformed Church in America for much of its history.

The kind of separated community the Reformed Church became during the pre-Revolutionary period was further shaped by a second dynamic. Regardless of what may have been its desire, the church could not be totally immune from the broader cultural currents within American society. During the first half of the 1700s, the American colonies were swept with what historians have labeled "the First Great Awakening." The Dutch Reformed churches in the colonies were molded by, but also contributed to, this new religious phenomenon.

In some ways, Reformed clergy were pivotal contributors to the Great Awakening. There was within colonial Dutch Calvinism a strand of "experiential theology" that accepted the creeds of the church but "emphasized the new birth, the conversion, and the sanctification of the believer" so that such a person might acquire "an experiential or personal knowledge of Christ's saving grace" (Osterhaven 1974, 180). Thus, one of the contributions the Reformed Church made to the Great Awakening was that it added to the American stream of thought "that awakening theology which marked the Pietists of the Netherlands and of northwestern Germany" (Tanis 1985, 114).

Moreover, two central figures in the Reformed Church both contributed to the revivalist impulse and played central roles in leading the Reformed Church to be open to the revivalist impulse. These men were Theodorus J. Frelinghuysen (1691-1748) and John Livingston (1746-1825). Both had studied at Utrecht in the Netherlands, where Gisbertus Voetius had established its university as the center of Dutch Voetian experiential theology. And both were "profoundly influenced by the warm personal tone and theological content of the Heidelberg Catechism" (Heideman 1976, 96).

Frelinghuysen and Revivalism

Frelinghuysen was a key figure in the First Great Awakening within America's Middle Colonies. Believing that true faith requires a kind of experiential knowledge of Jesus Christ, Frelinghuysen attacked all manner of formalism. Accordingly, he placed at the center of his preaching and pastoral activity the new birth and sanctification of the believer and called for individuals to surrender themselves to God and the service of God.

While Frelinghuysen and other revivalists generally assented to the predestinarian tenets of the Synod of Dort, they "continually struggled with the seeming contradictions implied in telling people that they must be born again on the one hand, and then telling them that the decisions regarding their ultimate salvation had already been made by God himself" (Tanis 1985, 117). Thus, while they affirmed the central Reformed doctrines of election and certainty of faith, they did eventually cast them in a new form. Frelinghuysen taught and preached passionately that religious life without true conversion was an abomination. Frelinghuysen's "summons to repentance" marked a break with Reformed theology as articulated in the Canons of Dort (Tanis 1985, 117). In the end, his "emphasis on conversion was to become highly influential in the Reformed church" (Janssen 2000, 50).

The theological and religious tensions that arose in the wake of Frelinghuysen's preaching were aggravated by the "intensely personal animosities" that had developed within Reformed churches in the Raritan Valley between those who followed Frelinghuysen's theology and those "more staid adherents of conservative orthodoxy and traditional ecclesiology" who opposed it (Tanis 1985, 116). This division anticipated a larger schism—one that divided the *coetus* and *conferentie* parties within the Dutch churches during the middle of the eighteenth century (Beardslee 1986, 11), and it eventually led the more experientially focused members of the Dutch Reformed Church to seek greater ecclesiastical independence from the Netherlands.

Frelinghuysen and those who sympathized with his evangelical point of view held that the geographical separation between the Netherlands and North American continent hindered the ministry of the Dutch churches in America. From their perspective, what was needed was an organizational body in America that could serve to enhance the effectiveness of the Dutch congregations locally. As a result, the *coetus* party sought to have a synod of elders and ministers that would meet periodically in America rather than follow the practice of having a few delegates from America serve as representatives to a broader synod in the Netherlands. The *coetus* party also believed it would be advantageous to have theological training for ministerial candidates in America, rather than sending them to Holland for theological training.

Those in the traditionalist party, the *conferentie*, opposed such "Americanization" and were "adamant in following the Dutch way precisely," as they sought to maintain the religious practices of the previous century when the Dutch government still controlled New York (Bruins 1985, 178). Between 1747 and 1771, these two groups were pitted against each other and locked in a bitter struggle related to the control of, and direction for, the denomination.

Both the *coetus* and the *conferentie* ministers did things the Dutch way, following the order and pattern of Dort (Bruins 1985, 178). The efforts of the *coetus* party were not simply a desire to "Americanize" the church, as is evident from the fact that it was not until 1762 that an English-speaking Dutch Reformed minister was brought from the Netherlands to enable some worship services to be conducted in English (Bruins 1985, 179). Yet, as time elapsed, some of the more zealous *coetus* clergy turned their efforts towards ecclesiastical independence from the Netherlands; later their efforts would also focus on political independence from England (Tanis 1985, 117).

Frelinghuysen's legacy is evident within the Reformed Church in America. The Great Awakening, and American revivalism more generally, challenged traditional theological tenets of the Reformed faith. Leaders of the pietistic movement within the Reformed Church upheld the Canons of Dort, but their preaching reflected an Arminian emphasis upon the individual's ability to accept grace and undergo conversion (Tanis 1985). Frelinghuysen served as an important bridge between tradition and change— enabling the Dutch Reformed Church to "remain true to their traditions while participating in the life of the New World" (Heideman 1976, 96). In so doing, the Reformed Church made its first move towards Americanization—a step taken over a hundred years before the immigrants who would comprise the CRC had even arrived in America.

Secondly, while subscribing to the confessional statements of the Reformed tradition, Frelinghuysen and the other Reformed pietists sought to make the Christian faith more vibrant and relevant to daily living. Despite the initial opposition to their work, Frelinghuysen's "emphasis upon the conversion...of the individual" has now become "a permanent fixture in the theology of his denomination as well as in the whole revival tradition in America" (Heideman 1976, 96).

Finally, Frelinghuysen's legacy is evident in terms of the emphasis on personal piety and lives of personal holiness. As a result, some have argued that the Reformed Church in the nineteenth century became less one of "Word and sacrament," and more one of "Word and personal holiness," as Reformed preaching during this period placed a heavier emphasis on personal piety than orthodoxy. Thus, "for all practical purposes, holiness....became for many the new mark of the true church in Reformed theology" (Breadslee 1986, 10-11).

Livingston and Ecumenism

The split between *coetus* and *conferentie* parties in the Dutch Reformed Church was finally healed in 1772 when the two parties were reunited largely by the efforts of John Livingston (1746-1825). In the course of his peacemaking, Livingston provided for a general body in America with powers to train and ordain ministers—all of which, until then, had to be done in the Netherlands.

By the time of the American Revolution, the Reformed Protestant Dutch Church, as it was then known, had ninety-eight congregations with forty-five thousand parishioners. The disruption caused by the Revolutionary War as well as a growing consciousness of "being American" further weakened the RCA's ties to the Netherlands. In fact, by the close of the Revolutionary War, some leaders of the RCA had come close to identifying America as "God's chosen and blessed land" (Kennedy 1976).

Given that the United States had become an independent country, ties with the Netherlands were neither very practical nor desirous. The church once again turned to Livingston, who was now asked to formulate a constitution for the Dutch churches. His efforts culminated in the Explanatory Articles of 1792, which embodied a new organizational pattern reflecting the Canons of Dort, as modified for the American scene (Bruins 1985, 180). In particular, the preface included an emphasis on "liberty of conscience" as well as an organizational pattern that acknowledged the American principle of voluntary church membership (in contrast to the Dutch pattern of basing church membership on geographical residence). As a result, the new constitution distanced itself from Dort in various places (Janssen 2000, 51).[5]

Given these important contributions,[6] Livingston can rightfully be called the "father of the Reformed Church." His legacy shaped the church's direction in three general areas. First, like Frelinghuysen and others, Livingston placed an emphasis upon the personal experience of faith. As a professor at New Brunswick Theological Seminary, he cast both theological studies and formal training in ministry more in terms

[5]   By accepting the American principle of voluntary church membership, it distanced itself from Article 36 of the Belgic Confession as well, an article on the relationship between the church and the magistracy.

[6]   Livingston was also instrumental in the preparation of the church's first hymnbook as well as establishment of the denomination's seminary (Janssen 2000, 51).

of faith and piety than academic inquiry. Secondly, Livingston placed an emphasis on the unity of the church, as was evident in his resolution of the *coetus-conferentie* controversy. Finally, Livingston helped move the Reformed Church out of its ethnic enclave by fostering a new evangelical thrust as "a basis for its full participation in American society, as well as in the foreign missionary movement" (Heideman 1976, 97).

As a result of this third facet of Livingston's legacy, the Dutch Reformed Church opened it doors during the first three decades of the nineteenth century to "full participation in the great mission of the Church in America, while providing just enough distance from others to allow continued loyalty to Dort" (Heideman 1976, 99). This opening enabled church members to join parishioners of other denominations in a host of interdenominational voluntary societies that sprang up during the Second Great Awakening in the early decades of the 1800s. These joint ventures were organized to promote a number of moral and religious causes (e.g., the burgeoning foreign and domestic mission initiatives; the study and distribution of the Bible; the campaign to advance personal morality and Sabbath observance; and, later, temperance and the abolition of slavery). Participation in these cooperative efforts ultimately moved members of the RCA outside the confines of their own denomination into broader ecumenical engagements.

However, such joint labors, along with various missionary endeavors along the frontier, created disagreements within the Reformed Church. Controversy surfaced initially in 1814, when the General Synod questioned the wisdom of receiving "licentiates for ordination from the Congregational Church...without examination" (quoted in Van Hoeven 1986, 20). During this time, "Hopkinsian theology" was gaining some prominence within American religious life. Jonathan Hopkins, a Congregational theologian, had been a student and friend of Jonathan Edwards, a central figure in the First Great Awakening and an ally of Frelinghuysen. While Hopkins had remained within the Reformed tradition, he and his colleagues "emphasized the freedom of the will more than Edwards, and thereby modified the doctrines of original sin, election, and limited atonement" (Van Hoeven 1986, 20). Clearly, without such an examination, there would be no way to know the extent to which those seeking ordination may have embraced Hopkinsian theology.

The quarrel resurfaced in 1822, this time as a major sectional conflict pitting the Albany Synod in the north against the New York

(City) Synod in the south. The southern group was largely concerned with orthodoxy and conformity in matters of doctrine and practice. The northern assembly, while adhering to Reformed standards, was strongly interested in "winning converts on the neighboring frontier to the west" (Van Hoeven 1986, 21). As a result, the Albany Synod was more open to evangelical Christianity and cooperative ventures with other churches within Reformed tradition (e.g., Presbyterian and Congregational churches), particularly with regard to frontier missionary efforts.

In part, this was due to the greater social changes occurring and the greater social challenges confronting Reformed churches in the northern region. The opening of the Erie Canal brought hosts of people migrating through the northern region on their way westward, and so it was much more influenced by the presence of the burgeoning frontier. In addition, the northern section of the church had experienced the loss of Dutch political and religious hegemony in the region along with increased intermarriage between the Dutch and English (Van Hoeven 1986, 27). As a result, in their effort to respond to this new situation theologically and programmatically, the northern portion of the church tended to temper its orthodoxy and be more open to American-style evangelicalism.

The church was not only adapting to America, it was also beginning to embrace America. The RCA was emerging into a "mainline" Protestant denomination. It sought to influence and preserve a nation that was "Protestant" as well as democratic, one that exhibited high moral standards. Moreover, it sought to do so through cooperation with other religious bodies. While the RCA did not officially abandon its confessions, it nevertheless was willing to tolerate more local and individual interpretations than those which some of its more orthodox members demanded (Van Hoeven 1986, 21).

Once again, these matters ultimately reached the General Synod, and once again, the synod attempted to walk a fine line between maintaining its allegiance to the old standards of confession while enabling participation in revivalism (Janssen 2000, 53). For those who held to a stricter reading of the Canons of Dort, however, the response of the Synod of 1822 was a deviation from doctrinal purity. As a result, twenty-four ministers and twenty-six churches seceded from the group to form the True Reformed Dutch Church. This early schism presaged the later split that produced the Christian Reformed Church; indeed, while several of these congregations remained independent, a handful eventually merged with the Christian Reformed Church in 1890.

Thus, by the middle of the nineteenth century, just as a new wave of Dutch immigrants began settling the Midwest, the RCA in the East had gone through nearly two hundred years of "Americanization." By then, nearly all church services were conducted in English, the organizational principles of Dort were adapted to an American setting, and American customs were widely accepted. After having participated in the First and Second Great Awakenings, those who were part of the RCA were no longer inclined to favor strict religious separation for the sake of purity. The spirit of the RCA was largely one of open engagement and ecumenical outlook for a distinctly Protestant America.

Enter the Christian Reformed Church

In order to understand the origins of the Christian Reformed Church, one must understand the religious experiences brought with them to America by many Dutch immigrants in the later half of the nineteenth century. During the early years of that century, different portions of Dutch society began to object to what they perceived to be liberal and unorthodox practices within the Hervormde Kerk, the state church of the Netherlands. In response, a number of congregations seceded from the national church, thus beginning the *Afscheiding*, the Secession of 1834.

While the Secession was by no means a homogeneous movement (TeVelde 2000, 85), it did reflect a strategy that separation and secession could be used as a means to restore and preserve the true church. Not surprisingly, the Hervormde Kerk did not respond favorably to such a "restoration effort." To split from the national church meant essentially "seceding from the nation"—almost as if one were denouncing one's citizenship or burning the national flag. And soon thereafter, those who seceded began to be persecuted.[7]

The Dutch Reformed Church in America was aware of these religious developments related to the Hervormde Kerk (Janssen 2000, 54-55). Beginning in the mid-1840s, a series of articles about the controversy in the Netherlands appeared in the *Christian Intelligencer*,

---

[7]   Moreover, many of the *Afscheiding* participants came from the lower classes (Bratt 1984, 12), and, as a result, they had been experiencing severe financial difficulties due to the major economic downturn in the Netherlands at the time.

a journal of the Dutch Reformed in America.[8] On the basis of these reports, it was clear that the "immigrants could expect a sympathetic hearing from the American church" (Janssen 2000, 55).

Consequently, in order to escape both economic hardship and religious persecution, many Dutch seceders decided to emigrate. In fact, some clergy, such as Albertus Van Raalte and Hendrik Scholte, offered to lead their entire congregations to the New World. Beginning in 1847, Dutch immigrants began to settle in the Midwest, and, with the promise of religious guidance, the number who chose to emigrate increased over the next decades. Moreover, while they had been a religious minority in the Netherlands, the seceders could establish relatively isolated religious colonies on the American frontier in which they were free to worship and structure communal life as they saw fit, thus maintaining a homogeneous society in their own small enclaves.[9]

Almost from the beginning of the arrival of the Dutch immigrants in 1847, there began a period of courtship between the eastern-based Reformed Protestant Dutch Church and the immigrant congregations that, under Van Raalte, settled in the area around Holland, Michigan. The "Holland immigrants" were welcomed initially by the Dutch Reformed Church when they arrived in New York's harbor in December 1846, and the church also assisted them on their journey westward. In 1847 and 1848, the General Synod of the church passed favorable resolutions about the new group, as well as noting with concern that they not be neglected.

In June of 1849, the Dutch Reformed Church's Board of Domestic Missions commissioned the Reverend Isaac Wyckoff, minister of the Second Reformed Church in Albany, New York (a church that was particularly helpful to Van Raalte's group on its westward trek), to open discussions with the churches of the new Dutch colony in Michigan with an eye toward a possible union. Wyckoff, in his report to the board, noted with regard to the immigrants' piety that "their religious habits are very strict and devout" and that in doctrine "a perfect agreement with our standards was found" (quoted in Eenigenburg 1986, 31).

In April of the next year, the Classis of Holland appointed Van Raalte to serve as its representative to the Particular Synod of Albany,

---

[8]   In addition, the *Intelligencer* also included an appeal by Albertus Van Raalte directed at the churches in America to assist those emigrants who chose to leave the Netherlands.

[9]   For a fuller discussion and description of this distinctive settlement pattern, see Luidens and Nemeth 2000.

with full power to facilitate a union with the Dutch Reformed Church. That meeting approved the organization of the Holland Classis and proposed union of the two groups to General Synod at its June meetings; the recommendation was adopted without debate.

Thus, the union that occurred in 1850 between the four immigrant churches of the Classis of Holland and the Reformed Protestant Dutch Church in North America was not something done hastily (Eenigenburg 1986, 31-32). A "courtship" had transpired over several years, during which relationships had been established and bonds of confidence, trust, and mutual respect had been forged.

However, the Dutch immigrant churches, given their experiences in the Netherlands, were somewhat suspicious of ecclesiastical domination. Whereas the RCA[10] had, over two hundred years of history in the country, gradually embraced America, many of the newly arrived Dutch immigrants came infused with a proclivity toward separatism. These immigrants left their homeland seeking to establish a "true church" and to practice their religious faith freely. This desire was cemented by the hardships of persecution, the emotional and economic stress of emigration, and the toils of survival in a new world. After all that they had expended emotionally, physically, and economically to form a pure church, many immigrants were very reluctant to compromise on even the smallest of details. The spirit in the distinctively Dutch "kolonies" of the Midwest was that they had given all, and now they desired all. It was the spirit of separatism that would, within ten years, become the Christian Reformed Church—in opposition to the open embrace of the Reformed Church in America.

The Secession of 1857

In the United States, Van Raalte and his followers found themselves in a different political and religious environment. Van Raalte understood that to be a Reformed Christian in America necessitated a certain amount of change and adaptation, but he was committed "to do so without losing sight of his ideal of moving the church 'back to Dort'" (Bruins 1985, 184). The new immigrants were weary of the internal disputes among the group, and they had "no desire to automatically project the Dutch Secession on an American screen" (TeVelde 2000, 87-88). Accordingly, Van Raalte promoted "Americanization" in his

[10]   At that time, the RCA was called the Reformed Protestant Church in North America.

colony, and, within the first five years, he had founded a school to teach English, had sections of the newspaper printed in English, and helped many colonists receive citizenship (Bruins 1985, 184). Van Raalte also prized ecumenicity and church union. Not only did he hold an "open attitude toward Presbyterians and Congregationalists," he maintained friendships with those from other Protestant traditions, including Methodists (Osterhaven 1986, 63).

However, Van Raalte's approach did not sit well with all of the Dutch in the Midwest. Gysbert Haan had worshiped in the East as well and complained that the churches there practiced open Communion, used choirs and hymns, and neglected preaching from the catechism. These objections paralleled those of earlier disagreements with the Hervormde Kerk: the singing of hymns, the preaching of the catechism, and the character of the classis had all been bones of contention in the Netherlands (TeVelde 2000, 89).

Haan's complaints raised, in part, the question of why those who had fought so hard for a "pure" church should now choose to unite with a church of questionable practices, rather than simply remaining loyal to the Seceder Church of the Netherlands (Swierenga 2000, 66). In time, four congregations presented letters of secession to the Holland Classis. While just one church listed any reason for departure (noting that the RCA did not show enough respect for the *Afscheiding*), it is clear that the leaders of this new secession held "to a stricter interpretation of the Dort Church Order than did Van Raalte and associates" (Swierenga 2000, 72).[11] They saw themselves as the preservers of the true church and believed that through their actions, the historic Reformed church of the Netherlands was being reborn (Zwanstra 1991, 9), an understanding made apparent in the first name of the new church: the True Dutch Reformed Church.

However, the Secession of 1857 was not based solely on theological and ecclesiastical considerations. Lurking behind the actions were cultural factors: the use of the English language and the speed of assimilation being experienced by the churches, particularly Van Raalte's promotion of Americanization (Osterhaven 1986, 62-63). Clearly, there were important cultural differences between the Dutch of

---

[11]   Van Raalte and his associates "asserted that the churches were free to change the Canons of Dort and adapt its contents to meet the needs of the times" (TeVelde 2000, 91). They criticized the seceders for ignorance in American customs and for an excessive attachment to tradition (Brinks 2000, 126).

western Michigan and those who had settled generations earlier in the East. The early group reflected the oldest church tradition in the nation, whose members spoke primarily English and were generally urban and urbane, while the new individuals were a band of immigrants, often farmers and artisans who spoke Dutch. One group boasted prominent national figures and important families—the Livingstons, the Roosevelts, and Martin Van Buren; the other lived precariously in log houses hewn from the remote forests along Lake Michigan. It is not surprising, therefore, that the two often felt considerable distance from each other.[12] These cultural differences were clearly evident in the Masonic Lodge conflict (Osterhaven 1986, 65-66) that served to establish the Christian Reformed Church as a separate organizational entity.

The Masonic Lodge Conflict

The Secession of 1857 was not an instant success among the immigrant churches of the Midwest. The fledgling denomination was weak for many years, having only one minister and five congregations, each of which was in turmoil. However, between 1867 and 1875, immigrants from the northern provinces of the Netherlands—the heart of the secessionist impulse—came to the burgeoning Midwest and tended to join CRC congregations rather than RCA affiliated ones (Swierenga and Bruins 1999, 98-103). Though such immigrants helped the CRC grow, its greatest increase in members occurred only after the Masonic Lodge conflict of the 1870s.

In Europe, the Masonic Lodge was largely composed of individuals bound together to spread Enlightenment ideals considered antithetical to the prevailing worldview of the Christian faith. In fact, in the Netherlands, one could not be both a member of the lodge and a member of the national church. However, Freemasonry was significantly different in America, where it was viewed "primarily as a fraternal and social organization," promoting the same morality as Christianity and

---

[12]   However, neither social class nor geographical origins appear to provide sufficient explanations for why some Dutch immigrants joined the RCA, while others formed the CRC (see Swierenga and Bruins 1999, 98-103). Rather, it appears that "RCA members acted like immigrants and CRC members acted like colonists," as CRC members desired to have "a little Holland, where they could continue life as they had known and valued it, but with a higher living standard" (Swierenga and Bruins 1999, 103).

employing the same foundational text (Bruins 1983, 56). As a result, by the beginning of the nineteenth century, Freemasonry had become a widely accepted institution in the United States, "highly regarded by many and, according to Masons, not considered to conflict with basic Christianity" (Swierenga and Bruins 1999, 111).

Within American society there had always been some opposition to secret societies on theological and social grounds, but Freemasonry was not a major issue within the RCA until 1867, when the Synod of the CRC banned membership in the lodge. Once this action was taken by the CRC, the immigrant churches of the RCA in the Midwest were not about to allow themselves to suffer by comparison. The Classis of Wisconsin therefore petitioned General Synod in 1868 to "declare that membership in the church and the lodge were incompatible and to condemn Masonry" (Swierenga and Bruins 1999, 114). But, in its deliberations of that year, the General Synod voted not to take any action on the matter.[13]

The next year, two midwestern classes (Holland and Wisconsin) again sent overtures to the General Synod calling for rejecting Freemasonry, and this time, the synod referred the question to a committee for further consideration. In 1870, the General Synod issued its decision, trying to strike a balance between the opposition to the Masons by the immigrants in the Midwest and the general acceptance of (and sometimes membership in) the Masons among church members in the East. The ruling conceded that, on the whole, membership in a secret society was not a good practice, and therefore it was not prudent for church members to belong, but at the same time, the General Synod would not rule that church law should forbid membership in the Masons (Swierenga and Bruins 1999, 115). In essence, therefore, it left Masonic membership to the decision of local consistories, arguing that to ban membership in the lodge would interfere with the local church prerogative of deciding who could and could not be a member of that congregation (Swierenga and Bruins 1999, 115).

On this issue, as with other questions, the CRC and RCA split over how much one was willing to tolerate differences within the church body. While Van Raalte disliked the Masons, he was willing to live with the synod's decision; at least on this front, church unity overrode church purity. However, when he died in 1876, Van Raalte's moderating

[13] Van Raalte was among the minority voting for synod action on this matter. The minority was outvoted eighty-nine to nineteen (Swierenga and Bruins 1999, 114).

voice was lost in the next round of the debate. Moreover, at about the same time, financial difficulties struck Hope College, an educational institution founded by the RCA in Holland, Michigan. The General Synod decided in 1878 to shut down Hope's theological education program because of its financial difficulties, an action interpreted by some immigrant churches as a Masonic plot by the eastern churches to undermine the immigrant clergy. Thus, the Masonic controversy once again reared its head, and the matter reappeared at the General Synod in 1880. This time it appeared that, if the 1870 decision was not reversed, secession would likely result. But the synod refused to change its earlier ruling, causing a flood of Reformed churches in the Midwest, including Van Raalte's own congregation, to leave the RCA and join the CRC.

The Masonic issue gave life to the Christian Reformed Church. Not only did it benefit numerically from the influx of former RCA members, but the church also began to benefit from the vast majority of new immigrants who elected to join the CRC rather than the RCA. In the aftermath of the Masonic controversy, the Seceder Church in the Netherlands officially switched its allegiance to the CRC, just as another wave of Dutch settlers was beginning to arrive in the Midwest. Thus, while the immigrant congregations of the RCA grew one hundred-fold between 1873 and 1900, the CRC grew eight hundred-fold over the same period of time. And despite the infusion of previous RCA members, the CRC became an even stauncher opponent of Americanization, adapting only cautiously and tentatively "in a manner that would not endanger its doctrinal and ecclesiastical purity." In contrast, the RCA continued to view schism, rather than adaptation, as the greatest evil to avoid (Bruins 1983, 72).

The 1890s to World War I

While the RCA and CRC elected to follow different paths, they continued to recognize their common roots and heritage. In the Netherlands, Abraham Kuyper was instrumental in creating a new seceder church in 1886, called the *Doleantie*, which shortly thereafter (1892) merged with the *Afscheiding*. These developments fostered several union discussions between the CRC and RCA in the late nineteenth century, but their differences remained too great. The RCA considered itself the true home of the CRC by virtue of its age and the fact that the CRC had left its fold; if there was to be a rapprochement, the RCA believed the CRC should rejoin them. The CRC believed their group was the true church by virtue of its purity; they were not willing to accept the questionable churches in the RCA "East," and would only merge with the "purer" midwestern congregations. As neither side was willing to budge, the talks broke down (Zwaanstra 1991, 13-15).

The general orientation of the CRC has never lent itself well to efforts at ecumenicity or church union. The only formal union in its history came in 1890 with the True Dutch Reformed Church, a church that had seceded from the RCA in 1822, espoused the same confessions, engaged in the same practices, and exhibited the same separatist attitudes as the CRC. However, even that union proved not to be very effective, as in 1908 all but three congregations of the True Dutch Reformed Church left the CRC.[14]

Dutch immigrants in the late 1800s and early 1900s were influenced greatly by the life and thought of Abraham Kuyper (1837-1920). Kuyper had a remarkable career as a pastor, journalist, politician, and professor. He first served as a pastor; he was then elected as a representative to Parliament, when he also began publishing a daily newspaper. Kuyper later founded both a political party and a university (the Free University of Amsterdam), and he served as prime minister of the Netherlands from 1901-1905.

Kuyper's newspaper writings and philosophical works led to the creation of three distinct "parties" within the CRC in America: the first supported one side of a Kuyperian paradox, a second party was in favor of the opposing argument to that same paradox, and a third rejected Kuyper's model in its entirety (Zwaanstra 1973, 68-70; Bratt 1984, chapter 3). Kuyper emphasized a fundamental difference (an antithesis) between the church and the world, because each emanated from very basically different principles. His philosophy called for the formation of separate Christian institutions in every field ("pillars") which would care for church members from cradle to grave. Kuyper's articulation and advocacy of this separatist ("Antithetical") model predominated during the first half of his career, a period of institutional formation (Bratt 1984, 19). In America, the Antitheticals embraced Kuyper's notion of separate Christian institutions, in part as a means to maintain isolation and purity.

---

[14]   Similarly, CRC talks with the United Presbyterian Church of North America between 1888 and 1898 about uniting the two groups dissipated for the same reasons. The CRC did not want to lose its Dutch distinctiveness and purity (Zwaanstra 1991, 12-13).

Later in his life, however, Kuyper advanced the notion of "common grace"—holding that unsaved individuals can do good things and possess useful knowledge; the doctrine "legitimized a certain amount of cooperation between the redeemed and unbelievers" (Bratt 1984, 20). Not surprisingly, this aspect of Kuyper's thought arose in the later years of his life, when his party and government in the Netherlands had to work in coalition with other political parties in managing public life (Bratt 1984, 19).

In America, those who were known as Positive Calvinists embraced the idea of common grace. They did not seek to shelter believers from the world; rather, they sought to prepare the faithful to go out and transform the world (Bratt 1984, 52). While they wanted to provide a distinctive Christian testimony within every sphere of life, they did not insist on doing so through separate organizational structures like the Antitheticals. Instead, separation was viewed to be a matter of "tactics, not principles" (Bratt 1984, 53).

Finally, the Confessionalists opposed both of Kuyper's formulations. They traced their roots back to the Seceders, not to the *Reveil*, the movement with which Kuyper had been associated. The Confessionalists were much more concerned about what was, and was not, "Reformed" (Zwaanstra 1973, 73). For them, Reformed principles were truths that their tradition "drew out of the Word of God and formulated in its confessions." They objected to the way in which Kuyper and his followers spoke of the confessions, believing that Kuyperians generally viewed these statements more as containing, rather than constituting, Reformed principles (Zwaanstra 1973, 75). The Confessionalist position, at least in its less sophisticated manifestations, probably reflected the viewpoint of the largest group of CRC Dutch Americans, with those espousing such positions best described as "inward-looking pietists" (Bratt 1984, 50).

Tied to these distinctions were subtle doctrinal differences. For example, the Confessionalists were "infralapsarians" who maintained that God performed election after the fall of man, while the two Kuyperian parties were "supralapsarians," contending that election occurred prior to creation itself. These relatively abstract theological debates had important ramifications in terms of the relationship between the church and salvation. For the "Supras," the elect were already redeemed at birth, and infant baptism therefore transpired on the assumption that regeneration had already occurred. Consequently, the "instruments of the church—preaching and sacraments—did not induce but simply confirmed regeneration" (Bratt 1984, 47). Such an understanding, however, languished after the CRC synod in 1906 declared infralapsarianism to be the more Reformed and thoroughly scriptural position. At least in this round, the Confessionalists had prevailed.[15]

Meanwhile, the RCA moved steadily towards mainline American Protestantism. Since the country was considered a Protestant Christian nation, they did not view Americanization as a problem. For example, histories written in the English periodical of the RCA "West," the *Leader*, displayed America's leaders and founders as stalwart Christians, largely ignoring past inconsistencies in their religious character (Voskuil 1986, 121-124). And, in the Dutch RCA community, the *Leader* was the voice of normative Americanization; it expressed hostility toward Catholicism, but also toward the CRC's Christian school movement (Bratt 1984, 44). The circle of those who wrote for the *Leader* came to resemble most closely the Reveil-evangelical party in the Hervormde Kerk: moralistic, genteel, willing to submerge strict "Reformed-ness" in general Protestantism in order to spread that faith over the entire nation (Bratt 1984, 44).

When the progressive movement appeared in American politics in the early part of the twentieth century, the *Leader* endorsed it with few exceptions. For progressives, "Moral action...proved the value of religion" (Bratt 1984, 68), which is why the "Prohibition won its strongest support from Reformed Church progressives" (Bratt 1984, 73).

World War I: Awakened Consciousness

The CRC and RCA approached the possible entrance into World War I in ways their respective orientations might suggest. The RCA largely supported the war effort; it was not only a just, but a "holy" war. The CRC likewise viewed the war in the typical manner of its general orientation: members largely saw it as a confirmation of "total depravity and divine punishment for national sins" (Bratt 1984, 85) and were reluctant to join the conflict. When war was finally declared, however, this attitude was strongly rebuked, first by the RCA and then by secular newspapers, as the church's separation and critique of American life

[15] It should be noted, however, that despite the fact that these three distinct parties existed within the CRC, they functioned within a broader community that served more to unite than to divide them (Bratt 1984, 54).

and culture were viewed as unpatriotic in the extreme nationalism of the day.[16]

In response to the criticism, the CRC began to recognize a problem in its separatist position. As the war closed, Christian Reformed veterans returned home who had fought alongside other Americans, further challenging the isolationist mentality. And the denomination faced another challenge—namely, the dwindling of Dutch immigration. These pressures led the CRC to do the very thing that it had so long opposed—engage in the process of Americanization (Swierenga 2001, 95).

The Reformed Church in America, on the other hand, found itself in the opposite quandary. Having placed its trust in the social optimism of Mainline Protestant progressivism, the RCA now found that optimism called into question. Many tenets association with Protestant liberal thought could not survive the horrors of the war. The church's American fervor had to be re-examined and, in the end, reduced. While the RCA continued to follow the mainline impulse toward hopeful progressivism, it did so with much more caution. Churches in the Midwest were particularly critical of this direction, and, because of them, the RCA failed two tests for mainline Protestantism: "toleration of theological liberalism and enthusiasm for denominational mergers" (Bratt 1985, 201). During WWI and after, the RCA became gradually more willing to offer social critiques, reassessing American society and the church's own position in it. The paradoxical consequence of WWI was that the CRC realized its need for Americanization while the RCA came to exhibit a greater willingness to stand apart from and critique American government and society. Each moved, in small ways, back towards the middle.

Between the Wars

The starting approaches of the CRC and RCA, though tempered, did not change much between the First and Second World Wars. When WWI ceased, the Christian Reformed Church began a series of internal battles among its different parties that reflected their contrasting visions for the church. Immediately after the war, both Confessionalists

---

[16] Such attacks were not simply verbal. The Christian schools linked to Christian Reformed churches were vandalized, and, as a result, parents had to take turns guarding the schools. In the press, such schools were attacked as being Prussian in nature and disloyal to the country (Bratt 1984, 87).

and Antitheticals were on the defensive based upon their opposition to the war.

One option that presented itself to the CRC was that of American fundamentalism, an option advocated by Harry Bultema. Fundamentalism was a loose movement of "co-belligerents united by their fierce opposition to modernist attempts to bring Christianity into line with modern thought" (Marsden 1980, 4), and fundamentalists drew largely on American revivalist impulses and were largely Anabaptist in their theological orientations. But the synod of 1918 reproved Bultema and turned away from the fundamentalist movement on confessional grounds.

Next, the Antitheticals accused Calvin Seminary Professor Ralph Janssen of theological liberalism because he adopted a higher criticism approach to biblical texts. During the latter parts of the nineteen century and the early years of the twentieth century, there emerged within American Christianity a strong liberal element which increasingly took a stance that stressed the incorporation of modern assumptions and paradigms within the Christian tradition (Hutchison, 1976). This element, for example, tended to stress the findings of German Higher Criticism as a means of interpreting biblical texts, an approach that incorporated the study of history, linguistic scholarship, and comparative religion. As a result, those advocating such an approach became convinced that the Bible contained both historical errors and scientifically untenable conceptions. In response, theological liberals began to downplay God's revelation of himself and emphasize the human discovery of God, downplay the fixed nature of revelation in the Bible and emphasize God's continuing nature of revelation in the world, downplay God's transcendence from the world and emphasize God's immanence within the world.

Before Janssen was convicted and deposed by the synod in 1922, he turned the tables on the Antitheticals for their rejection of common grace. The Confessionalists, who had joined ranks with the Antitheticals to convict Janssen, then reversed course against them when Herman Hoeksema (a prominent leader among the Antitheticals) was charged with denying common grace in 1924. Confessionalism again predominated within the CRC, standing in opposition to the two great enemies of the time, Modernism and worldliness. However, the separatist impulse of antithetical ideas settled into the background of Christian Reformed mentality, remaining a strong force in the church's search for purity. As Bratt explains, "The antithesis was transformed from a principle into an instinct" (Bratt 1984, 18).

This instinct of separation was evident in the CRC's relationship with other religious bodies. The CRC joined the Federal Council of Christian Churches in 1918, but it did so for purely practical reasons: the Federal Council was virtually the only agency that could place chaplains in the military during WW I. Six years after joining, the CRC pulled out (Zwaanstra 1991, 21-23). Likewise, when invited to discuss a merger with five other Protestant churches in 1930, the CRC turned away, seeking instead to draw lines of separation between itself and the world (Zwaanstra 1991, 23-24).

In 1943, however, the denomination joined the National Association of Evangelicals (NAE), reflecting its closer ties to the separatist fundamentalists than to the theological liberalism found within mainline churches. But calls for ecumenical engagement continued to clash with the CRC instinct for separation, and, in 1944, the synod made an official ecumenical pronouncement. The adopted position called for engagement with other Christian churches, but its specified method of outreach reflected the CRC emphasis on purity and separation: the CRC could unite, but it could not compromise (Zwaanstra 1991, 33). Because it was the "true" and "pure" church, the CRC should first work to purge others of their non-Reformed principles, *then* join them in organic union. Ecumenical councils and associations remained noticeably absent from the entire report.

Even the CRC association with the NAE was troubled from the start. Every year after joining, calls resounded in the church's press and pulpits for separation. In 1951, only eight years after joining the NAE, the CRC left, drawing a theological line between itself and fundamentalism (Zwaanstra 1991, 38-48).[17]

The RCA's willingness to "Americanize" and display a greater ecumenical openness allowed it to more readily engage in fellowship with other denominations. Unlike the CRC, the Reformed Church did not closely critique another group's precise doctrinal stance before engaging them; the RCA was less worried about "contamination," and, as a result, the RCA developed charter memberships in the American Bible Society, the World Alliance of Reformed Churches, the Federal

---

[17] However, in 1988, the CRC chose to rejoin the National Association of Evangelicals. Despite efforts to try to offer an alternative "third way," the CRC found it necessary to "choose a side" as American Protestantism increasingly became divided into evangelical and mainline camps.

Council of Churches, the National Council of Churches, and the World Council of Churches (Kromminga 1985, 141-142). The Reformed Church's strategy, though strained by the harsh events of the twentieth century, still looked with a balance of optimism and realism towards effecting ecumenical engagement and societal benefit.

Each denomination maintained its distinct mentality, but each functioned from the middle of the spectrum. The Christian Reformed Church leaned towards fundamentalism on one side but ultimately separated itself from complete association, while the Reformed Church in America continued its presence in mainline Protestantism but operated as a conservative critic.

World War II and Post-War Immigration

Like World War I, World War II shook both denominations, forcing them to re-evaluate their identities. This time the groups exchanged places in their approach to the war. The lessons the RCA learned from its "repentance for the 'excesses' of the last war" were not forgotten, and it tended to celebrate "a rather innocent patriotism" and avoid "grandiose conceptualizations" of the theological implications of the hostilities (Bratt 1984, 153). The CRC, on the other hand, embraced WWII in patriotic fervor.

Emigration from the Netherlands following WWII brought more than twice as many immigrants to Canada than the United States, due in part to the U.S. quota-based immigration policy (Van Ginkel 1996, 139). These new individuals were highly influenced by the social structures and cultural patterns that had emerged in the Netherlands following Kuyper. Known as *verzuiling*, different confessions and world views were visibly evident in the formation of parallel institutional "pillars" throughout the country. In the Netherlands, different religious communities would establish (and the state would partially fund) community structures such as educational institutions, media programming outlets, labor unions, and political parties for their own separate groups or religions. This heritage led the post-WW II wave of Dutch immigrants to create their own churches, their own schools, and their own social and political organizations in their new country as well.

In the face of this influx of Dutch Calvinists, the U.S.-based Christian Reformed Church sent "home missionaries" to Canada with the charge of welcoming and encouraging the new immigrants to join the CRC (Kits 1991, 340). Moreover, given the Christian Reformed experience in the United States, the CRC representatives who were sent to Canada thought that the Canadian CRC should be "'indigenized' at a more rapid pace than the American churches had been" (Van Ginkel 1996, 141). However, this pressure to assimilate was resisted and tensions arose—not only between the American home missionaries and their newly arrived Dutch charges, but between recent and earlier immigrants, and between the Canadian and American parts of the CRC (Kits 1991, 340). In response to the disagreements, discussions were held that enabled a consensus to emerge, and a denominational split along national lines was precluded (Van Ginkel 1996, 142).

The Beginnings of Change

Following World War II, there were intimations of important changes in orientations transpiring in both denominations. Members of the CRC, having worked together with other Americans in the war effort, once again came to recognize the church's relative isolation. This awareness reopened the battle among its internal factions as to the future direction of the denomination. Controversy swirled around the church-sponsored Calvin College and Calvin Seminary, and in 1952 all but one of the seminary faculty members was forced to resign; a younger crowd with fresh ideas, led by Henry Stob, replaced them. Stob contended that three types of thought were present within the CRC-the militant mind, the mind of safety, and the positive mind-and he opted for the last. This restaffing of the seminary signaled the CRC's move towards progressive Calvinism (Swierenga 2001, 96-98).

As the years advanced, progressives gained strength and Confessionalists lost ground through the gradual dismantling of traditional institutional and theological constraints. The first break with strict adherence to traditional practices by the CRC synod occurred in 1951. Worldliness, though still considered a great enemy, was beginning to lose its place of fear. Outreach was expanding, and some missionaries and others challenged the traditional emphasis on limited atonement due to its stifling impact on evangelical outreach. In the wake of the debate, "The Confessionalists' dominance was...broken on the official level" (Bratt 1984, 207). The breakdown of legalism within the CRC continued in future decisions of the General Synod, such as the 1966 ruling reversing the 1928 decision against movie attendance. Progressives taught "permeation" rather than separation, and they were gaining ground (Bratt 1984, 206-208).

While the direction of the progressive movement was clear, the weakening of classic Christian Reformed separatist mentality occurred only haltingly. For example, in a 1957 essay written for the centennial celebration of the founding of the CRC, John Kromminga, president of Calvin Seminary, reiterated much of the same long-held, separatist view. In an admittedly celebratory article, Kromminga praised the Secession of 1834 in the Netherlands, which the CRC has always claimed to be its origin. When speaking of the immigrants, Kromminga noted that though "...small in number, in culture, in power, they were heirs of the faith, defenders of the faith, and lovers of the faith" (Kromminga 1957, 22). To paraphrase, heirs of this legacy were the remnant: small, but right. Even after one hundred years of life in America, Kromminga praised purity of profession as the outstanding feature of the CRC, perhaps indirectly critiquing the RCA for failing the purity test.

Yet, at the same time, Kromminga demonstrated he was not bound by the separatist past. Joining with the new progressive movement, he called for a greater engagement and application of faith in the modern culture (Kromminga 1957, 41). As he critiqued the historic introversion of the CRC, Kromminga referred the denomination towards ecumenicity and union (Kromminga 1957, 57). Continuing this thought, two decades later Kromminga (1974, 114) showed an even greater willingness to question the CRC past. While still serving as president of Calvin Seminary he reanalyzed the split of 1857 and noted that it would be difficult to deny that "a spirit of separatism" was present and operative in those who left the RCA more than a century before.

The CRC was also beginning gradually to open its arms ecumenically. The Reformed Ecumenical Synod, an association of Dutch Reformed churches, all of which boasted Seceder origins, met for the first time in 1946. The CRC's role in the synod would gradually become that of moderator, holding together the more liberal elements with the more conservative in the interest of ecumenical fellowship (Zwaanstra 1991, 79-84).

In 1958, the CRC General Synod increased the call for ecumenicity and church union, though there were few immediate results. Due to the growing strength of its progressive movement, the CRC was no longer being invited to national assemblies of other more traditionalist Reformed denominations who had become wary of the CRC's purported "liberal" tendencies. In 1956, the Reformed Presbyterians approached the CRC for the purposes of seeking union, and, despite their overt appeal, the CRC elected not to join specifically because the Reformed Presbyterians were too separatist in their theology, believing in complete political dissent (Zwaanstra 1991, 51-52). Meanwhile, the CRC had approached the Orthodox Presbyterian Church about the possibility of merging. The two churches came close to union in 1966, following ten years of discussion. But, in the following year, the Orthodox Presbyterians brought charges of liberal tendencies against the CRC. And, by 1971, all discussions of merger were dead; the CRC was simply too progressive for the Orthodox (Zwaanstra 1991, 52-56).

During the years following WWII, the actions of the CRC revealed the first cracks in the separatist mentality that had more or less guided every denominational decision until that point. The CRC was critically examining its "spirit of separatism" and, for the first time, critiquing the underlying principles of that worldview. Legalism began to disappear, and there were calls for increased engagement and ecumenicity. As mentioned before, the synod of 1958 called for ecumenicity—but it also revised Article 36 of the Belgic Confession, essentially Americanizing the strict confessions of the church—something the RCA had done many years before, in 1792.

During this same time, the Reformed Church had rediscovered its own "Netherlandic past." In so doing, it had experienced something of a "theological renaissance" (Bratt 1984, 196), while still maintaining the momentum of its American and ecumenical orientations. It sought to emulate the national church (the Hervormde Kerk) of the Netherlands, desiring to be a broad, yet confessing, church that addressed matters of concern to the entire nation.

The revitalized economy that followed World War II increased mobility among Americans, opening up contact between members of many previously sheltered Dutch Reformed congregations and other churches and cultures. The result of these interactions was an increasing fervor for ecumenicity, church union, and church growth. The RCA willingly and consciously de-emphasized denominational distinctiveness and positioned itself increasingly as a mainline denomination, even as mainline Protestantism as a whole was beginning to see its share of the religious market diminish. In the process of this alignment on the religious spectrum, the RCA made strides toward becoming a "national" denomination, with church growth efforts in the South and West, where numerous RCA families were moving (Nemeth and Luidens 2001). In the process, the church became even more self-consciously an "American" denomination in its theology and programs.

Clearly, in both denominations, the traditional mentality of the church was gradually diminishing and evolving. For the Reformed Church, the major changes came after WWI, when its hyper-Americanization caused realignment in theological and doctrinal perspectives. With the decline of progressive optimism and theological liberalism, the RCA had to re-evaluate itself and revive its confessional standards. Subsequently, in the period following WWII, the RCA increased its theological awareness and productivity, while remaining committed to church growth, evangelism, and ecumenical fellowship.

The Christian Reformed Church, on the other hand, experienced relatively few cracks in its separatist mentality until after WWII. Only then did progressive Calvinists begin calling for a new engagement, a new ecumenicity, and a new involvement in the modern culture; only then did the legalism designed to protect against "worldliness" begin to disappear. In 1951, a new and progressive faculty was installed at Calvin Seminary, and while it would take at least a decade for this new attitude to make a significant impact in the life of the CRC, the church had, by the 1960s, modified its separatist attitude and begun to look outward towards the wider world. The degree of its isolation ebbed as the church began calling for a new strength—a strength in union, fellowship, and engagement.

A Social Profile of the CRC and RCA
At the Turn of the Millennium

Given the history of the Christian Reformed and Reformed churches, how do the two denominations compare today in terms of the demographic and social characteristics of their members? Based on the historical background of the two denominations, one would anticipate a higher geographical percentage of RCA members in the eastern portion of the United States, a higher percentage of Canadians within the CRC than the RCA, with the bulk of members within both denominations today residing in the midwestern portion of the United States.

These expectations are verified by the data presented in Table 2.1, drawn from statistics presented in the yearbooks of each denomination in 2000.[18] At the turn of the millennium, somewhat more than a

---

[18]   For the CRC, the data for Canada are drawn from Classes Alberta North,

quarter (29 percent) of all RCA members resided in the East, compared to only a handful (4 percent) of the CRC parishioners. At the same time, Canadians constituted nearly a quarter (24 percent) of all CRC members, but Canadians comprised less than one in twenty (3 percent) of all RCA members. As anticipated, nearly three-fifths of the parishioners of both the CRC and the RCA resided in the American Midwest (57 percent and 59 percent, respectively). Thus, while the bulk of the members of both denominations are located in the same geographical region of the United States, the remaining members of the two denominations are concentrated in distinctly different regions of North America.

Table 2.1
The Geographical Distribution of CRC and RCA Members
at the Turn of the Millennium

Region	CRC	RCA
Canada	24%	3%
United States		
Midwest	57	59
East	4	29
Rest	15	13
Total	100%	100%

These distinctive "minority" components result in each denomination continuing to be pulled in decidedly different directions.

Alberta South/Saskatchewan, British Columbia North-West, British Columbia South-East, Hamilton, Huron, Niagara, Quinte, and Toronto. For the RCA, the data are drawn from the Regional Synod of Canada.

For the CRC, the data for the East are drawn from Classes Atlantic Northeast, Hackensack, Hudson, and Southeast U.S. For the RCA, the data for the East are drawn from the Regional Synod of Albany, the Regional Synod of the Mid-Atlantics, and the Regional Synod of New York.

For the CRC, the data for the Midwest are drawn from Classes Chicago South, Georgetown, Grand Rapids East, Grand Rapids North, Grand Rapids South, Grandville, Heartland, Holland, Iakota, Illiana, Kalamazoo, Lake Erie, Lake Superior, Minnkota, Muskegon, Northcentral Iowa, Northern Illinois, Northern Michigan, Pella, Thornapple Valley, Wisconsin, and Zeeland. For the RCA, the data for the Midwest are drawn from the Regional Synod of the Great Lakes, the Regional Synod of the Heartland, and the Regional Synod of Mid-America.

For the CRC, the data for the West are drawn from Classes Arizona, California South, Central California, Columbia, Greater Los Angeles, Pacific Hanmi, Pacific Northwest, Red Mesa, Rocky Mountain, and Yellowstone. For the RCA, the data for the West are drawn from the Regional Synod of the Far West.

Whereas the eastern membership of the RCA draws the overall theological and political character of the church in a more "liberal" direction, the Canadian population of the CRC presses the theological and political character of that denomination in a somewhat different direction than its American members. The RCA still looks to the East when there are concerns about denominational unity; by contrast, the CRC stretches its institutional embrace to incorporate members from Canada.

Other differences in the membership of the two denominations become evident from the data presented in Table 2.2, based on responses to the laity surveys conducted in each denomination at the turn of the millennium.[19] Members of the CRC are more solidly Dutch in their background than are members of the RCA; while 80 percent of the Christian Reformed Church members report that their ethnic heritage is Dutch, only half of Reformed Church parishioners do so. The German element of the two denominations (whose history is not discussed in this chapter[20]) is significantly more pronounced in the RCA than in the CRC, as nearly one in six (15 percent) RCA members reports German as a primary ethnicity.

Table 2.2
Membership Characteristics in the CRC and RCA
at the Turn of the Millennium

	CRC	RCA
Ethnicity:		
Dutch	80%	50%
German	3	15
Denomination at Age 16		
RCA	4%	39%
CRC	71	12
None	4	10
Level of Attendance at Age 16		
Regular	89%	75%
Mean length of membership in denomination	40 yrs.	29 yrs.
Mean length of membership in congregation	23 yrs.	24 yrs.

Members of the RCA are less likely than members of the CRC to have been raised in the specific denomination of which they are now

[19] A description of these studies can be found in the Appendix.
[20] For a discussion of the Ostfrisian components of the two denominations, see Brinks (1983) and Beuker (2000).

a part. In fact, as can be seen in Table 2.2, fewer than two in five RCA members (39 percent) report that their denominational affiliation at sixteen years of age was RCA, while nearly three out of four CRC members (71 percent) report that they were affiliated with the CRC at that age. In terms of denominational migration, the RCA benefits more frequently from former CRC members joining its congregations than vice versa, as nearly one in eight RCA members (12 percent) reports an affiliation with the CRC at sixteen years of age, while only one in twenty-five CRC members (4 percent) reports RCA an affiliation at that age.

Since a higher proportion of CRC than RCA laity hold life-long membership in the denomination, one might anticipate the average length of membership in one's denomination would be greater for CRC than RCA members. Indeed, this is case. On average, CRC members have been part of their denomination for forty years, while RCA members have averaged only twenty-nine years of membership. At the same time, length of denominational membership has little relationship to length of time as a member of a specific *congregation*. Members of both denominations tend to be linked to their local congregations for an equally long time, as the mean number of years of membership is virtually identical for the two denominations (twenty-three years versus twenty-four years for the CRC and RCA respectively).

However, in terms of other social characteristics, the members of the two denominations are relatively similar, as can be seen from Table 2.3. Members of the CRC tend to be slightly younger than RCA members. A quarter (26 percent) of CRC members report that they are under forty years of age, but one-fifth (20 percent) of RCA members do so. Conversely, RCA members are somewhat more concentrated than CRC members in the older age brackets. Nearly half of all RCA members (48 percent) are older than fifty-six years, while slightly more than two out of five CRC members (41 percent) fall in that age bracket.

Both the CRC and RCA are composed of larger numbers of females than males, with the RCA having a somewhat higher percentage of women among its membership. In both denominations, a similar percentage of parishioners (roughly 80 percent) report that they are currently married. The somewhat younger age composition of the CRC is also mirrored in the higher percent of "never married" congregants found in the CRC than the RCA (9 percent versus 4 percent, respectively).

Table 2.3
A Social Profile of CRC and RCA Members
at the Turn of the Millennium

	CRC	RCA
Age		
Under 40	26%	20%
41-55	33	32
56-69	20	25
70+	21	23
Sex		
Male	44%	40%
Female	56	60
Marital Status		
Never married	9%	4%
Currently married	81	80
Currently widowed	7	10
Currently separated or divorced	3	5
Educational Attainment		
High school diploma or less	33%	28%
Some college or vocational training	27	28
College diploma or more	40	44
Family Income		
Under $30,000	20%	21%
$30,000 to $49,999	30	26
$50,000 to $74,999	24	26
Over $75,000	26	27
Community Size		
Farm or rural community under 2500 persons	21%	19%
Town (not suburb) of 2500 to 20,000 persons	19	25
Town (not suburb) of 20,000 to 60,000 persons	16	16
City of 60,000 to 250,000 persons	21	15
Large city of more than 250,000 persons	10	8
Suburb of a large city	15	17

Educational attainment and family income are also relatively similar across the two denominations. Two-fifths or more of the members in both denominations report that they are college graduates, while roughly three in ten report that they hold a high school diploma or less. In both denominations, those members who are older are less likely to report having obtained a college diploma (data not shown). Given the relative age of members of both denominations, such reported levels of post-high school educational attainment tend to be fairly impressive.

As income tends to be related to levels of educational attainment, it is not surprising that the reported levels of family income in the two denominations are also remarkably similar. While approximately one-fifth of CRC and RCA members report that their family income is under $30,000 per year, more than one-quarter of the members of both denominations report family income in excess of $75,000 per year.

Finally, a majority of members of both denominations are located in small towns or cities (fewer than 60,000 people) or in rural communities, including approximately one in five members for each denomination who reside in a farm or rural community under 2,500 people. It is noteworthy that the relatively rural composition of the RCA today reflects a shift in the RCA membership base from the eastern urban centers of New York City, Albany, and Philadelphia to the Mohawk and Hudson River valleys as well as the plains of the Midwest. According to the U.S. census of 1916, the RCA ranked as the third most urban denomination in the country (Nemeth and Luidens 1994, 88). But, as the old, inner-city RCA congregations in the East have waned in size over the last several decades, the shift in base membership has moved westward—so that today the RCA is relatively rural and small town in nature, resulting in a residential profile that is virtually identical to that within the CRC.

Conclusion

The Reformed Church in America boasts a legacy of almost four centuries in the "New World," dating its origins to 1628; by contrast, the Christian Reformed Church traces its beginnings to 1857, with a secessionist impulse borne of years of prior experience. Their common roots in the Netherlands belie their contrasting evolution while in North America. While the RCA struggled early with its "American" identity, adapting to the home-spun evangelical web of colonial and post-Revolutionary revivalism, the CRC did not come to that challenge until two centuries later. For the RCA, theological issues were attributed less import than ecumenical cooperation and accommodation. By contrast, the CRC was born in the quest for theological and congregational purity, and assimilation into the broader American religious scene has been more hesitant and disruptive.

Despite divergent historical experiences, the RCA and CRC shared much in common by the end of the twentieth century, including their demographic composition. Both were centered in the small towns and rural communities of the Midwest with predominantly female and aging populations, and both were solidly cast in the middle of the socioeconomic spectrum.

But differences between the two groups continue. While they share a Dutch heritage, that ethnic lineage is more eroded in the RCA than the CRC. Perhaps most importantly, each has a sizable minority constituency that represents polar opposites. The RCA continues to look east towards New York and New Jersey, while the CRC's attention is focused on Canada.

Clearly these demographic characteristics present important challenges to each denomination. The historical components of growth in membership size in both denominations—namely, immigration from the Netherlands and high fertility rates—are no longer operative. Members are not only aging, but younger families within each denomination are less likely to have as many children as families had several decades ago. Moreover, the economic life that sustains many congregations of both denominations is facing serious challenges, as many small towns find it increasing difficult to survive as farm sizes increase and agribusiness replaces farming as a way of life. Larger and larger farms deplete the population in rural areas, thereby diminishing the religious vitality of many congregations in small town and rural life. As members of the congregation age, generational replacement is unable to keep pace with the displacement of members that occurs through the death of its current members.

It is unclear, as the twenty-first century unfolds, just what these historic narratives and demographic characteristics may portend for possible cooperation between the two denominations. It may be that the different historical experiences and proclivities of the two denominations, their different institutional structures, and their different religious identities may incline and enable each to remain as separate denominations. But, it is also true that the demographic trends found within each denomination will likely encourage greater cooperation between the two denominations, regardless of whether or not possible merger is part of that discussion.

However, the future relationship between the two denominations will not be shaped simply by whatever common legacy they may share or demographic similarities they may exhibit. It will also be shaped, in part, by the extent to which the two hold common theological perspectives and understandings today. Whatever may have been the theological commonalities of the past, any relationship between the two denominations will be shaped by the similarities and differences evident today. Consequently, we now turn our attention to theological beliefs to better answer the question of unity and division found both within and across the two denominations today.

CHAPTER 3

'Faith of our Fathers Living Still'?
Religious Beliefs within the CRC and RCA

Denominations can differ in a variety of ways. They can vary, for example, in terms of their ecclesiology (church structure or order) or in terms of their liturgy (worship practices). They can also diverge in their central emphases. For some, the core is the Eucharist; for others, it is spiritual experience. For Reformed Christians, the primary emphasis has historically been, and continues to be, doctrine. As John Hesselink (1983, 279), former president of Western Theological Seminary (RCA), has stated, Reformed Christians have been characterized by a "theological approach to life and an appreciation of doctrine, the life of the mind, and education."

Some might argue that there is greater theological diversity than unity within both the CRC and RCA, making it impossible to speak of any common theology that unites all clergy or laity within either body. Indeed, there has been, and will continue to be, pluralism with regard to the theological beliefs held within the Reformed perspective. Nevertheless, there is a broader Reformed theological tradition that provides some basis of unity, both within and across the two denominations. Thus, in comparing and contrasting the CRC and RCA at the turn of the millennium, a logical starting point is an examination of the religious beliefs and doctrinal stands of the clergy and laity.

Theological Positions: CRC and RCA Clergy

In the Reformed tradition, clergy are required to have theological education in order to serve as pastors or ministers of the Word. Ministers are to be educated "shepherds" who instruct and train their congregants in the proper understanding and application of God's Word to his[1] people.

An examination of CRC and RCA clergy in the late 1980s (Guth et al. 1997, 44-46) revealed several patterns in the theological orientations of pastors within the two denominations. First, both CRC and RCA clergy were highly orthodox theologically. Secondly, the theological positions of clergy of the two denominations were positioned midway between the more theologically liberal positions of mainline Protestant ministers and the even more highly orthodox stance of evangelical Protestant clergy. Finally, CRC pastors were found to be somewhat more orthodox theologically than those in the RCA. Given that theological understandings are not likely to change dramatically over one's lifetime and that a number of the clergy surveyed in 1989 were also questioned in a more recent 2001 study, we anticipate that the patterns found in the late 1980s will likely continue to hold in the most recent survey as well.

We begin our examination of theological orientations by comparing responses given by clergy and laity to various theological questions in the 2001 survey. This study examined a range of theological matters, including broad questions related to historic understandings of the Christian faith, as well as more specific items gauging Reformed interpretations of Christian faith and the ways that the Reformed Christian faith relates to the world in which we live. This examination, therefore, addresses matters of general theology, Reformed theology, and social theology.

General Theology

Table 3.1 reports responses from CRC and RCA clergy on six questions related to matters of general theology: three questions about the life and work of Jesus of Nazareth, and one each regarding the existence of the Devil, the historicity of Adam and Eve, and the nature of biblical authority. As is evident in the table, ministers in both

---

[1]   This book will adopt the conventional practice of employing the masculine pronoun when making a reference to God.

denominations continue to be highly orthodox on questions related to the life and work of Jesus and to the existence of the Devil.[2] More than five out of every six RCA, and nine out of every ten CRC pastors affirm that Jesus was born of a virgin, that he will return to earth again, that there is no other way to salvation than through Jesus Christ, and that the Devil actually exists. Relatively few respondents expressed either uncertainty or disagreement with such historic understandings of the Christian faith.

It is also clear that, on these four items, CRC pastors continue to be somewhat more orthodox in their theological expressions than RCA clergy. While there is almost universal acceptance of these positions among the CRC ministers, roughly nine in ten RCA pastors express acceptance as well. As a result, there is approximately a 10 percent difference between clergy of the two denominations. Clearly, RCA pastors are highly orthodox in their theological expressions; CRC clergy are somewhat more so.

Among the "general theology" questions on the survey, the greatest difference between CRC and RCA clergy centers on whether Adam and Eve are to be viewed as real, rather than symbolic, figures. Nine in ten CRC pastors (90 percent) accept their historicity, but fewer than three in five RCA pastors (58 percent) believe them to be real people. These differences in interpretation about the historicity of Adam and Eve do not, however, stem simply from differences in approaches to biblical authority. Despite these sizable differences between CRC and RCA pastors on the matter of Adam and Eve, the clergy of the two denominations stand much closer together on the nature of biblical authority. When asked to express their level of agreement or disagreement with the statement that the Bible constitutes the inerrant Word of God, 58 percent of CRC clergy and 45 percent of RCA clergy expressed agreement with the statement. Thus, while some differences in interpreting the historicity of Adam and Eve may result from differences in how such pastors interpret the nature of scripture, not all such differences do so.

It should be noted, however, that Reformed theology has historically differentiated between the infallible and the inerrant nature of scripture, with the former (the Bible as the infallible Word of

[2]   To examine how the positions of CRC and RCA clergy compare to those of clergy in other major evangelical and mainline Protestant denominations in the United States, see the various chapters found in Smidt (2004).

Table 3.1
Theological Positions of CRC and RCA Clergy
at the Turn of the Millennium
(Percent agreeing)

	CRC 2001	RCA 2001
General Theology		
Jesus was born of a virgin.	98%	89%
Jesus will return to earth.	98	90
The Devil actually exists.	98	87
There is no other way to salvation but through Jesus Christ.	96	84
Adam & Eve were real persons.	90	58
The Bible is the inerrant Word of God.	58	45
Reformed Theology		
God gives faith and repentance to those he has selected to be saved.	94%	79%
Humans can successfully resist the Holy Spirit's call to conversion.	16	40
Those saved can lose their salvation by failing to keep their faith.	9	14
Social Theology		
All great religions of the world are equally good and true.	2%	4%
Most churches today are not concerned enough about social justice.	66	60
Most churches are too concerned with organizational as opposed to spiritual issues.	57	71
Evangelism is the most important task of the church.	63	71
If enough people were brought to Christ, social problems would disappear.	29	41

God) being the standard interpretation of biblical authority.[3] Reformed theology has always emphasized that the Bible is the basis of religious authority and is fully trustworthy (without falsehood) relative to humanity's salvation and God's redemptive actions. Inerrancy goes further, stating that the Bible is accurate in all matters of science and history; this stance is a relatively recent doctrinal perspective for understanding the nature of biblical authority (Marsden 1980, chapter 13). This differentiation between inerrancy and infallibility is reflected in the responses given by CRC clergy to a 1993 random survey of the denomination's pastors. Respondents were asked whether they agreed with two different, but related, statements: (1) "The Bible is without errors not only in matters of faith, but in historic and scientific matters," and (2) "The Bible is an authoritative guide to salvation, but it is not necessarily authoritative in historical and scientific matters." While 33 percent of CRC pastors agreed with the first statement, 64 percent expressed agreement with the latter assertion. Moreover, among the two-thirds of CRC clergy who held that some errors related to historic and scientific matters might be contained in the Bible, nearly all (90 percent) nevertheless agreed that it is still an authoritative guide to salvation (data not shown).

Reformed Theology

As noted in chapter 2, the CRC emerged, in part, because many new Dutch immigrants in the nineteenth century believed the RCA was not sufficiently Reformed in its emphasis. Many of these early seceders felt that the RCA had become more broadly evangelical in its theological focus, reflecting the revivalist undercurrents associated with the American frontier and the Second Great Awakening. Given this historical divergence, one might anticipate that CRC clergy would adhere more fully than RCA pastors to historic Reformed doctrines, while the RCA ministers would express more general evangelical sentiments than their CRC counterparts.

---

[3] The classical formulation of the inerrancy position was only published in 1881 by Hodge and Warfield, two orthodox Calvinists teaching at Princeton Seminary. The inerrancy position argues that the scriptures not only contain, but are, the Word of God—and, consequently, are errorless in all their elements and affirmations. This emphasis upon the verbal inerrancy of scripture was obviously related to the Protestant principle of *sola scriptura*, but, in addition, it was augmented upon principles of Common Sense philosophy and Baconian science (Marsden, 1980: chapter 13).

The Reformed faith has been summarized frequently in terms of the five major points of Calvinism commonly labeled by the acronym of TULIP: Total depravity, Unconditional election, Limited atonement, Irresistible grace, and Perseverance of the saints. According to this framework of doctrinal interpretation, Reformed theology emphasizes that God elects those whom he would save, those whom God elects cannot resist his call, and those truly called by God cannot fall from grace and lose their salvation (i.e., they persevere).

These doctrinal perspectives are examined in the second portion of Table 3.1, which assesses the relative level of agreement expressed by CRC and RCA respondents in 2001 on three matters related to Reformed theology. First, in an effort to assess the doctrine of election, clergy were asked whether they agreed with the statement that "God gives faith and repentance to each individual he has selected to be saved." Second, in order to appraise the doctrine of irresistible grace, pastors were asked whether they agreed that "human beings are able to successfully resist the Holy Spirit's call to conversion." Finally, to analyze the doctrine of perseverance of the saints, ministers were asked whether "those who are saved can lose their salvation by failing to keep their faith." A Reformed position would be reflected by a response of agreement with the first statement, while a Reformed position in relationship to the second and third assertions would be signaled by a reply of disagreement.

As is evident in the second portion of Table 3.1, both CRC and RCA pastors are Reformed in their theological perspectives, but Christian Reformed clergy are somewhat more so than their Reformed Church counterparts. Basically four of five RCA ministers (79 percent) agree that "God gives faith and repentance to each individual he has selected to be saved," while nearly all CRC clergy (94 percent) responded in the same manner.[4] Likewise, relatively few CRC or RCA respondents claimed that those who are saved can lose their salvation, though slightly more RCA ministers (14 percent) than CRC clergy (9 percent) did so. Thus, in terms of the doctrines of election and perseverance of the saints, both

---

[4]   Clergy of both denominations were provided an opportunity to respond to the theological issue of election in a somewhat different fashion—namely, whether they agree with the statement, "Faith in Christ is not freely given but is part of God's gift of salvation." When using this wording, CRC ministers are still slightly more Reformed in their theology than RCA pastors, but only marginally so—as two-thirds of CRC respondents (67 percent) express agreement with the statement compared to three-fifths of RCA participants (61 percent) doing so.

CRC and RCA pastors overwhelmingly express agreement with these historic understandings of Reformed doctrine, though CRC clergy generally stand in somewhat stronger agreement than those in the RCA clergy. The clearest difference in Reformed theology emerges between the two groups in assessing their opinion about an individual's ability to resist the Holy Spirit's call to conversion. Two out of five Reformed Church clergy (40 percent) believed that human beings are able to resist that call, while only about one in six Christian Reformed pastors (16 percent) expressed such agreement.

In summary, both CRC and RCA clergy overwhelmingly stand in agreement with Reformed theology on matters of salvation, but RCA pastors are somewhat less inclined than CRC ministers to agree with perseverance of the saints. Just why there is a greater divergence between CRC and RCA clergy on this particular matter and not the previous two statements on Reformed theology is not clear. Perhaps it results from a stronger general evangelical orientation evident among the Reformed Church in America clergy. The extent to which this may be the case will be assessed more fully through the remaining portions of this chapter.

Social Theology

Table 3.1 also addresses "social theology," or perspectives on the role of the church in the world (Guth et al. 1997, 12). Generally speaking, CRC and RCA clergy adopt relatively similar positions on such matters, although some interesting minor differences emerge.

First, pastors of both denominations overwhelmingly reject the notion that "all great religions of the world are equally good and true." Fewer than one in twenty respondents in either denomination report agreement with the statement. Both CRC and RCA ministers clearly view the Christian faith as distinctive and reject placing other religious faiths on equal footing or to be judged equally true as the Christian faith.

In addition, the vast majority of clergy in both denominations tend to agree that "most churches today are not concerned enough about social justice." Interestingly, despite the RCA's affiliation with the National Council of Churches (NCC) and the NCC's historic emphasis on the "social gospel," Christian Reformed Church pastors are more likely than Reformed Church clergy to express agreement with the statement (66 percent versus 60 percent, respectively). The lower inclination of RCA pastors to affirm that churches today are insufficiently concerned about matters of social justice need not necessarily reflect a lower level of commitment to the issue of social justice itself; rather, it could simply be a reflection of the fact that they are more likely than their CRC counterparts to perceive their denomination as already emphasizing social justice to a sufficient degree.

Nevertheless, a majority of clergy in both denominations express a sense of frustration with organizational structures. While RCA ministers are more likely than CRC clergy to agree that most churches are "too concerned with organizational as opposed to spiritual issues," a majority of clergy in both denominations stand in agreement with the statement (71 percent versus 57 percent, respectively). Again, the statement does not permit us to discern whether this frustration is directed at congregational, denominational, or ecumenical structures. But, it is clear that many pastors perceive organizational matters as diverting attention away from what they deem to be a need for a more properly balanced emphasis on "spiritual issues."

While a majority of clergy in both denominations believes greater emphasis needs to be given to social justice, it does not see any need to do so at the expense of the evangelical mission of the church. Pastors of both denominations generally stand in agreement that "evangelism is the most important task of the church," with RCA clergy somewhat more likely than CRC pastors to assert this (71 percent versus 63 percent, respectively). Similarly, RCA clergy are more likely than their CRC counterparts to believe in the transformational power of evangelism. When asked whether they agreed that "if enough people are brought to faith in Jesus Christ, social problems would disappear," a majority of Christian Reformed pastors (54 percent) but only a plurality of Reformed Church ministers (43 percent) *disagree* with the statement (these specific percentages are not shown in the table).

Theological Positions: CRC Clergy and Laity

Thus far, we have examined the theological beliefs of CRC and RCA clergy. But just where do the laity stand in relationship to the clergy of their denomination? The extent to which the theological perspectives of clergy and laity mirror each other within a denomination is important because major gaps between the two can suggest a "gathering storm" that may destabilize the community. Some differences between clergy and laity are to be anticipated. Reformed clergy generally hold a higher level of educational attainment than the laity, putting the ministers in a stronger position to know and understand the nuances of the Reformed theological heritage. As a result, one might anticipate that the laity and clergy of the two denominations may well reflect similar levels of agreement with the *general theological* tenets of the Christian faith, but that the parishioners may be less likely than the pastors to espouse stands reflecting the particular historic *Reformed understandings* of the faith. Moreover, because ministers are more uniformly educated than the people they serve, one might anticipate greater levels of cohesion among clergy than members in terms of the stands they adopt on *social theology*.

Table 3.2 compares the theological stands of CRC clergy and laity at the turn of the millennium and analyzes the extent to which there may be a gap between the positions expressed by the two groups within the Christian Reformed Church. The three categories and their related questions examined in Table 3.2 are the same as those previously analyzed in Table 3.1, and therefore the percentages reported for CRC clergy in Table 3.2 are the same as those shown in Table 3.1.

General Theology

Christian Reformed Church clergy and laity stand in virtual unanimity concerning the historic tenets of the Christian faith. Nearly all pastors and parishioners agree that: (1) Jesus was born of a virgin, (2) Jesus will return to earth again some day, (3) the Devil exists, and (4) there is no other way to salvation but through Jesus Christ. Clergy exhibit a somewhat higher level of orthodoxy on these matters than church members, but both exhibit high levels of consensus, as 95 percent or more of both clergy and laity agree with these broad statements of the Christian faith. The only matter that reveals some difference between the two groups relates to the historicity of Adam and Eve. CRC laity stand in less agreement than CRC clergy about the literal existence of these biblical figures. Nevertheless, even on this matter, the vast majority of CRC members (82 percent) believe that Adam and Eve were real, rather than symbolic, figures.

Reformed Theology

With regard to Reformed theology and social theology, greater differences emerge between CRC clergy and laity. CRC clergy tend to be much more conventionally Reformed in their theological orientations than the members of the church. These differences are reflected in the

Table 3.2
Theological Positions of CRC Clergy and Laity
at the Turn of the Millennium
(Percent agreeing)

	CRC Clergy 2001	Laity 2001
General Theology		
Jesus was born of a virgin.	98%	96%
Jesus will return to earth.	98	95
The Devil actually exists.	98	95
There is no other way to salvation but through Jesus Christ.	96	96
Adam & Eve were real persons.	90	82
Reformed Theology		
God gives faith and repentance to those He has selected to be saved.	94%	72%
Humans can successfully resist the Holy Spirit's call to conversion.	16	44
Those saved can lose their salvation by failing to keep their faith.	9	34
Social Theology		
All great religions of the world are equally good and true.	2%	5%
Most churches today are not concerned enough about social justice.	66	44
Most churches are too concerned with organizational as opposed to spiritual issues.	57	30
Evangelism is the most important task of the church.	63	68
If enough people were brought to Christ, social problems would disappear.	29	42

22 to 28 percent difference between the two groups in their stance on Reformed theological matters. To varying degrees, pastors and parishioners tend to agree on the doctrine of election; 94 percent of clergy and 72 percent of laity acknowledge that "God gives faith and repentance to those he has selected to be saved." At the same time, and seemingly in contradiction with this basic tenet of predestination,

Christian Reformed Church laity are more in tune with popular evangelicalism's emphasis on the responsibility of individuals to shape their own eternal destiny. Accordingly, they are less distinctively Reformed in their positions on irresistible grace and perseverance of the saints. Nearly one-half of CRC laity believe that human beings can resist the Holy Spirit's call to conversion, and over a third agree that those who have been saved can lose their salvation by failing to keep their faith.

Social Theology

CRC clergy and laity agree on some matters of social theology, but disagree on others. Both reject the notion that all great religions of the world are equally good and true, and both generally agree that evangelism is the most important task of the church—although the parishioners are slightly more likely to affirm this priority than the ministers (68 percent versus 63 percent, respectively).

The most pronounced differences between Christian Reformed ministers and lay members emerge in assessments of the church's need to promote social justice and its emphasis on organizational, as opposed to spiritual, matters. Nearly two-thirds of CRC pastors (66 percent) agree that "most churches today are not concerned enough about social justice," while fewer than half of CRC laity (44 percent) do so. While almost three-fifths of the clergy (57 percent) assert that most churches are too concerned with organizational matters, fewer than one-third of the members (30 percent) feel the same. Finally, less than one-third of CRC ministers, but a little more than two-fifths of CRC parishioners, express confidence that Christian conversions would solve most social problems (29 percent and 42 percent, respectively). Again, this higher level of agreement expressed by CRC laity than clergy reflects the greater tendency among the laity to adopt positions reflecting broader cultural understandings of popular evangelicalism today rather than positions that reflect more distinctively Reformed understandings.

Theological Positions: RCA Clergy and Laity

We now turn our attention to the Reformed Church in America and address the same issue that we have analyzed in relationship to the Christian Reformed Church—namely, the extent to which clergy and laity stand in agreement in terms of their theological perspectives.

Table 3.3 compares the theological stands of RCA clergy and laity as reflected in 1999, and, once again, the table reports the respondents' answers to questions on general theology, Reformed theology, and social theology. However, the particular questions examined in Table 3.3 are not identical to those analyzed in the previous two tables. The RCA surveys, constructed by Luidens and Nemeth in consultation with

Table 3.3
Theological Positions of RCA Clergy and Laity
at the Turn of the Millennium
(Percent agreeing)

	RCA Clergy 2000	Laity 1999
General Theology		
God is not responsible for all the evil in the world.	85%	79%
Humans are by nature sinful.	96	89
Jesus Christ brings me into a new covenant with God.	98	94
I regard the Bible as totally authoritative for my faith.	92	85
I believe in a divine judgment after death.	85	80
Reformed Theology		
Though there is suffering in the world, God is in charge.	97%	94%
Our salvation is determined by God before we are born.	77	65
My behavior will determine whether or not I will be saved.	9	47
Social Theology		
The church should bring Christ to the whole world.	95%	85%
The primary purpose of this life is preparation for the next.	26	55
All Christians should belong to one church.	23	16
Success in this world is a sign of one's salvation.	1	6

the RCA, raised similar issues, but with different questions, than those used in the CRC surveys. Nevertheless, given that identical questions were posed to both RCA clergy and laity, one can therefore assess the extent to which they stand in agreement on theological matters.

General Theology

Reformed Church in America pastors and parishioners exhibit patterns similar to those present within the CRC. Generally speaking, RCA clergy and laity conform closely to established doctrine in terms of general theology, with ministers being slightly more orthodox than the laity on these broad measures. For example, almost all clergy (98 percent) and laity (94 percent) affirm that "Jesus Christ brings me into a new covenant with God." Overwhelming numbers of ministers and members agree that "humans are by nature sinful" (96 percent and 89 percent, respectively) and that "the Bible is totally authoritative for my faith" (92 percent and 85 percent, respectively). Sizable majorities of both groups (85 percent of pastors and 80 percent of members) respond that they "believe in a divine judgment after death where some shall be rewarded and some punished." And, similarly high numbers of clergy and laity report agreement that "God is not responsible for all the evil in the world" (85 percent and 79 percent, respectively).

Reformed Theology

The questions included in the 1999 RCA clergy and laity survey that permit an examination of adherence to uniquely Reformed theology are somewhat less direct measures than those examined in the previous two CRC tables. However, there are three items that seek to address three different historic theological understandings related to the Reformed faith: first, its assertion of the sovereignty of God; second, its emphasis on election; and third, its insistence on human depravity.

As was true for the Christian Reformed Church respondents, RCA clergy are more Reformed in their theology than RCA laity, although the extent to which they differ in their "Reformedness" varies with the particular theological issue examined. There is almost universal agreement about God's sovereignty, as both pastors and parishioners stand uniformly in accordance that "though there is suffering in the world, God is in charge" (97 percent and 94 percent agreeing, respectively). Somewhat greater disparity begins to arise when assessing the doctrine of election. More than three-quarters of RCA ministers (77 percent), but less than two-thirds of members (65 percent) believe that "our salvation is determined by God before we are born." But with regard to human depravity, there is even greater divergence, as less than one-tenth of RCA pastors (9 percent) affirm that human behavior in some way affects one's salvation, while nearly half (47 percent) of RCA lay members do so.

Social Theology

RCA clergy and laity tend to differ more in terms of their stands on social theology than in terms of their positions related to general theology—a pattern similar to that found within the CRC. The greatest differences between RCA pastors and members lie in their contrasting understandings of the primary purpose of life on earth. While a majority of Reformed Church members (55 percent) express agreement that "the primary purpose of this life is preparation for the next," only about one-quarter of the ministers do so (26 percent). Important, but less dramatic, differences separate the two groups on the importance of world evangelism. Virtually all RCA pastors (95 percent) and an overwhelming majority of RCA parishioners (85 percent) agree that "the church should bring Christ to the whole world." Nevertheless, this 10-percentage-point difference on this matter is greater than any gap found on statements about general theology. Somewhat smaller disparities exist with regard to the importance of church union, as relatively few RCA clergy and laity express agreement that "all Christians should belong to one church." On this ecumenical issue, Reformed Church ministers are more prone to agree than are their church members (23 percent versus 16 percent, respectively). Only on an item tapping orientations toward the "health and wealth" gospel do we find widespread agreement between clergy and laity; both groups overwhelming reject the notion that "success in this world is a sign of one's salvation."

Theological Positions: CRC and RCA Laity

Thus far we have analyzed similarities and differences between CRC and RCA clergy, between CRC clergy and laity, and between RCA clergy and laity. We have found that there is considerable consensus within and across these groups when examining basic Christian theology. Differences between CRC and RCA clergy were primarily evident in terms of Reformed and social theology, with CRC clergy being somewhat more conventionally Reformed in their theology than RCA clergy. Clergy in both denominations were also somewhat more Reformed in their theology than the laity within their respective denominations. Given these patterns, we would anticipate that CRC laity would be more Reformed in their theology than RCA laity, but it is unclear just how much so. Neither is it clear just how identical are the theological stands of CRC and RCA laity in terms of general theology or social theology. So it is to these matters that we now turn our attention.

To facilitate comparisons with the theological stands of RCA laity, the CRC laity survey of 2001 included various questions that had been asked in the RCA laity survey of 1999. As can be seen from Table 3.4, these identical questions are the very same questions just analyzed in Table 3.3. As a result, the percentages presented for RCA laity in Table 3.4 are the same as those presented in Table 3.3 and are simply reported again for ease of comparison with CRC laity.

General Theology

Christian Reformed and Reformed Church members adopt relatively similar general theological positions. Both tend to be highly orthodox on these broad measures of Christian faith, with the CRC respondents being slightly more orthodox than those from the RCA. For example, almost all (96 percent of CRC laity and 94 percent of the RCA laity) affirm that "Jesus Christ brings me into a new covenant with God." Furthermore, while nearly all CRC parishioners (97 percent) agree that "humans are by nature sinful," almost all RCA members (89 percent) do so as well. Similar patterns prevail in terms of views of biblical authority, as nearly all CRC laity (95 percent) responded that they agreed that "the Bible is totally authoritative for my faith," while almost all RCA did so as well (85 percent). CRC laity were somewhat more likely than RCA laity to indicate that they "believe in a divine judgment after death where some shall be rewarded and some punished" (91 percent versus 80 percent, respectively), while relatively similar numbers report agreement that "God is not responsible for all the evil in the world" (84 percent and 79 percent, respectively). Clearly, on these matters of general theology, almost all CRC and RCA laity exhibit high levels of orthodoxy, with CRC laity generally responding in a somewhat more orthodox fashion than RCA laity.

Table 3.4
Theological Positions of CRC and RCA Laity
at the Turn of the Millennium
(Percent agreeing)

	CRC 2001	RCA 1999
General Theology		
God is not responsible for the evil in the world.	84%	79%
Humans are by nature sinful.	97	89
Jesus Christ brings me into a new covenant with God.	96	94
I regard the Bible as totally authoritative for my faith.	95	85
I believe in a divine judgment after death.	91	80
Reformed Theology		
Though there is suffering in the world, God is in charge.	97%	94%
Our salvation is determined by God before we are born.	84	65
My behavior will determine whether I will be saved.	21	47
Social Theology		
The church should bring Christ to the whole world.	93%	85%
The primary purpose of this life is preparation for the next.	42	55
All Christians should belong to one church.	18	16
Success in this world is a sign of one's salvation.	6	6

Reformed Theology

As expected, CRC members are more Reformed[5] in their theology than the RCA, though the extent to which this is the case varies with the particular theological issue at hand. There is almost universal agreement among the laity of both denominations concerning God's sovereignty, as both CRC and RCA believers stand uniformly in agreement that "though there is suffering in the world, God is in charge" (97 percent and 94 percent, respectively). Greater differences emerge on the doctrine of election where five in six of CRC respondents (84 percent) report that "our salvation is determined by God before we are born," while slightly fewer than two-thirds of RCA laity (65 percent) agree. However, the greatest variation arises when questions are raised about the doctrine of human depravity and the extent to which behavior helps to determine salvation. Less than one quarter of Christian Reformed believers (21 percent) respond that one's behavior helps shape one's salvation, while nearly half of all Reformed Church members (47 percent) hold this conviction.

Social Theology

With regard to social theology, differences between CRC and RCA members tend to be somewhat less pronounced than that found with regard to Reformed theology. Both Christian Reformed and Reformed Church members reject the "health and wealth" gospel with equal vigor, as only six percent of parishioners in both denominations report that "success in this world is a sign of one's salvation." Similarly low numbers of laity in both groups agree that "all Christians should belong to one church" (18 percent versus 16 percent for CRC and RCA, respectively). And, both CRC and RCA members (93 percent and 85 percent, respectively) strongly believe that "the church should bring Christ to the whole world."

Only with regard to one item do differences between CRC and RCA laity exceed 10 percent on such matters of social theology. While

---

5   As noted previously, the theological items used in the RCA laity survey of 1999 were somewhat less direct measures of adherence to Reformed theology than those previously examined for CRC clergy and membership (see Table 3.2). Still, three items address theological matters related to the Reformed faith—namely, the sovereignty of God, election, and human depravity—and enable us to compare adherence to Reformed theology among laity in the two denominations.

a majority of RCA members (55 percent) express agreement that "the primary purpose of this life is preparation for the next," fewer than half the CRC laity (42 percent) respond this way.

Patterns in Theological Orientations

Having examined and compared the theological beliefs of CRC and RCA clergy and membership as a whole, we now turn our attention to two additional issues that will be the focus of the remainder of this chapter. First, do important differences exist between sub-groups within either the ranks of the clergy or the laity? And, secondly, are there notable changes to response patterns over the latter decades of the twentieth century?

While a variety of factors may contribute to differences in the theological positions among clergy and laity, such factors are not necessarily likely to be the same for both groups. For example, while differences in the level of educational attainment may well affect responses given by parishioners to theological questions, schooling will likely have less effect in accounting for differences among clergy as their levels of education attainment exhibit much less variation. Likewise, while there may be notable regional differences in the theological positions of CRC and RCA members (particularly within the RCA), the mobility of clergy from congregations in one region of the country to another may well mute regional differences within their ranks. On the other hand, age is one factor that may have a profound impact on the theologies of both clergy and laity. As the historical narrative in chapter 2 suggests, there has been a gradual edging away from the Reformed heritage in both the RCA and, more recently, in the CRC. Given such erosion of tradition over time, are younger pastors and parishioners then less orthodox and Reformed than the older generations they are replacing?

Clergy

Table 3.5 examines patterns of general theological orthodoxy and support for Reformed doctrine found among Christian Reformed and Reformed Church clergy and laity broken down in terms of different age groups. As identical questions were not asked of all the respondents, two different assessments of general theological orthodoxy as well as Reformed doctrine must be presented. These different assessments reflect the different belief statements presented in Table 3.1 and Table

3.4. However, while this limitation prohibits any direct comparisons of the absolute levels of orthodoxy (or Reformed doctrine) across these two different approaches employed for each theological orientation, the use of two different approaches for each does provide an added benefit—namely, it allows us to assess whether the pattern evident with the use of one battery of statements is also evident when a different battery of statements is used. If similar patterns are evident, regardless of the specific measures employed, then there is greater confidence that the patterns reflect real patterns and are not simply a function of the particular statements employed to assess levels of adherence to orthodoxy or Reformed doctrine.

Clearly, CRC clergy are highly orthodox and generally Reformed in terms of their theology and tend to be somewhat more orthodox and Reformed in theological stands than their RCA counterparts. On broad tenets of Christianity as measured by the first four "general theology" questions found in Table 3.1, nearly all Christian Reformed clergy (97 percent) can be classified as orthodox, while more than four out of five Reformed Church clergy (81 percent) are similarly grouped. And while more than half of CRC ministers (57 percent) are fully Reformed in their theological stands based on the three queries assessing Reformed theology shown in Table 3.1, only about one third of RCA respondents (35 percent) can be so classified.

However, what is more revealing are the patterns of orthodoxy and Reformed doctrine when examining clergy based on their years in the ministry. What is noteworthy is that the most recent Christian Reformed and Reformed Church ministerial graduates, rather than those who have served in the ministry longer, are among the most orthodox and Reformed in their doctrinal positions.[6] Among RCA clergy, the percentage of those who are most orthodox and Reformed in their doctrinal positions *declines* as one moves from those who have served in the ministry for less than twelve years to those who have served twenty-five years or more. But all CRC clergy, despite their length of tenure, are strongly orthodox on these measures of "general theology."

This pattern of the more newly ordained clergy being more orthodox than clergy who have served longer in the ministry also reflects the patterns found regarding historic Reformed doctrine. As can be seen in the bottom portion of Table 3.5, both CRC and RCA clergy who have served twelve years or less in the ministry are more likely than

---

6   Actually, this pattern is not unique to CRC and RCA clergy; it tends to be true among Protestant clergy as a whole (Smidt 2004, chapter 23).

Table 3.5
Longevity Patterns in Theological Orientation
Among CRC and RCA Clergy and Laity
(Percent agreeing)

| | Clergy | | | Laity | |
	CRC	RCA		CRC	RCA
Historic Orthodoxy #1*	97%	81%		95%	x
Years in Ministry			*Age*		
12 years or less	98%	86%	Under 40	93%	x
13 thru 24 years	94	82	40-59	94	x
25 years or more	99	75	60+	97	x
Historic Orthodoxy #2**	x	89%		89%	75%
Years in Ministry			*Age*		
12 years or less	x	92%	Under 40	84%	75%
13 thru 24 years	x	89	40-59	90	77
25 years or more	x	86	60+	93	74

Historic Reformed #1+	57%	35%		27%	x
Years in Ministry			*Age*		
12 years or less	63%	47%	Under 40	21%	x
13 thru 24 years	58	34	40-59	26	x
25 years or more	51	29	60+	33	x
Historic Reformed #2++	x	80%		74%	44%
Years in Ministry			*Age*		
12 years or less	x	83%	Under 40	70%	43%
13 thru 24 years	x	82	40-59	75	47
25 years or more	x	75	60+	77	40

* Based on agreement with the first four items under general theology found in Table 3.1

** Based on agreement with the first four items under general theology found in Table 3.4

+ Based on agreement with the three items on Reformed theology found in Table 3.1

++ Based on agreement with the three items on Reformed theology found in Table 3.4

more experienced pastors to subscribe to positions reflective of historic Reformed doctrine. While the nature of the questions asked affects the relative level to which clergy express agreement with such statements,[7] the pattern is consistent. Despite the different formulations of such statements, less experienced ministers are more likely to subscribe to these statements of Reformed doctrine than are those who have served longer in the ministry.

Laity

Table 3.5 also examines differences in the theological positions of CRC and RCA laity within three age groups (under forty years, those forty to fifty-nine years of age, and those sixty years and older). Consistent with the patterns evident in Tables 3.1 and 3.4, Christian Reformed and Reformed Church members tend to be less orthodox on the general theology and Reformed theology measures than are their pastors. However, when examined in terms of "Historic Orthodoxy #1," virtually all CRC parishioners (95 percent) can be classified as orthodox based on the four statements of general theology found in Table 3.1, a level of widespread adherence that is comparable to that found among CRC clergy (97 percent). Using slightly different items (i.e., "Historical Orthodoxy #2"), a somewhat greater difference was found between RCA ministers and members. A higher percentage of RCA pastors than parishioners (89 percent versus 75 percent, respectively) stand in agreement with the statements used to assess Christian orthodoxy.[8]

But identical items can be used to compare CRC and RCA laity ("Historic Orthodoxy #2"). In so doing, members of the CRC are found to be slightly more orthodox than their RCA counterparts in their doctrinal positions, with 89 percent of CRC versus 75 percent of RCA laity being classified as theologically orthodox. This difference in levels of theological orthodoxy found among laity in the two denominations

---

[7]   This can be seen by comparing the relative level of agreement among RCA clergy on those questions contained in what is labeled "Historic Reformed #1" with the level of agreement among the same RCA clergy on those questions contained in what is labeled "Historic Reformed #2."

[8]   Again, one must be cautious in interpreting the absolute level of adherence to Christian orthodoxy, since it depends to some extent on the nature of the specific questions asked. Compare, for example, the relative level of orthodoxy found among CRC laity when the questions comprising the first measure of Christian orthodoxy are used (ninety-five percent) rather than the questions associated with the second measure of orthodoxy (eighty-nine percent).

is a function of the lower levels of orthodoxy expressed by those RCA members in the East, as only fifty-five percent of RCA members along the eastern seaboard can be classified as "orthodox" on these basic tenets of Christian tradition (data not shown).

However, CRC and RCA laity tend to diverge more substantially when assessing their relative levels of adherence to Reformed doctrine. While RCA laity are clearly orthodox in terms of Christian faith, they are much less "Reformed" in their doctrinal positions than their CRC counterparts. Whereas 74 percent of Christian Reformed parishioners can be classified as subscribing to Reformed doctrine based on their level of agreement to the three questions relating to Reformed theology in Table 3.4, less than half that number (44 percent) of the Reformed Church in America laity fall within that grouping (with only 24 percent of RCA laity in the East being so classified).

Finally, there is another important pattern evident in Table 3.5. Whereas clergy with fewer years in the ministry (and therefore, in many cases, younger in age) are the most orthodox and Reformed, it is the older segments of the laity who are the most orthodox and Reformed. This is most clearly evident in the CRC. In the RCA, there are fewer differences among age groups. However, such age differences become somewhat more evident when regions of the country are examined. Among RCA members in the Midwest, orthodoxy increases as age increases, but in the East, the middle-aged RCA parishioners are the most orthodox. And, in terms of Reformed doctrine, the middle-aged laity exhibit the highest level of adherence regardless of region (data not shown).

Creeds and Confessions

To this point we have examined the extent to which CRC and RCA clergy and laity express agreement with statements related to historic Christian interpretations and more specifically Reformed theological traditions. Another approach to assessing theological beliefs and positions in the confessional Reformed tradition is to ask respondents about their level of awareness of, and the amount of importance they attribute to, historic confessional documents. Down through the ages, Christians have attempted to formulate distinct statements of their unique theological beliefs and perspectives.[9] Sometimes these

9   Of course, members of some religious traditions have rejected the notion of confessions as a way of seeking Christian unity—promoting instead fundamental statements such as "no creed but Christ."

affirmations are relatively broad and encompassing, emphasizing foundational beliefs for all Christians in all circumstances. At other times, their assertions are attempts to reflect distinct theological emphases and perspectives within the Christian faith that respond to peculiar historic contingencies.

Both the CRC and RCA recognize confessional statements from each of these categories. On the one hand, both denominations share with churches throughout Western Christendom adherence to the Apostles' Creed as a seminal confessional profession of Christian faith. But, along with these broader ecumenical affirmations,[10] both denominations recognize confessional statements that articulate uniquely historic Reformed theological understandings. As mentioned in chapter 2, the CRC and RCA share three confessional standards: the Belgic Confession, the Heidelberg Catechism, and the Canons of Dort. In fact, so central are these creedal statements that, in order to be ordained in either denomination, one must affirm adherence and loyalty to these three standards of unity.

Outside observers may suspect that clergy and lay members of the RCA do not take these standards very seriously. But, according to John Hesselink (1983, 278), former president of Western Theological Seminary (1973-1985), the Reformed Church in America has, in recent years, seen a greater "stress on Calvin, our standards and our Reformed heritage than when I was a student at Western (1951-53) or when my father attended Western (1921-24)!" Consequently, regardless of whatever differences may have existed previously, Hesselink (1983, 279) maintains that the graduates of Calvin and Western Seminaries today "share a similar training in the same confessions." Thus, any differences in loyalty to these confessional statements that may have existed previously between clergy of the two denominations has, in all likelihood, narrowed considerably—at least in the Midwest.

To what extent, then, are CRC and RCA clergy and laity familiar with these creeds and confessions? To what extent do they deem them to be important? And have there been any changes in awareness of, and loyalty to, these statements on the part of clergy and laity over time? It is to these questions that we now turn our attention.

---

[10]   These are not the full list of all the confessional statements recognized by the two denominations. Besides the Apostles' Creed, the two other major ecumenical creeds are the Nicene Creed and the Athanasian Creed.

CRC and RCA Clergy

Christian Reformed and Reformed Church ministers were asked about the relative level of importance the historic Apostles' Creed and the three Reformed confessions hold in their own personal religious faith. Specifically, clergy were asked the extent to which these four confessions were viewed to be "extremely" or "quite" important to their faith.[11] As is evident in Table 3.6, considerable differences exist among CRC and RCA pastors with respect to the relative importance attributed to the four confessional standards. Clearly, the most highly valued statement of faith among both CRC and RCA clergy is the Apostles' Creed, with approximately nine in ten ministers reporting that profession to be extremely or quite important to their faith (93 percent versus 87 percent, respectively). Ranking second in influence among pastors of both denominations is the Heidelberg Catechism.

Table 3.6
Creedal Awareness and Creedal Salience
of CRC and RCA Clergy and Laity
at the Turn of the Millennium
(Percent agreeing)

	Clergy		Laity	
	CRC	RCA	CRC	RCA
Heard of:				
Apostles' Creed	x	x	99%	98%
Heidelberg Catechism	x	x	97	77
Belgic Confession	x	x	93	43
Canons of Dort	x	x	89	34
Relative Importance of:				
Apostles' Creed	93%*	87%	89%	87%
Heidelberg Catechism	87	77	82	68
Belgic Confession	70	41	61	54
Canons of Dort	51	30	44	38

* percentage reflects those who answered either "extremely" or "quite" important
x question not asked in survey

---

[11]   Other options provided included "fairly" important, "not too" important, or "not at all" important.

And clergy in both denominations similarly ranked the Belgic Confession and the Canons of Dort in descending order in terms of their relative importance.

While clergy of both denominations are, generally speaking, equally supportive of the Apostles' Creed, CRC clergy are slightly more likely than their RCA counterparts to attribute prominence to the Heidelberg Catechism. More than five of six CRC pastors (87 percent) report that the catechism is important to their faith, but so do more than three-quarters of all RCA ministers (77 percent).

However, differences between the CRC and RCA clergy become much more pronounced with regard to the Belgic Confession and the Canons of Dort. Whereas seven out of ten CRC clergy (70 percent) indicate that the Belgic Confession is extremely or quite important to their faith, barely four of ten RCA pastors (41 percent) express the same. And while a bare majority of CRC ministers (51 percent) report the Canons of Dort to be of importance, less than one-third of RCA respondents (30 percent) do so.

CRC and RCA Laity

The Apostles' Creed holds, among CRC and RCA laity, a unique position compared to the other confessional statements. First, it is the only major creed that is universally recognized; virtually all of CRC and RCA members (99 percent and 98 percent, respectively) report having heard of the Apostles' Creed. Second, it is almost equally valued across both denominations—as nearly nine out of ten members of each denomination who have heard of the creed view it to be either extremely or quite important to their faith.

However, when one moves to confessions that are more explicitly associated with the Reformed faith, significant variations emerge. Almost all CRC members indicate that they have *heard of* the three Reformed confessions, with the Canons of Dort receiving the lowest recognition level (89 percent). But CRC parishioners do not attribute equal value to these confessional statements. While an overwhelming majority of CRC members (82 percent) indicate that they value the Heidelberg Catechism as being important to their faith, fewer than half of Christian Reformed laity (44 percent) who have heard of the Canons of Dort attribute importance to it in their religious life.

Significantly, these three confessional statements do not have the same stature in the RCA as they do in the CRC. While the vast majority of RCA members (77 percent) report having heard of the Heidelberg

Catechism, only small segments of the group recognize either the Belgic Confession (43 percent) or the Canons of Dort (34 percent). Of the RCA members who have heard of these Reformed confessional statements, only the Heidelberg Catechism holds notable significance to their belief; two-thirds (68 percent) report it as being important to their faith. Of the one-third of RCA laity who are familiar with the Canons of Dort, only a small segment (38 percent) view it as having any relative importance to their faith.

Given these particular levels of awareness and attributed importance, the question arises as to whether these levels reflect a decline in awareness and salience of these creedal statements over time. We do not have data to assess changes among CRC clergy and laity (who show remarkably strong allegiance to the creeds in any case); we do have data that enable us to compare the responses of RCA clergy and laity at the turn of the millennium with the responses provided in earlier surveys. These data are reported in Table 3.7.

Table 3.7
Creedal Awareness and Creedal Salience
of RCA Clergy and Laity
at the Turn of the Millennium
(Percent agreeing)

	RCA Clergy			RCA Laity		
	1986	1991	2000	1986	1991	1999
Heard of:						
Apostles' Creed	x	x	x	#	99%	98%
Heidelberg Catechism	x	x	x	#	82	77
Belgic Confession	x	x	x	#	50	43
Canons of Dort	x	x	x	#	41	34
Relative Importance of:						
Apostles' Creed	87%*	91%	87%	#	86%	87%
Heidelberg Catechism	74	77	77	#	67	68
Belgic Confession	29	36	41	#	55	54
Canons of Dort	20	25	30	#	39	38

x   question not asked
question asked in a different format which precludes direct comparisons
*   percentage reflects those who answered either "extremely" or "quite" important

Several interesting patterns are evident among RCA ministers and members. First, among Reformed Church in America clergy, the relative importance attributed to the Apostles' Creed and the Heidelberg Catechism has remained constant. In each of the surveys over the past fifteen years, nine out of ten RCA ministers rank the Apostles' Creed, and three out of four RCA pastors include the Heidelberg Catechism, as being extremely or quite important to them.

However, noticeable changes are evident among RCA clergy in the levels of influence they assign to the Belgic Confession and the Canons of Dort. Thus, the second significant pattern is that, over the past two decades, there has been a growing appreciation of these historic Reformed Confessions among RCA pastors. While the RCA clergy still rank below CRC ministers in the levels of importance they attribute to the Belgic Confession and the Canons of Dort (see Table 3.6), it is likely, however, that such differences have narrowed considerably over the past fifteen years.

Third, in contrast, there has been a noticeable decline in awareness of these historical Reformed confessions among the RCA laity. Over the 1990s, there was a 5 to 7 percent decline in recognition of each of the three Reformed creeds among RCA parishioners, signaling a gradual loss of connection with the foundational standards of the Reformed tradition among members of the denomination. Nevertheless, among those RCA parishioners who continue to recognize these historic confessions, there is a remarkable consistency in the importance they attribute to these historical Reformed confessions.

Conclusion

Several important conclusions can be drawn from the analysis presented in this chapter. Some conclusions offer considerable comfort about the health and vitality of the two denominations; other conclusions may be viewed as more troubling in nature.

First, with regard to the thesis of secularization, the data drawn from the laity surveys of the CRC and RCA suggest little, if any, decline in adherence to basic tenets of the Christian faith. Members of the CRC and RCA continue to express overwhelming levels of agreement with a number of historic and important tenets of orthodox Christian interpretations of the faith. The life, death, and resurrection of Jesus Christ continue to be the foundation of those who are members of the two denominations, as CRC and RCA laity almost uniformly subscribe to such doctrinal tenets that Jesus Christ was born of a virgin, is the foundation of our salvation, and will be coming again in glory. And there is almost near unanimity about the central role and importance that the Apostles' Creed plays in the religious faith of members of both denominations.

Second, there is little evidence of any major gap in the perspectives of clergy and laity within either denomination—gaps that might suggest some "gathering storm" within the body. While one should expect some differences between the viewpoints of clergy and parishioners based on their different levels of education and theological training, such differences, though apparent, do not appear to be of sufficient magnitude to suggest any critical divergence in the basic theological understandings and positions of clergy and laity within either the CRC or RCA.

Third, these data reveal that CRC and RCA clergy continue to be highly orthodox in their theological viewpoints. When compared to the theological views of clergy in other Protestant denominations, CRC and RCA clergy fall between those doctrinal positions reported by clergy in other evangelical and mainline denominations.[12] Perhaps this is not too surprising, given the nature of the Reformed faith, with its emphasis on theological reflection within the bounds of historic orthodoxy. Clergy in the CRC and RCA continue to command much of the middle ground theologically—standing between those clergy from more evangelical, and more "theologically conservative," denominations and those clergy from more mainline, and more "theologically liberal," denominations.

Fourth, the data reveal that younger clergy are both more orthodox and Reformed than older, more experienced, clergy. Regardless of whether or not one might view the survey formulation of the doctrinal positions investigated as being too simplistic an expression of that doctrinal understanding, the data provide some assurance that newly ordained CRC and RCA clergy are *not* standing *outside* the historic interpretations of the Reformed Christian faith. At worst, clergy are less willing to articulate more nuanced positions and more willing to subscribe to relatively simplistic statements; at best,

[12] This can be discerned from examining the tables on theological views found in the separate chapters of Smidt (2004). Though each chapter is devoted to analyzing a specific denomination, the questions in the second table of each chapter examine identical questions related to the theological stands of clergy in that particular denomination. By comparing the responses of clergy across the sixteen denominations surveyed that fall within either evangelical or mainline Protestantism, one can discern this pattern.

clergy who graduated from seminary since 1989 continue to be equally, if not more strongly, rooted in their Christian faith and Reformed understanding of that faith than those clergy who entered the ministry roughly between 1960 and 1989.

Fifth, the data analyzed in this chapter reveal that there is considerable similarity in the theological viewpoints of both CRC and RCA clergy and CRC and RCA laity. There appears to be wide consensus within these denominations about the central tenets of Christianity; what might be called a "generic Protestantism" is a given in the lives of both pastors and lay members. The primacy of Christ, born of a virgin, source of salvation, and coming again in glory, is widely held. While more variation exists between the RCA and CRC clergy on biblical interpretation, there is much less variance between the laity from the two denominations on the authority of scripture.

However, more troubling may be the findings related to the historic Reformed articles of faith. Greater differences between the denominations—and between clergy and laity within each denomination—are apparent on these doctrinal understandings. Similarly, there is divergence among the responding groups on matters of social theology and the appropriate ethical implications of their beliefs. In all these variations, the CRC ministers and members are more conventionally Reformed than their RCA counterparts.

The most significant differences among the groups are seen in their awareness of and support for the historic creeds of the Reformed tradition. The Heidelberg Catechism receives recognition and support from the vast majority of CRC and RCA members and ministers. However, there has been a substantial drop in awareness of the Reformed creeds among RCA members over the past ten years, and among those who are aware of such creeds, the Belgic Confession and Canons of Dort are more unevenly assigned importance by members of the two denominations. Once again, the pattern observed earlier is apparent: CRC clergy and laity show greater support for these tenets of faith than do RCA respondents, and within each denomination, the clergy rank them to be more important than do the laity.

Thus, this analysis of faith and beliefs within the CRC and RCA shows the groups to hold much in common. Yet, it is also important to recognize that the greatest similarities are on those matters that might be considered more general to North American Protestantism—most specifically evangelical Protestantism. On more classically Reformed measures, whether those involving specific tenets of faith or those assessing knowledge of and allegiance to the historic creeds of the Reformed tradition, divergences are more apparent. Of course, some of these differences between the two denominations can be attributed to the regional differences found within the RCA. But the regional character of the RCA cannot be ignored; it has been, and will continue to be, an important facet of the character of denominational life in the RCA.

CHAPTER 4

'Oh, For a Closer Walk with Thee'? Religious Practices and Loyalties within the CRC and RCA

While their distinctive histories have resulted in different denominational structures, the common theological roots of the Christian Reformed Church and the Reformed Church in America remain. As revealed in the previous chapter, the theological positions of clergy and laity on basic matters of the Christian faith are relatively similar, both within and across the two denominations. And, though there are varying degrees of support for the traditional creeds of the Reformed faith across the two denominations, only minor variations in stands on orthodoxy or Reformed doctrine are evident. Finally, some evidence in the previous chapter suggests that there may be growing convergence in the theological positions of CRC and RCA clergy and laity over time, as the RCA becomes more orthodox and the CRC moves out of its historic separatism.

This chapter shifts the focus from the theological beliefs to the religious practices of laity and clergy of the two denominations. Not only are religious practices distinct from theological beliefs, but the former reflect a certain level of personal investment of time and energy that the latter do not. Consequently, an analysis of the religious practices of Christian Reformed and Reformed clergy and members provides a glimpse into the relative levels of commitment clergy and parishioners exhibit in relationship to their faith. Of course, it is true that these assessed levels of relative commitment depend, in part, on the specific kinds of religious practices one chooses to analyze. But, in analyzing the religious practices of CRC and RCA clergy and laity, we report simply those patterns for which we have comparable data.

This chapter, therefore, compares and contrasts the religious practices and levels of commitment reported by laity and clergy from both denominations. In addition to making comparisons within and between denominations, we will examine trends over time and make comparisons with religious practice and commitment found among other Protestant communions. Finally, we will explore factors responsible for the differences in religious practices between the two denominations.

Religious Practices
Comparing CRC and RCA Laity and Clergy

While surveys of CRC clergy did not inquire about their religious practices, the surveys of CRC laity and of RCA clergy and laity did. As a result, we are able to provide information on four basic measures of religious practice: Bible reading, prayer, church attendance, and family devotions. Respondents were asked to indicate the frequency with which they participate in each of these religious activities. Basic comparisons can be made between and among the three groups—RCA laity and clergy and CRC laity—for each of these measures of religious involvement.

The data presented in Table 4.1 suggest a number of similarities as well as some distinct differences among the three groups. Reformed Church ministers (as one might expect) are more likely to pray than either of the lay groups. Nevertheless, daily prayer is uniformly high among parishioners of both denominations, as the overwhelming

Table 4.1
Religious Practices of RCA and CRC
Members: 2000
(Percent reporting)

	RCA Clergy	RCA Laity	CRC Laity
Pray Daily	95%	84%	89%
Read the Bible daily	76	33	58
Attend church weekly	NA	73	88
Conduct family devotions	38	26	63

NA = not applicable; question not asked of RCA clergy.

majority of CRC and RCA laity report praying daily. Between the two groups of laity, a higher percentage of CRC than RCA lay members pray daily (89 percent versus 84 percent, respectively). This pattern—namely, that CRC laity are more likely that RCA laity to report that they engage in the religious practice under examination—is one that continues throughout these comparisons.

Regular church attendance among RCA and CRC laity is also extraordinarily high, with more than seven out of ten RCA members reporting weekly church attendance and an astonishing nine out of ten CRC members doing so. Once again, while both groups report high levels of church attendance, the participation level among CRC members is somewhat higher than among RCA parishioners.

Table 4.1 also reveals clear differences among the three groups in terms of their regularity of Bible reading. Over three-fourths of RCA clergy report that they read their Bibles daily; again, it is not surprising that RCA ministers significantly out-pace laity from either denomination on this particular religious practice. Between the two lay groups, however, the established pattern reappears—nearly twice as many CRC lay members report reading their Bibles daily than do RCA laity (58 percent versus 33 percent, respectively).

Important differences also appear between the two denominations when examining daily family devotions. Christian Reformed laity engage in daily family devotions far more frequently than either RCA ministers or members (63 percent, 38 percent, and 26 percent respectively). However, one explanation for the denominational differences with regard to this particular practice is embedded in the manner by which the question was phrased in each survey. Christian Reformed Church members were first asked whether there was anyone living in their household with whom they could have family devotions. Respondents who answered affirmatively were then asked the frequency with which they held family devotions. In the RCA surveys, all respondents were asked how often they had family devotions, with "daily" as one of the options. Thus, a substantial portion of the difference observed between CRC and RCA members is due to the phrasing of the survey items, as the RCA survey captured segments of the laity that were excluded from the CRC data. Despite these limitations, however, it is still likely that CRC members display a higher level of participation in family devotions than do RCA members, given the differences between CRC and RCA laity revealed in the other religious practices examined in the table.

The data in Table 4.1 provide a snapshot of religious practices among Reformed members at the turn of the millennium, and they suggest some distinct differences in religious practice. First, CRC members are more active in their religious practices than are RCA members; and second, clergy are more active than laity. On the face of these data, there appears to be a higher level of religious involvement prevailing in the CRC than in the RCA.

However, one might anticipate that the relative level of frequency with which these religious practices are conducted by laity within each denomination is shaped, in part, by a number of other factors. In particular, one might anticipate that the age and geographical location of the respondent might play a part. Older people are more likely than younger people to devote time to prayer and Bible reading. The same may be true for church attendance, but it is likely that the practice of regular church attendance is less affected by the age of the respondent than the practice of daily Bible reading. Perhaps, then, some of the differences in religious practices between the two denominations found in Table 4.1 is a function of different age or regional groups within the ranks of CRC and RCA members. Consequently, Table 4.2 examines the relative levels of reported daily prayers, daily Bible reading, and weekly church attendance by laity in each of the two denominations according to the age and regional location of such respondents.

Several important patterns emerge from the data presented in Table 4.2. First, some, though not all, differences in denominational patterns are related to sociodemographic differences within the ranks of members of the two denominations, as denominational differences in religious practices do not disappear entirely when one compares similar age categories or similar regional locations of lay members of each denomination. For each of the age groups and for each of the regional groups analyzed, CRC members are still more likely than RCA members to report that they pray daily, read their Bible daily, or attend church weekly.

Second, the oldest members within both denominations are the most likely to report that they engage in such religious practices, while the youngest age groups are the least likely to do so. There is a monotonic increase in the percentage of people reporting that they pray daily, read the Bible daily, or attend church weekly, as one moves from those less than forty years of age, to those "middle aged," to those sixty years or older—regardless of denominational membership.

Third, the youngest members of the CRC and RCA are the most

Table 4.2
Religious Practices of RCA and CRC Members in 2000
by Age and Regional Location
(Percent reporting)

	CRC Laity	RCA Laity
Pray Daily	89%	84%
Less than 40 years	82	79
40 to 59 years	88	81
60 years plus	96	88
Midwest	92%	87%
East	91	74
Rest	85	88
Read Bible Daily	58%	33%
Less than 40 years	32	19
40 to 59 years	59	26
60 years plus	85	46
Midwest	58%	37%
East	56	21
Rest	60	39
Attend Church Weekly	88%	73%
Less than 40 years	78	63
40 to 59 years	89	71
60 years plus	95	79
Midwest	88%	79%
East	92	59
Rest	84	74

alike in terms of their religious practices. When differences in religious practices are examined by age groups, the magnitude of the differences between CRC and RCA members is smallest for the youngest age category. Thus, while there are still important differences between the religious practices of the youngest CRC laity and their RCA counterparts, such differences appear to be narrowing as younger generations replace the older generations of laity within the two denominations.

Fourth, the different regional composition of each denomination also contributes to the divergent levels of religious practices observed across the two denominations, but it does not fully account for such differences. While the magnitude of differences in the level of reported religious practices found between CRC and RCA laity is smallest among those members who reside in the Midwest, there are still differences in reported levels of religious practices among midwestern CRC and RCA laity. Thus, differences in regional distribution contribute to, but do not fully explain, denominational differences in reported levels of daily prayer, daily Bible reading, or weekly church attendance.

However, this static picture of religious involvement presented in Tables 4.1 and 4.2 can be enriched if it is compared to data from previous years. Trend data allow us to examine possible long-term continuities or changes in the religious practice among the members of the two denominations. As data related to reported levels of Bible reading, prayer, church attendance, and family devotions are available for RCA members in clergy in 1986, 1991, and 2000, and for CRC members in 1992[1] and 2000, these data are examined in Table 4.3.

Given the often-heard remarks that religious commitment in American public life is declining, one might expect a decline in this

Table 4.3
Trends in Religious Practices of RCA and CRC Respondents
(Percent reporting)

	RCA Clergy			RCA Laity			CRC Laity	
	1986	1991	2000	1986	1991	2000	1992	2000
Pray Daily	92%	95%	95%	77%	80%	84%	86%	89%
Read the Bible daily	74	76	76	31	31	33	64	58
Attend church weekly	NA	NA	NA	70	70	73	89	88
Conduct family devotions	56	46	38	29	30	26	60	63

NA = not applicable; question not asked of RCA clergy.

---

[1] The 1992 CRC laity survey was primarily a survey assessing laity evaluation of various denominational agencies. It did contain a few questions relevant for analysis in this chapter. However, because the survey did not examine other topics addressed in this volume, it is not used in other chapters.

religious practice. But it is obvious that the importance of private prayer has *not* declined within these Reformed denominations in recent years. Indeed, while private prayer has remained very strong among RCA clergy (with more than nine out of ten pastors praying daily), it may actually have *gained* in importance within both lay groups over the period under study.

The same pattern is true of CRC and RCA members with regard to reading the Bible on a daily basis. The level at which laity of both denominations report reading the Bible daily has not changed significantly over the past fifteen years. While one might expect Bible reading to remain high among the clergy (and it has, as three-quarters of RCA clergy report daily Bible reading), the absence of any decline among the laity is rather surprising. The pattern of stability in levels of reported daily Bible reading is consistent with the findings on private prayer. In neither case is there any evidence of erosion of religious activity for members of either denomination.

But this general pattern of stability is not limited to personal devotional activities. Reported weekly church attendance also continues to be high among CRC and RCA members, and there is no evidence of any decline in recent years. Nearly nine out of ten CRC members and seven out of ten RCA members report attending church at least four times a month. Thus, while there is a consistent 10-20 percent difference in reported weekly church attendance between CRC and RCA members, what is particularly noteworthy is that, for both groups, reported church attendance has been stable over time. Each denomination has a distinct set of cultural norms relative to this dimension of religious involvement.

Trend data on family devotions are also presented in Table 4.3. As previously reported in the "snapshot" discussion above, the data reveal that, when compared to CRC members, RCA clergy and laity have a history of lower involvement in family devotions. In 1986, only about one-half of RCA clergy and fewer than one-third of RCA laity held family devotions daily. Uniquely among these measures of religious involvement, there has been a decline in this practice among the RCA clergy. By the early 1990s, the percentage of RCA clergy having daily family devotions was substantially lower than the percentage for CRC laity (46 percent and 60 percent respectively). RCA clergy are today about as likely *never* to hold family devotions as they are to report holding them daily. Although the percentage of RCA lay members holding daily family devotions has never been as high as it has been for CRC laity, neither lay group has changed much over the past fifteen years.

This overview of the religious practices of CRC and RCA members over the past fifteen years reveals that there has been little change in the religious practices reported. The level of Bible reading, private prayer, church attendance, and family devotions has not varied markedly among either clergy or laity during this period. The only discernable decline in religious practices is the growing infrequency of daily family devotions among the RCA clergy, perhaps reflecting a society-wide shift in family activities away from the dinner table and to the soccer fields, or perhaps reflecting a graying of the clergy. Overall, however, the continuing high levels of observance of these basic religious practices would seem to contradict arguments of increasing secularization in America, at least among Reformed laity.

CRC, RCA, and Mainline Protestant Comparisons

Our analysis now moves from comparing CRC and RCA members to examining differences between these Reformed groups and the mainline Protestant community. Two new sets of data will help us make these comparisons. One is the 1998 General Social Survey (GSS), which provides data from a national sample of Americans. The second is the 2000 Cooperative Congregations Study Project (CCSP). This latter study (described in the appendix) provides information on more than forty denominations in the United States, data that are comparable to those gathered from the two Reformed denominations.

Most scholarly attempts to categorize Protestant denominations place the CRC within the evangelical Protestant tradition and the RCA within the mainline Protestant tradition (see, for instance, Roof and McKinney, 1987).[2] Given these academic categorizations, it would be expected that members of the CRC observe religious practices at a level higher than members of the RCA (a pattern suggested above). At the same time, due to the strong influence of evangelical piety in the life of the Reformed Church in America (see chapter 2), we would expect that members of the RCA would report higher levels of personal and public forms of religious practice than many others categorized as mainline Protestants. The GSS and CSSP data should provide us with

---

[2]   The primary basis for this differential classification is that the CRC is a member of the National Association of Evangelicals, while the RCA a member of the National Council of Churches.

information to help us ascertain whether these expectations are well founded. They may also help us discover whether the position occupied by the RCA serves as a bridge between evangelical and mainline Protestantism, in that the RCA is categorized as being closer to its Reformed sibling than to its mainline counterparts.

We begin by examining a broad range of religious involvement patterns in the RCA and CRC in comparison to those affiliated with mainline Protestant churches (using GSS data). These data allow comparisons to be made with the following four items: church attendance, Bible reading, private prayer, and contributions to charities. As has been established in the RCA and CRC surveys, private prayer is widely practiced throughout these Reformed communities. As Table 4.4 reveals, however, CRC and RCA members are significantly more likely to pray on a daily basis than are their counterparts in mainline Protestantism. On this measure, the CRC emerges at the high end of participation (89 percent) and the Protestant mainline at the other end

Table 4.4
Religious Practices of Lay Members of the RCA, CRC,
and Mainline Protestant Denominations
(Percent reporting)

	RCA	CRC	Mainline Denominations GSS-1998
Private Prayer			
Daily	84%	89%	67%
Weekly	12	7	24
Rarely/Never	5	4	9
Church Attendance			
Weekly	73%	88%	33%
Monthly	21	9	39
Infrequently/Never	6	3	28
Bible Reading			
Daily	33%	58%	12%
Weekly	41	32	39
Infrequently/Never	26	9	48
Contribute to Charity			
Yes	89%	91%	84%
No	11	9	16

(67 percent). While occupying the middle ground on this measure of frequency of praying, the RCA is located much closer to the CRC figure than to that of the mainline denominations.

The comparisons in Table 4.4 also indicate that the RCA and CRC both rank high in church attendance relative to the mainline pattern. Again, the CRC exhibits the highest levels of church attendance, with the RCA located in between the CRC and those falling within the mainline Protestant group. Similar to the pattern found for daily prayer, the RCA exhibits an attendance pattern much closer to that of the CRC than that of mainline Protestantism more generally.

The data on Bible reading presented in Table 4.4 reveal a similar relationship among the CRC, RCA, and other mainline Protestant denominations. The CRC has the highest percentage of members reading the Bible regularly with over 90 percent doing so at least weekly, while the mainline denominations have barely 50 percent of their members reporting weekly Bible reading. The RCA falls between the other two groups with nearly three-fourths reporting weekly Bible reading. This figure again puts the RCA much closer to the CRC than to the Protestant mainline.

The final measure of religious piety included in the General Social Survey (GSS) data assesses patterns of giving to charitable causes, including religious organizations. Table 4.4 provides the relevant data on each group's observance of this practice. Although all three groups exhibit a high level of charitable giving, with only seven percent separating the CRC from the Protestant mainline, the expected pattern among the responding denominations is again evident on this dimension of religious practice. Although the RCA is again situated between the other two groups, the percentage of RCA members giving to charitable causes (89 percent) is much closer to CRC members than to members of the Protestant mainline.

Next, religious practices in the Reformed denominations will be compared to those found in three Protestant denominations that have recently entered into agreement of greater cooperation with the RCA. In 1997 the Reformed Church signed a "Formula of Agreement" with the Presbyterian Church (USA), the Evangelical Lutheran Church of America, and the United Church of Christ.[3] The relationship

---

3   According to the official website of the RCA [www.rca.org/aboutus/
    partners/formula.html], the "Formula of Agreement is a historic measure
    designed to heal the rift between the largest branch of the Lutheran church
    and several Reformed denominations." In particular, the agreement

among the ethical emphases of congregations of the RCA, CRC, and the denominations included in the Formula of Agreement (FOA) are examined in Table 4.5. Data for these comparisons come from the 2000 CCSP key informant survey, in which a single survey was sent to a "key informant" (usually the senior minister) in each congregation. This person was asked to characterize the congregation along various dimensions, including the level of emphasis placed within congregation on various behavioral practices. Since the RCA is a member of FOA, it is interesting to see just how closely the RCA parallels the other members of this pact in terms of members' ethical perspectives.

On every dimension, the reports for RCA congregations fall between the reports for CRC and FOA congregations. For instance, according to the CRC informants, almost all CRC congregations (88 percent) place either a "great deal" or "quite a bit" of emphasis on personal prayer. Reports for RCA congregations place such an emphasis just below that of the CRC informants (at 83 percent), while congregations linked to the FOA report a still lower level of emphasis (at 77 percent). Moreover, RCA congregational scores are marginally

Table 4.5
Ethical Emphases of Congregations of the
RCA, CRC, and FOA Denominations:
2000 Cooperative Congregations Study Project
(Percent of congregations reporting
"Great Deal" or "Quite a Bit of Emphasis")

	RCA	CRC	FOA
Personal Prayer	83%	88%	71%
Scripture Study/Devotions	48	70	37
Abstaining from Premarital Sex	41	52	24
Sunday Activity Restrictions	26	32	15

states that such traditional denominational practices as baptism, communion, and ordination of clergy will be recognized across all the partner denominations. However, it is also explicit that the agreement "is not a plan to merge; the four denominations continue to maintain their distinctive traditions and identities." The first celebration of the agreement came on World-Wide Communion Sunday, October 4, 1998.

closer to CRC scores than they are to the figures provided from the FOA-group of denominations, suggesting (once again) that the pattern of religious behavior among RCA members fall much closer to their CRC peers than to those within other mainline congregations.

A significant regional component also exists within RCA congregations. As was discussed in chapter 2, the RCA has been divided between its longer established eastern synods, which date to colonial days, and the midwestern synods, which were founded in the last half of the nineteenth century. At the same time that RCA midwestern classes and synods were being formed, the CRC was establishing itself in the United States, also predominantly in the Midwest.

Table 4.6 compares the responses to these personal religious practice items from informants in the midwestern RCA and the CRC. What becomes apparent quickly is the remarkable similarity in patterns between midwestern RCA congregations and those from the CRC. Indeed, with the exception of the scripture study/devotions item, the differences are statistically insignificant. On these measures of congregational emphasis, the Midwest RCA and CRC congregations are virtually identical. It would appear that the culture that produced the CRC and the midwestern RCA churches has produced remarkably similar religious practices among its members. Clearly, the differences that appear between RCA and CRC laity are shaped, in large part, by the significant split in the religious practices between eastern and midwestern RCA members.

Table 4.6
Emphases of Midwestern RCA Congregations and the CRC:
2000 Cooperative Congregations Study Project

	Midwest RCA	CRC
Personal Prayer	86%	88%
Scripture Study/Devotions	61	70
Abstaining from Premarital Sex	54	52
Sunday Activity Restrictions	29	32

Summary

Our examination of the religious practices of CRC and RCA parishioners reveals that, although CRC members score higher than RCA members on most measures, the differences are usually not very great. Moreover, over the past two decades, there has been no significant drop in the levels of religious practices for members in either denomination. However, while there are certain discernable differences between CRC and RCA members in frequency of Bible reading, church attendance, and family devotions, there are no significant differences in the frequency of prayer, contributions to charitable causes, and the emphasis placed on personal religious practices within CRC and RCA congregations. When the two Reformed groups are compared to denominations from the Protestant mainline, the differences between them shrinks in comparison. And, when RCA members living in the Midwest are isolated and compared with CRC members living in the Midwest, nearly all differences in the levels of religious practice dissipate, though they do not disappear.

Institutional Loyalty

Religious affiliation for most Americans is primarily a reflection of congregational involvement. It is in the congregation in which they gather that churchgoers live their religious lives, worship God, experience religious community, and build long-term relationships. For many, if not most, worshipers, one's entire religious experience is wrapped up within the walls of one's local congregation. Often, it would seem, these expressions of religious life take place with little or no consciousness of the denominational traditions of which the congregation is organizationally a part (Hoge, Johnson, Luidens, 1994). Indeed, many parishioners' connections with their denominations are extremely tenuous.

In the context of the current study of the Reformed Church in America and the Christian Reformed Church, this basic sense of congregational identity begs a number of questions: Does the unique (largely ethnically Dutch and Calvinist) history of these two groups promote denominational identity? Has there been any change over time? Are the patterns the same for both denominations? Is there any carry-over from congregational identity to denominational identity?

The remaining section of this chapter will examine the ways in which denominational identity is related to congregational identity as well as to other dimensions of RCA and CRC members' religious lives. The data suggest that there are portions of both communions for whom direct loyalty to their denomination is a matter of paramount concern. For most individuals in these groups, denominational loyalty corresponds strongly with congregational allegiance.

However, what will be equally clear is that these forms of direct loyalty are but one dimension of a multi-faceted "web of loyalties" that binds RCA and CRC members to their denominations. Indeed, numerous strands of affinity are found in both groups, among both clergy and laity, and these different stands have existed over an extended period of time. "Denominational loyalty" is much more than a matter of overt and direct commitment to the RCA and CRC. These "ties that bind" are complex and allow for people of very different family backgrounds, very different theological and ideological perspectives, and significantly divergent religious life experiences to find common cause within each denomination. To the extent that denominations expect to retain their viability, they will have to respond to these overlapping—and sometimes conflicting—strands of allegiance. This will not always be easy to accomplish, as the threads are each being pulled by a particular constituency, every group expressing its allegiance to the denomination in its own way. Thus, denominational loyalty is not a single dimension; rather, churchgoers are "loyal" to a complex web of visions for the denomination.

Direct Lines of Loyalty

Martin Marty has written about two "parties" competing for the allegiance of Protestant denominations throughout American history. On the one side stand "personal pietists" who are recognized by their intense involvement in personal and collective acts of worship and spiritual formation. This segment has often been associated with conservative emphases, especially focusing on correct thinking and worshiping. On the other end of the spectrum are "public activists," who are known for their engagement with the larger social scene, especially through the mechanisms of political and social service expression. Public activists have generally been associated with contemporary cultural movements and thus have been perceived as more "liberal" in their interests. According to Marty (1970), these two groups regularly have found themselves striving for the hearts and souls of the large segments in the middle, often stretching the denomination to the left or the right.

Previous research on the Reformed Church in America found evidence that both of these parties are present within the laity and clergy of that denomination (Luidens and Nemeth 1987), though there was also a significant minority of members who expressed consistently "loyalist" feelings toward the RCA. This third, loyalist, "party" appears to be distinct from the other two parties. While the personal pietists are united primarily by their theological conservatism and the public activists by their political liberalism, the central unifying factor for the loyalist segment is their commitment to the denomination as a religious agency. Moreover, such loyalists within the RCA are split between those who have long-standing, familial roots in the RCA and those who are or have been significantly involved in the institutional infrastructure of the denomination (Luidens and Nemeth, 1998). As will be discussed below, these loyalists, a unifying contingent, may hold the prospect for preserving cohesion in the Reformed Church in America.

Many Protestants—including many members of the RCA and CRC—have expressed a very strong sense of identity with their denominations, here called "direct lines of loyalty." In informal interviews, these loyalists point to their family trees, to their intense involvement in the governance of "their" denomination, and to their inability to conceive of themselves as belonging to any another denomination. These direct lines of loyalty within the Reformed and Christian Reformed churches continue to be important in understanding denominational identity for both clergy and laity. In order to assess these denominational lines of loyalty, respondents were asked how important their denominational membership was to their faith. As is apparent in Table 4.7, the majority of respondents in each of the responding groups indicate that, at least until recently, their denominational membership is either extremely or quite important.

However, when comparing these groups over time, clear distinctions in the degrees of direct denominational loyalty are evident. First, as might be expected, clergy in both denominations are consistently more committed to their denominations than are laity. For instance, in 1986, about one-half of RCA laity (53 percent) responded that their denominational affiliation was "extremely" or "quite" important, while more than three-quarters of the RCA clergy responded in a similar fashion (77 percent). However, the magnitude of this difference had diminished slightly by 2000, when 48 percent of the RCA laity and 56 percent of the RCA clergy affirmed their denominational memberships. Among the CRC, 54 percent of the

Table 4.7
Denominational Loyalties: RCA Laity and Clergy, CRC Laity and Clergy

How important would you say your DENOMINATIONAL MEMBERSHIP is to you?

	RCA Laity			RCA Clergy			CRC* Laity	CRC* Clergy
	1986	1991	2000	1986	1991	2000	2000	1997
Extremely Important	18%	17%	17%	28%	18%	16%	18%	21%
Quite Important	35	35	31	49	48	40	36	61
Fairly Important	29	30	32	16	23	31	28	17
Not Too or Not at All	18	18	20	8	11	14	17	1

* Data for CRC are limited to the 2000 laity survey and the 1997 clergy survey.

laity in 2000 and a decidedly healthier 82 percent of the clergy in 1997 indicated strong denominational loyalty.

Secondly, over time, there has been a cooling of denominational ardor within the RCA, among both laity and clergy. Lay support within the Reformed Church has eroded over the past fifteen years by about five percent (from 53 to 48 percent strong affirmation), while among clergy the drop has been a precipitous 21 percent (from 77 to 56 percent). While data are not available for the CRC over time, the remarkably parallel scores between RCA and CRC members in 2000 suggest that similar patterns may be occurring in the CRC as well.

Changes have also taken place in congregational allegiance, although to a much less pronounced degree. Table 4.8 reports the data for respondents' feelings of congregational loyalty over time. While the erosion has not been as severe among RCA laity (the shift has been from "extremely" to "quite" important rather than to even lower levels of approval), laity were more tentative in their loyalty to their congregations than were clergy. The anomaly in this study is the response of RCA clergy in 1991, when there was a surge of support for congregational membership (with 97 percent indicating "extremely" or "quite" important levels of support[4]). But, by 2000, such responses receded to levels lower than that found in 1986.

For many members of the Reformed and Christian Reformed churches, denominational identity seems to arise from congregational identity. Within both the RCA and the CRC laity, approximately four-fifths of those who identified their denominational membership

Table 4.8
Congregational Loyalties: RCA Laity and Clergy,
CRC Laity and Clergy

How important would you say your CONGREGATIONAL MEMBERSHIP is to you?

| | RCA Laity | | | RCA Clergy | | | CRC Laity* |
	1986	1991	2000	1986	1991	2000	2000
Extremely Important	35%	32%	32%	48%	73%	35%	34%
Quite Important	38	40	42	39	24	39	42
Fairly Important	19	20	19	8	2	18	17
Not Too or Not at All	8	8	6	5	<1	8	8

* Data for CRC are limited to the 2000 laity survey and the 1997 clergy survey.

as extremely or quite important evaluated their congregational memberships similarly. Among these RCA laity this relationship has not changed significantly over time. Among RCA and CRC laity who have strong affinities with their congregations comes a strong affinity with their denominations. Similarly, congregational loyalty is strongly related to denominational loyalty among the RCA clergy. However, its importance appears to have diminished slightly in recent years. In 1986, 83 percent of clergy expressing high denominational loyalty also indicated high congregational affinity. These numbers dropped to 70 and 73 percents in 1991 and 2000, respectively.

---

[4]   This apparent anomaly is hard to explain, although in 1990 the denomination ended a longstanding debate about the status of women in ministry. The resolution was that individual congregations would decide whether or not to call women, thereby affirming—in a very un-presbyterial fashion—the importance of congregation-level decision-making in the denomination.

Finally, those who have been long-time members of the denomination reflect their years of involvement by their strong allegiance to the denomination. Significantly, this relationship has grown weaker among RCA laity between 1986 and 2000. Fewer long-term members today harbor strong denominational ties. Most remarkably, the number of years of membership is only weakly related to denominational loyalty among RCA clergy.

Indirect Lines of Loyalty

Claims of "direct" denominational loyalty, while prevalent among roughly half the laity and clergy of the RCA and CRC (see Table 4.7 above), present an incomplete picture of the strands that bind members and pastors to their respective denominations. In order to see if there were other patterns of identity that seem to characterize denominational memberships, a number of statistical analyses[5] were undertaken using the RCA and CRC data from lay and clergy respondents. Among the items included were religious belief, involvement, and practice measures as well as questions about respondents' perspectives on secular issues. Analysis suggests that there are significant clusters of variables which, separately and uniquely, seem to relate to levels of denominational loyalty among members of the CRC and RCA. Moreover, the consistency of these clusters across both samples and time suggests their importance in identifying the ways in which these denominations have maintained the loyalty of their adherents.

In 1986, for both RCA clergy and RCA laity, the most statistically important group was those with a high sense of loyalty to the denomination and to its historic creeds. Indeed, this "loyalist party" was sufficiently strong to offset those who pulled the denomination either to the left or to the right. While they shared the generally orthodox theology of the more conservative branch of the denomination, their primary concern was the survival of the denomination. Smaller groups of RCA members were characterized by their high level of personal religious practice (with the "conservatives" being a significant component of this group) and those who were older but having no

---

[5]   In order to look at "clustering" of variables around the same (statistical) themes, factor analysis was used in this section. While this technique of data manipulation generates "factors" that hang together statistically, it must be tempered by conceptually logical interpretations. What follows in chapter 4 is based on factors which made good theoretical sense as well as solid statistical probability.

unifying pattern of theological or religious practice. Finally, a less significant group was characterized by its strongly conservative political and social agenda.

But dramatic changes were afoot. By 1991, among the laity, the loyalists had lost their foothold and had been replaced by the religious conservatives as the most important subgroup within the RCA. By 2000, they had fallen behind all of the other three subgroups. Among RCA clergy, a similar collapse of the loyalists had taken place; they, too, moved from the most prominent subgroup in 1986 to a much less important status. Among RCA clergy, the most prominent groups by 2000 were those who were most theologically and politically conservative.

Few similar measures exist for analysis within the CRC. However, in 2000 a set of comparable items was included. Significantly, the most important cluster within the CRC includes items related to age and tenure of CRC members. As has become the case with much of the RCA, CRC members are most characteristically recognizable by their elderly caste. Moreover, among CRC laity in 2000, measures of denominational and congregational loyalty fall well down on the list of characteristic clusters—also mimicking the pattern within the RCA.

Conclusion

What is to be made of these patterns? What do they suggest about denominational identity in an era of increasing institutional fragmentation? First, when compared to other mainline Protestant denominations, the personal religious practices of CRC and RCA members appear to be remarkably similar. Although CRC laity score slightly higher on several piety measures (e.g. family devotions), the differences between members in these two denominations on most religious practices is only marginal.

Second, over the past two decades, there has been a remarkable level of stability in terms of the reported religious practices of CRC and RCA laity. Levels of religious practice in terms of daily prayer, daily Bible reading, and weekly church attendance were both relatively high and relatively stable between 1986 and 2000. Thus, for all the talk of growing secularization within American society, there appears to be little drop off in the levels of reported religious practices among members of these two Reformed denominations.

Third, it would appear that loyalty to the RCA, among both laity and clergy, has been eroding during the past fifteen years. This has meant that other forms of institutional identity have been thrust to the fore as the RCA struggles to retain its dwindling numbers and resources. Among laity, the growing importance of long-term RCA affiliation, paralleled by the secondary rise in importance of a cluster of RCA heritage measures, suggests that the RCA is increasingly relying on its longevity for denominational identity. In an era of low birth rates and increasing competition from other denominations, the RCA continues to rely upon internal growth for new members. Meanwhile, there appears to be a homogenizing of social/political conservatism along with confessional conservatism. Theological and political progressives have either left the RCA or have been absorbed into the larger conservative mix. The dramatic drop in membership in the eastern regions of the denomination argues for the former explanation; the RCA has become more like the CRC because it has lost the involvement of eastern progressives.

The departure of eastern progressives has been especially pronounced among the clergy. As a result, a conservative sociopolitical agenda has been growing more prominent among RCA clergy at the same time that an emphasis on traditional confessionalism has resurged. Together, these trends have led to a homogenizing of the clergy; there are fewer divergent perspectives within their ranks. Ironically, levels of RCA loyalty have been dropping at the same time. While there has been an increasingly narrow ideological range of perspectives among RCA clergy, this has not been reflected in a narrowing of demographic sources from which these clergy are being drawn. Nevertheless, such historic demographic factors as ethnicity and RCA lineage have decreased in importance in recent years among clergy in relationship to long-term membership within the RCA, while their conservative ideological perspective has increased in importance.

While there are no parallel trend data for CRC clergy, it is instructive that CRC laity in 2000 displayed a pattern of institutional identity that closely paralleled that of the RCA laity in that year. This infers some close historic parallels have been taking place among that denomination's membership as well.

Loyalty to a religious denomination, as a factor central to one's religious identity, has been under assault as the religious marketplace has become increasingly competitive. This has certainly been true for the Reformed and Christian Reformed churches. In the brief span of fifteen years, loyalty has dissipated as the most important unifying characteristic of the denominations' memberships. In both cases, personal commitment and loyalty has given way to inertia, as the mere persistence of membership now primarily explains variation in denominational loyalty. In light of this, the question for these denominations—indeed for all Protestant denominations—becomes, What will be the staying power of denominational identity when direct loyalty is eclipsed by age and length of membership or by political correctness? The lessons of the RCA and the CRC point to the need for multiple strands of allegiance, a veritable "web of loyalties," to overcome this decline. The task for these denominations in the future is to nurture and strike a successful balance among these competing strands.

CHAPTER 5

'Jesus Shall Reign'?
The Politics of CRC and RCA
Clergy and Laity

Analyzing continuity and change in the politics of Christian Reformed Church and Reformed Church in America clergy and laity requires considerable detective work, since data on the topic are fragmentary and vary in quality across time. Furthermore, those data that are available are more complete with respect to ministers of the two denominations than they are with respect to its members. Nevertheless, there is enough good information available to permit an analysis of this topic and allow us to arrive at some interesting, and potentially important, conclusions.

There are several reasons why a study of the politics of Christian Reformed and Reformed Church ministers and congregants may be informative. First of all, each denomination has a strong tradition of political and social involvement. Certainly it is notable that two presidents of the United States—Martin Van Buren and Theodore Roosevelt—have been drawn from the ranks of the Reformed Church in America, despite its being a relatively small denomination. But also notable is the social and political involvement of the Reformed laity of the church, stemming in part from the theological perspectives found within the Reformed tradition. Certainly, one important factor in this tradition of engagement with culture, rather than withdrawal from it, reflects the influence of nineteenth-century Dutch theologian and politician, Abraham Kuyper. Kuyper's emphasis on the importance of political action as a means of "transforming" social structures has encouraged generations of Reformed Christians to engage in politics as a way of improving political and social institutions. In this sense, Reformed Christians differ markedly from evangelical Protestants who, for much of the twentieth century, eschewed political and social involvement, viewing such activity as ineffectual or undesirable (Henry 1974; Oldfield 1996). Of course, not all Reformed Christians share Kuyper's vision; indeed there remains a strong pietist tradition in both the CRC and the RCA that places greater emphasis on individual spirituality and right living than on political and social involvement. Conversely, there has been among American evangelicals an awakening of political involvement in recent years (Wald 2003, chap. 7; Fowler et al. 1999, 40).

A second reason to study this topic is that Reformed thought has played an important role in shaping American political culture. This effect dates back as far as the Puritans, who embraced Reformed theology and social ethics. It has continued in recent years with the political thought and writings of such Reformed scholars as Marshall (1984), Monsma (2000), Mouw (1976), and Skillen (1990). While it is easy to exaggerate the impact of any religious tradition or group of scholars, it is fair to state that the recent evangelical political re-engagement owes a significant debt to the Reformed tradition of political involvement that is embodied in today's CRC and RCA.

A final basis for studying CRC and RCA politics is that there has been renewed talks of merger of the two denominations (Vander Zicht 1983, Honey 2002, Jesse 2002), despite the fact that the two denominations have been organizationally separated since 1857. Should any union occur, it would have to deal not only with nearly 150 years of theological disagreement between the two denominations, but also with any interdenominational differences in political and social attitudes which may have arisen over that period as well. Moreover, any such merger efforts would also have the potential for highlighting, if not exacerbating, various intradenominational political divisions (for instance, between regions or between clergy and laity) that may have developed over time.

As was noted in chapter 2, recent surveys of the CRC and RCA reveal that both denominations tend to be populated by white, middle-class, well-educated persons living in small towns or suburban areas.[1] On

---

[1]   For example, the CRC and RCA member surveys of 2000 revealed that fewer than 4 percent of RCA members and less than 1 percent of CRC

this basis alone, one would expect members of the two denominations to be politically (as well as culturally) conservative. Nevertheless, there are also good reasons to believe that a closer examination would reveal some important intra- and interdenominational differences as well. In order in insure that any such differences do not stem simply from living under different political systems and cultural contexts, we limit our analysis in this chapter to CRC and RCA clergy and laity within the American political system.[2]

What political differences might be expected in terms of the two denominations? In the first place, one might expect clergy and laity of the RCA to be more politically liberal than those of the CRC. Through its membership in the Federal Council of Churches and later the National Council of Churches, the Reformed Church in America has more closely associated itself with theologically and culturally liberal "mainline" denominations than has the Christian Reformed Church. Indeed, as discussed in chapter 2, the CRC seceded from the RCA in part over concerns about "liberal" cultural and theological drift in the older denomination. Moreover, although both the CRC and RCA have struggled with issues of self-identity and accommodation to American culture, the Reformed Church did so much earlier than the Christian Reformed Church (Eenigenburg 1959, Brown 1982, Japinga 1992, Luidens 1993). In this light, it is not surprising that the CRC has felt more comfortable associating itself with more conservative evangelical and Reformed denominations. An important cross-denominational

---

members identify themselves as African-Americans. Nearly three-fourths of the members of each denomination report having at least "some college" education, and approximately half of the families in each denomination have family incomes of $50,000 or more. Only 11 percent of CRC and 8 percent of RCA members live in large cities of 250,000 or more. One notable *difference* between the two denominations concerns the percentage of members claiming "Dutch" as their primary ethnic group: while 81 percent of CRC members do so, only 45 percent of RCA laity report their primary lineage is from the Netherlands.

2   While a separate comparison theoretically could be done of CRC and RCA clergy and laity in Canada, several practical considerations make such an assessment very problematic. Basically, the relatively few RCA clergy in Canada, as well as the small number of Reformed Church laity in Canada that would be captured through a random sampling procedure, makes any resulting percentages highly unstable, as the inclusion of one or two additional cases could dramatically change the percentages obtained.

study of American Protestant clergy after the 1988 presidential election lends support for this expectation (Guth et al. 1997). In this study of clergy in four evangelical and four mainline denominations, Christian Reformed and Reformed Church clergy fell in the middle of the ideological spectrum, with CRC clergy tending to be somewhat more conservative, on balance, than RCA clergy.

Secondly, one might expect to find important regional political differences, particularly within the RCA. Data presented in chapter 4 revealed some of the differences that exist in the RCA between the more theologically and culturally liberal eastern wing and a more conservative midwestern wing, reflecting some of the historic differences in patterns of settlement and immigration (Bratt 1984; Van Engen 2002). Unlike the established eastern segment of the RCA, the midwestern branch contains higher percentages of "newly arrived," culturally conservative Dutch immigrants. Thus, one might expect to find greater political liberalism in the East than in the Midwest, at least within the Reformed Church in America.

A third anticipated difference relates to life-style issues, particularly those regarding Christian education and educational choice. The CRC has long supported the creation and maintenance of distinctively Christian schools at all levels, while the RCA has tended to be less supportive of such schools (Hesselink 1983). This pattern may lead to higher levels of support for political proposals such as tuition vouchers for private and parochial school students among the CRC clergy and laity than among their RCA counterparts.

Finally, one might anticipate that within each denomination there would be some important differences between the clergy and laity over political values and issues. More than three decades ago, Hadden (1969) highlighted a growing gap between activist, politically liberal, mainline Protestant clergy and their more conservative congregants, suggesting that such differences were producing a "gathering storm" in the churches. However, Luidens and Nemeth (2003) found that, during the 1970s and 1980s, the "gap" between RCA ministers and members had been "filled" in a creative way: while clergy retained their more liberal social and political perspectives (compared with the laity), they also experienced growing theological orthodoxy, making them more traditional on that dimension than the laity. Nevertheless, RCA ministers remain more politically liberal than their lay counterparts. Certainly, one might suspect that different levels of theological training between clergy and laity might produce some differences, but the situation is likely more nuanced than education alone can explain. Recent research on CRC ministers, for example, suggests that important age-related, attitudinal differences are evident *within* the clergy on political and social issues (Penning et al. 2001). So, at the very least, one must be cautious in explaining what serves to account for any difference that may appear between clergy and laity.

This chapter, therefore, examines the politics of Christian Reformed and Reformed Church ministers and members over time, focusing on several key issues. First, it analyzes the basic political beliefs, identifications, and practices of CRC and RCA clergy and laity. Second, it examines whether changes have occurred in these beliefs, identifications, and practices over time. Finally, it assesses whether key inter- or intradenominational differences appear across or within the two groups.

General Clergy Orientations toward Politics

We begin our analysis by examining Christian Reformed and Reformed Church clergy within American society and their reported orientations toward politics and political life. In general, ministers from the two denominations tend to exhibit similar patterns of orientation toward religion and politics. Pastors in both denominations report relatively high levels of interest in politics: when asked in 2001 to indicate their relative level of interest in politics on a seven-point scale (ranging from a value of 1 indicating "very interested" to a value of 7 indicating "not at all interested"), approximately one-half of clergy in both denominations (52 percent for CRC clergy and 47 percent for RCA clergy, respectively) reported scores of either "1" or "2" (data not shown).

Similar patterns are further evident from Table 5.1, which examines the social theology of those CRC and RCA ministers serving congregations in the United States at the turn of the millennium. As one might expect, overwhelming proportions of both groups agree that religion "has a positive effect on American social and civic life." Substantial, though less pronounced, support is also given to the proposition that "religion has a positive effect on American political life." Overall, pastors in both denominations perceive a positive connection between religion and politics.

Nevertheless, these same CRC and RCA ministers also perceive problems for people of faith in the current American political environment. For example, large majorities of both CRC and RCA

Table 5.1
Positions on "Faith and Politics" among
CRC and RCA Clergy at the Turn of the Millennium
(Percent agreeing)

	Clergy	
	CRC	RCA
Religion has a positive effect on American social and civic life.	92%	90%
Religion has a positive effect on American political life.	77	66
Religious freedom in the U.S. is threatened by those opposing religion.	70	62
It is better to compromise and achieve something than to stick to one's principles at the risk of achieving little.	50	36
Government must take special steps to protect America's religious heritage.	48	45
Churches should not try to lobby public officials.	39	31
The U.S. was founded as a Christian nation.	37	42
Civil liberties are threatened by those imposing religion.	23	28
On most political issues there is only one correct Christian position.	11	11

pastors (70 percent and 62 percent, respectively) agree that "religious freedom in the U.S. is threatened by those opposing religion." Nearly half of the clergy from each denomination agree that "government must take special steps to protect America's religious heritage." In contrast, barely a quarter of the pastors (23 percent of the CRC and 28 percent of the RCA) perceive religion as threatening the fabric of the political system.

The data in Table 5.1 also clearly reveal that CRC and RCA clergy are wary of simplistic, triumphalist approaches to politics. Only about one in ten (11 percent) agree that "on most political issues there is only one correct Christian position." Moreover, half of CRC clergy and over a third of their RCA counterparts take the pragmatic position that it is "better to compromise and achieve something than to stick to one's principles at the risk of achieving little." Finally, a majority of clergy from each denomination rejects calls for the church to avoid lobbying public officials. Thus, overall, it is readily apparent from these data that ministers within both the Christian Reformed and Reformed Church are widely attuned to the political scene and perceive religion as having an important role to play in the course of political events.

Ideological Orientations of CRC and RCA Clergy

Shifting from these more general notions about politics to a more specific focus on ideological orientations, three particularly important questions are examined. First, do CRC and RCA ministers tend to classify themselves as political conservatives, as political liberals, or as political moderates? Second, have the political orientations of the clergy changed over time and, if so, in what direction? Finally, are there key ideological differences between ministers in the two denominations,

Table 5.2
Ideological Orientations and Political Party Identification
among CRC and RCA Clergy over Time

	CRC			RCA		
	1989	1997	2001	1989	1997	2001
Ideological Orientation						
Liberal	25%	30%	17%	32%	34%	25%
Moderate	26	17	21	24	18	21
Conservative	48	54	63	45	49	54
(N)	(364)	(247)	(398)	(371)	(251)	(367)
Partisan Identification						
Strong Democrat	3%	6%	3%	10%	6%	8%
Weak Democrat	5	4	4	7	8	6
Independent, Leaning						
Democrat	15	9	9	19	19	17
Independent	10	11	9	13	13	12
Independent, Leaning						
Republican	36	35	22	22	23	14
Weak Republican	16	18	26	15	15	21
Strong Republican	15	17	28	14	16	22
(N)	(342)	(251)	(397)	(374)	(253)	(369)

and, if so, are the differences of such a magnitude that they may create a potential barrier to dialogue and future organizational merger?

Ideologically, Reformed clergy tend to be a conservative group. Table 5.2 reveals that clergy in both denominations are far more likely to identify themselves as political conservatives than as political liberals. Furthermore, between 1989 and 2001, the percentage of both CRC and RCA clergy identifying themselves as political conservatives has increased, while the percentage identifying themselves as political liberals has decreased. Over this same time period, those who fall in the "center" also appear to have declined slightly within both denominations. Significantly, for a substantial number of pastors, it is inconceivable that liberalism and Christianity can even co-exist. In the 2001 clergy survey, 36 percent of CRC ministers and 28 percent of RCA clergy either "strongly agreed" or "agreed" with the statement, "It would be hard to be both a true Christian and a political liberal."

Table 5.2 also demonstrates that, regardless of the survey year examined, Christian Reformed clergy tend to be more ideologically conservative than their counterparts in the Reformed Church. The most recent data available (2001), for example, reveal that nearly two thirds of CRC ministers identify with the political right, while only slightly more than half of RCA pastors do so. Nonetheless, overall differences between the two groups of clergy are not exceedingly great, and the variation between CRC and RCA pastors are largely attributable to clergy in the RCA's eastern region being far more politically liberal than their midwestern counterparts.[3]

Partisanship and Voting Behavior of CRC and RCA Clergy

Although we lack good data on the party identification and voting behavior of CRC and RCA laity, that is not the case with respect to clergy. Table 5.2 reveals not only that the basic party identifications of Christian Reformed and Reformed Church ministers are remarkably similar but that the patterns of change in their partisan identifications are also exceedingly uniform across the two denominations. In each of the post-presidential years examined, majorities of both CRC and RCA pastors classified themselves as identifying with or "leaning toward" the Republican Party, while only minorities reported identifying with

---

[3]   In 2000, for example, while fully 32 percent of RCA clergy residing in the East identified with the ideological left, only 15 percent of those living in the Midwest did so.

the Democratic Party or being "independent" politically. Although Democrats are somewhat more common in the RCA than in the CRC, Republicans clearly dominate among clergy in both denominations.

Moreover, the percentages of both Democrats and independents appear to have decreased slightly over time, while the percentages of those ministers identifying themselves as Republicans have increased. For example, between 1989 and 2001, CRC clergy who identified with or leaned toward the Republican Party increased from 67 to 76 percent while the comparable percentage in the RCA increased from 51 to 57 percent.

Nevertheless, CRC and RCA ministers recognize that each political party possesses distinctive major strengths and weaknesses, and pastors in both denominations tend to assess these strengths and weaknesses in a similar fashion. Drawing on responses to our 1997 survey (data not shown), both CRC and RCA clergy perceived Republicans as being particularly strong with respect to "national defense," "supporting family values," and "maintaining economic growth," while Democrats are perceived by both groups as being particularly strong in "protecting the environment," "representing minorities," and "aiding the disadvantaged." At the same time, majorities of clergy in both the CRC and RCA report that neither party was better than the other with respect to such issues as "protecting free speech" and "fighting crime." Given the partisan breakdown of the two groups of clergy noted above, one might rightfully expect that Christian Reformed Church ministers would prove slightly more likely than Reformed Church clergy to give high marks to the Republican Party.

Regardless of their personal identifications, ministers from both denominations seem reasonably content with the current party system. At the very least, they clearly reject the idea, proposed by some Christian dissidents, that the United States needs a distinctively Christian political party. In the 1997 clergy survey, for example, only sixteen percent of CRC pastors and only six percent of RCA clergy agreed with the statement, "The United States needs a Christian political party" (data not shown).

Not surprisingly, these patterns of party identification are reflected in the self-reported presidential voting behavior of CRC and RCA ministers. In the four recent presidential elections (1988, 1992, 1996, and 2000), the Republican presidential candidate received overwhelming support from clergy in the Christian Reformed Church, earning no less than 74 percent of the vote in any year. Furthermore, the tendency of CRC ministers to support Republican presidential nominees appears to have increased over time: while George Bush, Sr., won approximately three-fourths of the CRC clergy vote in 1988, his son, George W. Bush, won an overwhelming 86 percent in 2000. In contrast, while Reformed Church clergy support for Republican presidential candidates has also been substantial, it has been somewhat less extensive than CRC support, ranging from 58 percent for George Bush, Sr., in 1988 to 67 percent for George W. Bush in 2000 (data not shown).

Ideological Orientations of CRC and RCA Laity

We are not only interested in the ideological and partisan orientations of CRC and RCA clergy, we are also interested in the orientations of laity, as it is the members who form the backbone of the church and provide it with the human and financial resources necessary for denominational survival and growth. Therefore, we examine the basic ideological orientations of CRC and RCA laity in the United States, and then we compare ministers and laity in the two denominations in terms of their ideological orientations. In particular, we seek to determine whether major ideological "gaps" exist between clergy and laity that may serve to produce a "gathering storm" in either or both denominations (Hadden 1969).

One might anticipate that members of theologically conservative, well-educated, middle-class denominations such as the Christian Reformed Church and the Reformed Church in America would tend to be ideologically conservative, and Table 5.3 reveals that this is, indeed, the case. The most recent data available (2000) indicates that large majorities of both CRC and RCA respondents label themselves

Table 5.3
Ideological Orientations among CRC and RCA
Clergy and Laity At the Turn of the Millennium

| | Clergy | | Laity | |
	CRC	RCA	CRC	RCA
Liberal	17%	25%	10%	20%
Moderate	21	21	17	20
Conservative	63	54	73	60

politically conservative, while relatively small percentages claim to be either moderates or liberals.

The data presented in Table 5.3 also demonstrates that CRC congregants are somewhat more ideologically conservative than their RCA counterparts. While 73 percent of CRC lay respondents classified themselves as conservatives in 2000, only 60 percent of RCA respondents did so. Nevertheless, the overall picture presented by the data is that both denominations are composed largely of members who classify themselves as political conservatives.

The table further reveals there is only a marginal difference between the ideological orientations of pastors and those of the parishioners in both the CRC and RCA, with members tending to be slightly more conservative than ministers. Indeed, at the turn of the millennium, 73 percent of Christian Reformed Church members reported identifying as political conservatives, while 63 percent of CRC clergy did so. Within the RCA, the pattern is similar, with 60 percent of the laity labeling themselves as political conservatives and 54 percent of clergy doing so.

However, with the RCA long having been divided culturally between its older, more established, eastern wing and its newer midwestern wing, it is possible that the variations in overall patterns of ideology between the two denominations may reflect, at least in part, significant regional differences *within* the RCA. Table 5.4 reveals that this, indeed, is the case. There are few regional differences in ideology within the CRC, as Christian Reformed Church members, regardless of region, tend to identify themselves as political conservatives. On the other hand, there is considerable regional variation in the ideological orientations of Reformed Church members. The percent of midwestern RCA parishioners who classify themselves as political conservatives (67 percent) is far greater than the percentage of RCA members living in the East who do so (44 percent), and it is nearly equal to the percentage reported by their CRC midwestern counterparts (73 percent). In both denominations, laity living outside the East or Midwest (those who are members of congregations in the South and Far West which, on the whole, reflect relatively younger congregations) also tend to place themselves in the conservative category, though such CRC members also proved to be somewhat more conservative than RCA members (73 percent versus 61 percent, respectively).

A comparison of surveys of Reformed Church members over time suggests that the regional differences in self-reported ideology

Table 5.4
Ideological Orientations among CRC and RCA
Clergy and Laity by Region At the Turn of the Millennium

	CRC				RCA			
	East	Midwest	Rest	Total	East	Midwest	Rest	Total
Liberal	7%	10%	8%	10%	32%	15%	19%	20%
Moderate	20	16	19	17	24	18	22	20
Conservative	73	74	73	73	44	67	61	60
Total	100%	100%	100%	100%	100%	100%	100%	100%

have increased rather than narrowed in scope. For example, in 1986 the percentage of RCA parishioners in the East who classified themselves as political conservatives was 47 percent, while in the Midwest it was 59 percent. However, by 2000, the corresponding percentages were 44 and 67 percent. Thus, not only is there a regional ideological gap among RCA parishioners, but this gap is growing, caused in large measure by the increasing conservatism of midwestern RCA members.

While the ideological differences between clergy and laity are worth noting, they certainly are not large and are not likely to be of sufficient magnitude to produce a broad, "gathering storm" in the two denominations. This assessment is further supported by data from several surveys in which CRC and RCA ministers were asked to report their perceptions of possible differences between their personal political ideology and that of their respective congregations (data not shown). In 1989, a majority of clergy from both denominations perceived an ideological "gap" between their congregations and themselves, with majorities of both CRC and RCA clergy reporting themselves to be "more liberal" than their congregations. However, over time, perceptions of these differences have diminished to such a degree that, in 2001, approximately half of the pastors from both denominations reported their views to be "about the same" as those of their congregations; this is true both for social and economic issues. Furthermore, among those clergy in 2001 who perceived some ideological difference between themselves and their congregants, the proportions perceiving themselves as either "more liberal" or "more conservative" than their congregations were approximately equal. In general, then, there appears to be growing ministerial-membership ideological convergence over time, with little support for any contention that there are growing ideological differences between clergy and laity in either the CRC or the RCA.

The available data on CRC and RCA laity do not permit any assessment of their partisan preferences. The best one can do is speculate that, given the ideological conservatism of most CRC and RCA laity, a majority of the members of both denominations would also tend to identify with the Republican Party. At the very least, we can state that this pattern is found among both the Christian Reformed Church and Reformed Church in America ministers.

Stands on Political Issues

To examine whether the CRC and RCA clergy are as politically conservative as their self-described ideological orientations and partisan identifications would suggest, we examined the issue positions of clergy on a variety of specific issues, dividing those issues into two broad agendas—a "moral reform" agenda and a "social justice" agenda. While some judgment is involved in assigning issues to these two categories, issues were placed in the "moral reform" category if they related primarily to matters of personal morality or to the rights of religious groups. In contrast, issues were placed in the "social justice" category if they relate primarily to matters of structural injustice, racism, or the rights of the dispossessed.

The Issue Positions of CRC and RCA Clergy

In 1997, when ministers within the Christian Reformed Church and the Reformed Church in America were asked to name the "greatest problem facing the United States today," a plurality of both groups tended to focus on issues of personal morality rather than issues of social structure or injustice (data not shown). Among CRC pastors, the three most common responses given to the question were "moral decay" (22 percent), "decline of family values" (8 percent), and "racism" (8 percent). Similarly, among RCA clergy, the three most common responses were "moral decay" (16 percent), "decline in family values" (11 percent), and "general values" (8 percent). Of these responses, only "racism" falls in the "social justice" category.

The issue agendas of CRC and RCA clergy can also be assessed by asking their opinions on a variety of key political issues. Table 5.5 reports the responses of clergy to a series of issue questions posed in the 2001 survey, and it reveals that CRC and RCA pastors are not as consistently conservative in their issue positions as their conservative ideological and partisan orientations might suggest. On certain topics (in particular, abstinence-based sex education, abortion, and welfare reform) majorities of clergy from both denominations adopt what might be labeled politically "conservative" positions, while on other issues (such as gun control, gay rights, prayer in public schools, and the necessity of Israeli concessions), they tend toward more "liberal" stances.

This issue "inconsistency" is not necessarily surprising, in that the relationship between one's expressed ideological orientation and one's positions on specific political issues can be rather tenuous, resulting either from a lack of understanding of the meaning of these ideological terms or from the result of the shifting meaning of "conservative" or "liberal" labels over time (Penning and Smidt 2002, chap. 6). Consequently, while pastors within both the CRC and RCA tend to label themselves as political conservatives, the positions on key political issues are not as consistently conservative as these ideological labels might suggest.

In general, CRC pastors tend to take somewhat more conservative positions on these issues than do their RCA counterparts, particularly

Table 5.5
Issue Positions among CRC and RCA Clergy
at the Turn of the Millennium
(Percent agreeing)

| | Clergy | |
	CRC	RCA
Moral Reform Agenda		
Sex education programs included in the curricula of public high schools should be abstinence based.	92%	82%
The government should provide vouchers to parents to help pay for their children to attend private or religious schools.	80	38
We need a constitutional amendment to prohibit all abortions unless to save the mother's life, or in case of rape or incest.	78	52
Government is providing too many services best left to private enterprise.	45	34
We need a constitutional amendment to permit prayer in public schools.	22	21

	Clergy	
	CRC	RCA
Social Justice Agenda		
A lasting peace in the Middle East will require Israel to make greater concessions to the Palestinians.	70%	60%
China should not have been given most favored nation trading status until it stopped religious persecutions.	66	62
Homosexuals should have all the same rights and privileges as other American citizens.	54	65
Public policy should discourage ownership and use of handguns.	54	56
Blacks and other minorities may need special governmental help to achieve an equal place in America.	50	48
More environmental protection is needed, even if it raises prices or costs jobs.	47	52
The federal government should do more to solve social problems.	46	61
We need government-sponsored national health care insurance.	41	48
The U.S. should spend more on the military and defense.	26	27
We still need more legislation to protect women's rights.	21	30
Education policy should focus on improving public schools rather than encouraging alternatives such as private and religious schools.	18	50
Current welfare reform laws are too harsh and hurt children.	15	22

with respect to the "moral reform" agenda. Indeed, some marked differences between the two groups of clergy appear over certain key questions asked in the "moral reform" section. For example, while over three-fourths of CRC clergy surveyed in 2001 favored banning all abortions, only about half of RCA clergy did so. The greatest difference between clergy on such "moral reform" issues, however, relates to government assistance to private schools, with CRC clergy giving substantially more support for the proposal than RCA clergy. While fully 80 percent of CRC clergy supported government vouchers to parents of children attending private or religious schools, only 38 percent of RCA clergy did so.

The degree of support given by both CRC and RCA clergy to the social justice agenda varied considerably from issue to issue. In general, ministers from each denomination tended to provide similar responses to social justice questions. The biggest difference in the "social justice" category that divided CRC and RCA pastors concerned education policy, with RCA clergy being far more supportive of public, rather than private or religious, schools. Other notable, though smaller, gaps appeared with respect to Israeli concessions, the proper role of the federal government, and gay rights. Pastors from the two denominations were evenly divided on the need for more environmental protection and for affirmative action, and they were united as well in their opposition to increased defense spending.

Issue Positions of CRC and RCA Laity

The limited available data on the issue positions of Christian Reformed and Reformed Church members necessitates some caution when comparing the issue stands of church members across the two denominations (as well as when comparing pastors and parishioners within each denomination). Nevertheless, there are some data that can enable us at least to begin to address these questions.

We begin by examining whether the issue positions reported by CRC and RCA laity are as conservative on such issues as they are in terms of ideology. Table 5.6 reports the issue positions of CRC and RCA laity given at the turn of the millennium, along with the responses given by RCA clergy in 1999 (the 2001 survey of CRC and RCA clergy did not contain these specific issue questions). The data reveal that there is considerable ideological diversity among CRC and RCA laity with respect to both the "moral reform" and "social justice" agendas. For example, with respect to the moral reform agenda, majorities of congregants from both denominations gave "conservative" responses concerning prayer in public schools, gay public school teachers, and genetic engineering. Yet, majorities of CRC and RCA members gave "liberal" responses concerning relative-assisted euthanasia. Thus, as was revealed earlier among clergy, consistency between a self-reported ideological perspective and responses to specific political and moral issues is not always present among the laity of the two denominations.

With respect to the limited number of "social justice" agenda items included in Table 5.6, majorities of members from both denominations gave "conservative" responses to each issue —forgiving debt obligations

Table 5.6
Issue Positions among CRC and RCA Laity
at the Turn of the Millennium
(Percent agreeing)

| | Laity | | Clergy |
	CRC	RCA	RCA
Moral Reform Agenda			
Permitting prayer in public schools	84%	83%	60%
Instituting tax deductions for private school tuition	73	43	51
Banning all abortions	77	50	50
Allowing next-of-kin to withdraw life-support systems	63	73	70
Imposing death penalty for persons convicted of murder	44	40	20
Religious people today need special protection	38	x	x
Allowing homosexuals to teach in public schools	19	26	48
Churches and clergy should stay out of politics	19	x	x
Social Justice Agenda			
Forgiving debt obligations of developing countries	28%	20%	x
Increasing gov. programs to deal with social problems	22	25	29
Seeking new applications of genetic engineering	17	15	32

of developing countries, increasing federal government efforts to solve social problems, and seeking new applications of genetic engineering.

On certain issues, however, clear differences emerged between parishioners of the two denominations. For example, CRC congregants were far more "conservative" on abortion than their RCA counterparts: while 77 percent of CRC congregants in the year 2000 favored a ban on all abortions, only 50 percent of RCA congregants did so. Large interdenominational gaps also appeared with respect to government assistance for private schools. CRC laity reflected their denomination's traditional support for Christian education, as nearly three-quarters (73 percent) agreed that the government should institute tax deductions for private education, while less than half (43 percent) of RCA parishioners did so.

Just as was true among CRC and RCA clergy, members within the two denominations also tend to self-identify as political conservatives. Similarly, the issue positions of laity in the two denominations are not nearly as conservative as their ideological orientations might suggest. These findings comport well with studies of the American electorate that demonstrate there is a lack of ideological consistency or attitudinal "constraint" among much of the American public (Campbell et al. 1964; Nie et al. 1976; Smith 1989).

Because there are relatively few questions on political issues that were asked in an identical fashion for both clergy and parishioners at approximately the same time, it is difficult to compare thoroughly the issue positions of clergy with those of laity. However, a limited number of identical questions were posed in the 1999 RCA clergy and laity study (some of which were then included in the 2000 laity survey of CRC members), and these clergy data are also found in Table 5.6. These data reveal that, at least for the RCA, the degree of clergy-laity issue agreement varies widely by the issue under consideration. On several topics, including abortion, increasing government spending on social problems, and allowing relatives to withdraw life-support systems, ministers and members within the RCA proved to be in close agreement. However, other survey questions revealed considerable differences between the two groups, including prayer in public schools, tax deductions for private school tuition, special protection for religious people, permitting homosexuals to teach in the public schools, and genetic engineering. Significantly, and in keeping with the previously mentioned study by Luidens and Nemeth (2003), these differences do not occur in a consistently liberal or conservative direction. On certain issues (such as prayer in public schools, capital punishment, permitting homosexuals to teach in public schools, and genetic engineering), the laity tend to give more conservative responses than do clergy, but with respect to other issues (specifically, tax deductions for private school tuition and permitting relatives to withdraw life support systems) the opposite is true.

Political Engagement

Ultimately, these ideological orientations, patterns of partisanship, and issue positions count for very little unless individuals involve themselves, directly or indirectly, in the political process.

Therefore it is important to examine more carefully whether clergy perceive themselves to be politically engaged and precisely what forms of political activity they believe to be legitimate and desirable.

Do CRC and RCA clergy see themselves as significant political actors, exhibiting confidence in their own ability to influence others (a confidence which political scientists sometimes label "political efficacy")? Although there are only limited data concerning this matter, the 1997 clergy survey included several questions on this matter, with the results presenting mixed findings regarding clergy political efficacy. On the one hand, a fairly large number of ministers seemed confused by the political process: when asked whether "it is difficult for ministers to know the proper political channels to use to accomplish some goal," nearly half of the CRC pastors (47 percent) agreed, as did well over a third (39 percent) of the RCA counterparts (data not shown).

On the other hand, in 2001, more than half of the ministers from each denomination (57 percent in the CRC and 59 percent in the RCA) agreed that "pastors have great potential to influence the political beliefs of their congregation"(data not shown). At the same time, only minorities of Christian Reformed Church (39 percent) and Reformed Church pastors (31 percent) expressed agreement that "churches and clergy should *not* try to influence or lobby public officials." Indeed, clergy in both denominations see value in promoting interdenominational political cooperation. When asked in 1997 whether "clergy of different faiths need to cooperate more in politics, even if they cannot agree in theology," approximately two-thirds of both CRC and RCA ministers concurred (data not shown).

In spite of these findings, CRC and RCA clergy do not accept the value of clergy political involvement uncritically. Indeed, approximately two-thirds of the ministers in both denominations who responded to the 1997 survey agreed that "some Christian leaders in America have gone too far in mixing religion and politics." But, when asked in 2001 whether "some clergy in *my denomination* have gone too far in mixing religion and politics," less than one-quarter of CRC pastors (22 percent) expressed agreement, while a little more than one-third of RCA clergy (36 percent) did so (data not shown).

It appears that ministers from both denominations tend to take relatively sophisticated approaches to politics and church-state relations, rejecting simplistic and ahistorical approaches. For example, in 2001, approximately one-half of responding CRC pastors (51 percent) and RCA counterparts (49 percent) *disagreed* with the position that the "the U.S. was founded as a Christian nation." In the same vein, overwhelming proportions of both CRC (77 percent) and RCA (76 percent) ministers rejected the dogmatic notion that "on most important political issues, there is only one correct Christian view" (data not shown).

The predominant view among clergy from both denominations is one favoring, rather than opposing, political engagement. Christian Reformed and Reformed Church ministers are unified in their rejection of the view that the Christian's task is exclusively spiritual. Indeed, in 1997, only seven percent of CRC clergy and six percent of RCA pastors expressed agreement with the proposition, "Christianity is clear about separating spiritual and secular realms and emphasizing spiritual values." Moreover, approximately half of both CRC ministers (48 percent) and RCA pastors (46 percent) indicated, in 2001, that they would like to be "more involved" in social and political activities than they currently are. Furthermore, in the same year, substantial percentages of CRC and RCA ministers (48 percent and 36 percent, respectively) also agreed that their particular denomination needed to be "more involved in social and political issues" (data not shown).

Issues Addressed from the Pulpit

Which issues do CRC and RCA ministers address most often from the pulpit? Are there differences in the political agendas of clergy from the two denominations, and have those agendas changed over time? Our clergy surveys from 1989, 1997, and 2001 reveal that there is tremendous variation in the frequency with which CRC and RCA ministers address various issues (data not shown). Some topics, including "abortion" and "hunger and poverty," are discussed relatively frequently, while others, including "gay rights" and "Israel," are not often addressed from the pulpit. In general, Christian Reformed Church clergy reported addressing "moral reform" issues somewhat more frequently than did their Reformed Church counterparts, while RCA clergy discussed "social justice" issues more often than the CRC clergy. Differences between CRC and RCA clergy on abortion and pornography proved to be particularly great, with CRC ministers indicating a much greater propensity to address these issues. On the other hand, RCA pastors proved far more likely to address the social justice issue of national defense.

Overall, the frequency with which clergy from the two denominations address various issues has not changed markedly over time. One exception in this regard is an overall pattern of apparent decline in CRC clergy addressing issues of national defense, possibly reflecting the end of the "cold war" and the demise of the Soviet Union.

Approval of Clergy Political Activities

Ministers can, of course, engage in a wide variety of political activities other than simply addressing issues from the pulpit. These activities range from relatively "easy" activities, such as signing a petition, to more "difficult" actions, as running for public office. Equally important, however, is the fact that pastors may hold varying opinions about the appropriateness of these numerous political activities. Table 5.7 explores the norms expressed by CRC and RCA pastors regarding the different ways clergy can become involved and engaged politically. Responses are grouped into two categories: "direct action activities," involving active participation in the political process; and "cue-giving activities," wherein pastors give verbal cues or other indications to congregants regarding their preferences of political candidates or stands on political issues.

Table 5.7 reveals that there is a remarkable level of agreement among CRC and RCA ministers concerning the appropriateness of clergy participation in various forms of political action. Among both Christian Reformed and Reformed Church pastors, the greatest degree of support was expressed for direct action activities, such as organizing a church study group to discuss public affairs, contributing money to a political cause, or organizing a church action group—as well as for such cue-giving activities as publicly (though not from the pulpit) supporting a political candidate or delivering a sermon on a controversial political issue. As might be anticipated, more controversial activities such as committing civil disobedience, running for public office, and (especially) endorsing a candidate from the pulpit received lower approval levels from the clergy. While endorsing candidates from the pulpit may be an accepted practice among some ministers, it is definitely frowned on by both CRC and RCA ministers. Overall, in both denominations, clergy support tends to be greater for direct action than for cue-giving activities.

The data in Table 5.7 further reveal that some important changes have occurred over the past decade in the extent to which clergy in the two denominations express approval of various forms of clergy political activities. There has been a pronounced decline in the level of approval

Table 5.7
Clergy Approval of Clergy Political Activities
by Denomination over Time
(Percent approving)

	CRC		RCA	
	1989	2001	1989	2001
Direct Action Activities				
Organize a study group in church to discuss public affairs.	92%	85%	93%	78%
Contribute money to a candidate, party, or PAC	89	78	84	68
Form an action group in church to accomplish some social or political goal	82	59	78	57
Participate in a protest march	78	70	67	65
Join a national organization to work for political beliefs	75	55	62	45
Commit civil disobedience to protest some evil.	52	26	54	22
Run for public office or be appointed to public office.	48	51	53	56
Cue Giving Activities				
Publicly (not preaching) take a stand on a political issue	x	79%	x	79%
Publicly (not preaching) support a political candidate	77	53	69	45
While preaching, take a stand on some political issue	60	44	60	46
Deliver a sermon on a controversial social or political topic	73	65	78	68
Take a stand while preaching on some moral issue	x	96	x	92
Endorse a candidate from the pulpit	7	x	5	x

x – question not asked in survey

reported by CRC and RCA pastors for clergy engagement in almost all forms of political involvement—regardless of whether it relates to direct-action or cue-giving activities. The extent to which there has been a decline in the approval of such activities tends to be consistently strong, as well. The only exception to these patterns of decline relates to clergy running for public office, where there was a slight increase in expressed approval.

It is one thing, of course, to believe that certain types of political involvement are appropriate for clergy political engagement; it is quite another for ministers actually to engage in them. Data from 2001 indicate that both CRC and RCA pastors proved more likely to engage in cue-giving activities than in direct political action (data not shown). This is not particularly surprising, since direct political action involves relatively greater expenditures of time and money than do simple cue-giving activities. For both Christian Reformed and Reformed Church clergy, the most frequently reported direct action was signing a petition and contacting a public official about some issue. Conversely, as one would expect, relatively few ministers of either denomination actually ran for public office. Both CRC and RCA ministers reported that they had quite frequently engaged in cue-giving activities, such as "touching on" a controversial issue, publicly taking a stand outside of church on a public issue, and praying publicly for candidates. However, relatively few pastors in either denomination reported that they had endorsed a political candidate from the pulpit.

When the reported political activity of CRC and RCA clergy in 1989 are compared with that reported in 2001, it is evident that there has been a consistent drop in all forms of political behavior between 1989 and 2001 among pastors of both denominations (data not shown). Whereas it might appear from media accounts that clergy have become more actively engaged in political campaigns, such increased involvement is not evident in terms of the responses of CRC and RCA ministers over time. Moreover, this pattern of decline in both the approval of and engagement in various forms of clergy political activity is not confined to only the CRC and RCA. These same patterns of decline are also evident among evangelical and mainline Protestant clergy over the same period of time, with such changes in political involvement linked, at least in part, to the growing theological conservatism among candidates who are entering the ministerial ranks today (Smidt 2004, chapter 23).

Nevertheless, these patterns of decline may have been reversed in the most recent presidential election of 2004. Certainly, "religion matters in American electoral politics and in the 2004 election it mattered particularly" (Smidt et al, 2006, 422). Given its importance in this most recent presidential election, it remains to be seen whether the patterns reported in Table 5.7 continue to hold or have been reversed in more recent political campaigns.

Conclusions

This chapter examines the politics of laity and clergy within both the Christian Reformed Church and the Reformed Church in America by focusing on several key issues. The first related to the primary political beliefs, identifications, and practices of the two groups. While data pertaining to laity are more limited than those for the clergy, it is fair to conclude that both members and ministers in the two denominations tend to be politically conservative in ideology and (for clergy) in party identification and voting behavior. The RCA, given its more politically liberal eastern wing, tends to be somewhat less politically conservative than the CRC.

A second issue addressed whether any major intra- or interdenominational political differences were evident in the issue positions taken by clergy and laity of the two denominations. When CRC and RCA pastors and parishioners tend to label themselves as political conservatives, their issue positions and group relationships are not nearly as consistently conservative as these identifications might suggest.

The issue positions adopted by Christian Reformed ministers and members on "moral reform" questions tend to be somewhat more conservative than those reported by their RCA pastors and parishioners. However, this pattern does not hold with respect to "social justice" issues, as there is greater agreement on such matters across the two denominations. CRC laity and clergy proved far more supportive of government aid to private schools than did their RCA counterparts; indeed, so great are these differences that one would expect that the two denominations would likely need to discuss them thoroughly prior to making any serious effort toward organizational unity. However, equally important as any differences between the CRC and RCA are the significant variations that appear within the Reformed Church itself. For example, in 2000, while nearly two-thirds (63 percent) of RCA members residing in the Midwest agreed that all abortions should be banned, only one-fifth (21 percent) of their fellow congregants in the East did so. No such regional gaps appeared within the Christian Reformed Church.

Finally, this chapter examined the political activities of CRC and RCA clergy. An examination focusing on both "direct action" and "cue giving" activities revealed similar patterns both between the two denominations and within each denominational body over time. In general, Christian Reformed Church and Reformed Church ministers tend to be politically efficacious and supportive of Christian political involvement. While the pastors reported that they engaged in some political actions quite frequently (principally signing a petition and touching on a political issue in a sermon), they generally avoided other forms of political involvement (such as running for public office or endorsing a political candidate from the pulpit). In general, "cue-giving" proved to be more common among ministers from both denominations than did "direct action," probably because the former generally requires less effort and entails less political and personal risk.

The overall pattern suggested by the data, then, is that both the CRC and RCA are generally conservative politically, both at the lay and at the clergy levels, with the CRC being somewhat more conservative than the RCA. Changes over the period of time examined here appear to have been in a more conservative direction, with growing political convergence between the two denominations. Indeed, some of the most important differences were found *within* the RCA rather than between the Christian Reformed Church and the Reformed Church in American or between the laity and clergy in either denomination.

CHAPTER 6

'How Lovely Is Your Dwelling Place, Oh Lord'?
Congregational Life in the CRC and RCA

Our analysis to this point has focused on the religious beliefs and behavior of individual CRC and RCA members and pastors. Now we shift our attention to the nature of congregational life within the Christian Reformed Church and the Reformed Church in America. This chapter seeks to ascertain the characteristics and practices of Reformed congregations in contemporary American life by examining congregational life within the two denominations in terms of their worship style, sermon content, member participation, and intrachurch conflict.

Congregations, as corporate bodies, attempt to accomplish various goals. They seek to express the most basic beliefs, values, and traditions held by their members, address different kinds of human needs both within and outside the membership, and provide their adherents with various opportunities to engage in acts of Christian ministry and service. Finally, congregations seek to establish and strengthen bonds of fellowship and Christian love among their members, while they also endeavor to attract new members, whether by transmitting their beliefs, values, and traditions to young children within their congregation or by appealing to those outside the church who may be drawn to participate in group life.

Congregations today confront a religious world in which traditional denominational loyalties have declined. In their place, a new individualism in religious life has emerged, tied, in part, to higher levels of education, greater geographical mobility, and increased exposure to broader cultural influences and ideas through the mass media. Largely gone are the old, socially cohesive, ethnocultural communities in which institutions of church, school, and family overlapped and reinforced shared values and norms.

How then are congregations to thrive in such an environment, where religious life is less a product of community socialization and more a matter of individual choice? The answer is that congregations frequently seek to succeed by "meeting people's needs," developing distinctive identities and ministries, and engaging in "niche marketing." Not long ago, the liturgy and worship style of CRC and RCA congregations tended to be relatively uniform across all churches. Such homogeneity, however, comes at a "cost." When the worship practices of congregations are identical, their appeal is to a relatively narrow segment of the religious "marketplace," limiting the denomination's outreach potential. A "market segmentation" approach (in which different congregations offer varying mission tasks, divergent worship styles, unique theological emphases, and distinct programs) provides potential members with increased choice and provides specific congregations within a denomination the ability to appeal to a wider, or at least a different, segment of the "market."

Associated with these changes have been a variety of efforts related to sharpening the distinctiveness of particular congregations. Today, many congregations have been encouraged to develop distinct mission statements and to form unique ministries. As a result, some congregations focus on forging a sense of community, others emphasize social justice or evangelism, and still others focus on worship. They differ in their mission emphases, the programs they offer, and the forms of worship they employ.

Thus, as religious affiliation in America is becoming much less "tribal" or ethnically tied, it increasingly reflects "the freedom of Americans to choose with whom they will congregate in service to their most basic values" (Warner 1993b, 1077). Conceivably, groups could still forge clear social and religious identities in spite of distinct ministries or unique styles of worship. But while growing diversity in congregational life (particularly in worship style, theological emphases, or mission efforts) provides opportunities for "church growth" within a denomination, it also creates a variety of new challenges for the denomination seeking to maintain some coherence among its various congregations.

The analyses of this chapter are drawn primarily from data collected through surveys of CRC and RCA congregations conducted in 1999 as part of the Faith Communities Today (FACT) study. The larger project gathered data from 14,301 congregations across forty-one different religious groups. Questionnaires were sent to key "informants," usually clergy, in each group. In the Christian Reformed and Reformed Church components of the study, questionnaires were sent to every congregation in both denominations located in the United States.[1] The survey included questions related to the congregation's emphasis on ministry, the nature of its worship services, and the characteristics of the congregation's regularly participating adults. Final survey results included responses from a total of 399 RCA congregations and 514 CRC congregations in the United States.

The analysis of contemporary Reformed congregational life will begin by examining the size and location of congregations in the CRC and RCA today. We then look closely at the different reported bases of authority within congregational life of the two denominations, the variations in their reported mission emphases, and the unique liturgical practices they follow. The focus then turns to the different kinds of social outreach programs provided by CRC and RCA congregations as well as the extent to which members tend to participate in such programs. Finally, the chapter concludes with an examination of conflict in the congregational life of the two denominations.

Reformed Congregations Today

Size and Location

As can be seen in Table 6.1, there are some important differences in the reported sizes of congregations in the CRC and RCA. The majority of bodies in both denominations fall between 100 and 399 professing members, with 53 percent of CRC and 59 percent of RCA congregations reflecting this membership size. There are more small RCA than CRC congregations, and more large parishes in the Christian

---

[1] In the CRC, surveys were also sent to all Canadian congregations; a total of 171 surveys were returned from Canadian churches. Depending on the question at hand, some analyses will include all CRC congregations, regardless of whether they are Canadian or American; at other times, only CRC congregations located in the United States will be compared to RCA congregations located in the United States.

Reformed Church than in the Reformed Church in America. Nearly one-third of RCA congregations (29 percent) report membership of fewer than one hundred individuals, while nearly one-fifth of CRC churches (17 percent) do so. Conversely, while three in ten Christian Reformed assemblies (31 percent) report having four hundred or more professing members, barely one in ten Reformed Church groups (12 percent) exhibit such size.

Table 6.1
Characteristics of CRC and RCA Congregations

	CRC	RCA
Size of Membership		
0- 99 members	17%	29%
100-199 members	26	32
200-299 members	15	16
300-399 members	12	11
400+ members	31	12
Total	101%	100%
Size of Community		
Rural	14%	13%
Town/Small City	31	37
Large City	35	29
Suburbs	21	21
Total	101%	100%

While the membership size of CRC and RCA congregations varies, the types of communities in which they are located tend to be similar. As can be seen from Table 6.1, the distribution of the two groups is virtually identical across their different contexts. The percentage of CRC and RCA congregations that are found in rural settings is nearly the same (14 percent versus 13 percent, respectively), and the percentage of congregations found in the suburbs is equal (21 percent). A plurality of RCA churches (37 percent) are found in towns or small cities, while a plurality of CRC assemblies (35 percent) are in large cities.

Not only are congregations from the two groups located in similar physical settings, their total professing membership is basically equivalent and their structures are located largely in the same geographic settings. Table 6.2 presents statistics drawn from official church records for 2000; these reveal 186,000 professing members in CRC congregations and 181,000 professing members in RCA congregations. A majority of the CRC's professing members (54 percent) are located in the Midwest, as are a majority of those in the RCA (61 percent). One-third of all CRC professing individuals (33 percent) and nearly one-third of all those in the RCA (29 percent) live in the state of Michigan. The biggest difference between the two denominations relates to the different proportions of members who reside in the East and in Canada. Whereas a quarter of all CRC professing members (26 percent)

Table 6.2
Professing Members and Geographical Location:
CRC and RCA in the Year 2000

	CRC	Total	RCA	Total
Total Professing Members	186,226		181,163	
Canada	48,519[1]	26%	3,875[5]	2%
East	8,915[2]	5	47,178[6]	26
Midwest	100,944[3]	54	111,009[7]	61
West	27,848[4]	15	19,101[8]	11
Grand Rapids	18,474	10%	15,918	9%
Grand Rapids/Grandville				
/Zeeland	9,377	16	25,908	14
Michigan	62,011	33	52,903	29

1. Alberta North, Alberta South/Saskatchewan, British Colombia North-West, British Columbia South-East, Chatham, Hamilton, Huron, Niagara, Quinte, Toronto
2. Atlantic Northeast, Hackensack, Hudson, Southeast U.S.
3. Chicago South, Georgetown, Grand Rapids East, Grand Rapids North, Grand Rapids South, Grandville, Heartland, Holland, Iakota, Illiana, Kalamazoo, Lake Erie, Lake Superior, Minnkota, Muskegon, Northcentral Iowa, Northern Illinois, Northern Michigan, Pella, Thornapple Valley, Wisconsin, Zeeland
4. Arizona, California South, Central California, Columbia, Greater Los Angeles, Pacific Hanmi, Pacific Northwest, Red Mesa, Rocky Mountain, Yellowstone
5. Regional Synod of Canada
6. Regional Synod of Albany, Regional Synod of the Mid-Atlantics, Regional Synod of New York
7. Regional Synod of the Great Lakes, Regional Synod of the Heartland, Regional Synod of Mid-America
8. Regional Synod of the Far West

are Canadians, only one in fifty RCA church members (2 percent) reside there. On the other hand, one-quarter of all RCA professing members (26 percent) live in the eastern United States, while only one in twenty CRC members (5 percent) reside in that region.

Authority and Mission

Congregations not only vary in their size and physical location, they can also vary in the bases of authority upon which they draw for

Table 6.3
Source of Authority by Denomination

How important are the following sources of authority in the worship and teaching of your congregation?

Level of Importance	Founda- tional	Very Imp.	Some What	Little/No Imp.	Total
Sacred scripture					
CRC	98%	2	*	0	100%
RCA	90%	10	0	0	100%
Historic creeds, doctrines & tradition					
CRC	20%	59	19	3	101%
RCA	15%	54	29	2	100%
Holy Spirit					
CRC	62%	30	7	*	99%
RCA	29%	52	17	3	101%
Human reason and understanding					
CRC	3%	41	48	8	100%
RCA	3%	32	55	11	100%
Personal experience					
CRC	3%	37	52	8	100%
RCA	1%	23	55	21	100%

* less than 1 percent

worship and teaching. Here we examine five different possible sources of religious authority: sacred scripture; historic creeds and doctrines; the Holy Spirit, human reason; and personal experience. The key informants were asked to assess whether each of the five sources was foundational, very important, somewhat important, or of little or no importance in their congregational life. Table 6.3 examines responses from both denominations.

The patterns reported by the key informants largely mirror each other across the two denominations (particularly if one merges the "foundational" and "very important" responses). Not surprisingly, the most frequently noted basis of authority within Reformed congregational life is sacred scripture. Virtually all key informants within the CRC (98 percent) and an overwhelming majority in the RCA (90 percent) cited scripture as a foundational source of religious authority. On the other hand, very few key informants from either group (3 percent or less) reported that either human reason or personal experience were foundational as sources of authority in their congregational life. Finally, the attributed levels of importance given to the historic creeds and doctrines within the life of their particular Reformed congregations are quite similar across the two denominations; 20 percent of the key informants within the CRC and 15 percent of those from the RCA report that creeds and doctrines serve as a foundational source of authority in their congregational life.

Some differences in emphases exist between the CRC and RCA. Most noteworthy is the divergent emphasis placed on the Holy Spirit as a source of authority. Nearly two-thirds (62 percent) of the respondents for the Christian Reformed Church reported that the Holy Spirit is a foundational source of authority within their congregational life, while less than one-third (29 percent) of Reformed Church respondents did so. Still, the Holy Spirit is viewed as a critical component within RCA congregations, as a majority of Reformed Church survey participants (52 percent) view the Holy Spirit to be very important; RCA key informants are simply less prone than those in the CRC to report the authority of the Holy Spirit to be foundational in nature. Second, while a majority of both CRC and RCA key respondents rated both human reason and personal experience as relatively minor sources of authority in congregational life, CRC survey participants were slightly more likely than RCA informants to attribute some level of importance to these factors.

Of course, the data presented in Table 6.3 do not reveal which one of these sources serves as the *most* important source of authority within congregational life. This issue is addressed in Table 6.4, which reveals clearly the central role played by scripture in Reformed congregational life: approximately nineteen out of twenty churches, regardless of denomination, report that the Bible is the primarily basis of authority. In fact, in contrast to the pattern in Table 6.3, a higher percentage of RCA than CRC key informants (97.5 percent versus 93.5 percent, respectively) reported that scripture is the most important source of authority within their congregational life. Respondents within the Christian Reformed Church were slightly more likely than those in the Reformed Church to cite the Holy Spirit (4.4 percent versus 1.3 percent, respectively) as filling that role.

Table 6.4
Most Important Source of Authority by Denomination
(Percent of importance)

The one source of authority that is most important in
your congregation's worship and teaching

	CRC	RCA
Sacred Scripture	94.5%	97.5%
Historic creeds, doctrines, and tradition	1.4	0.5
Holy Spirit	4.4	1.3
Human reason and understanding	0.2	0.3
Personal experience	0.5	0.5
	100.0%	100.1%

If the source of authority for congregational life is basically identical across the two denominations, then do churches in the CRC and RCA also see their congregational missions similarly? Table 6.5 examines the extent to which different statements about congregational "mission" serve to describe the lives of Reformed congregations in the American context. These data explore whether there are more apparent differences between the two denominations in relationship to their congregational "mission" than in terms of the primary basis of authority within the congregation. In other words, do some congregations choose to focus specifically on social justice, others on denominational distinctiveness, and still others on deepening relationships between congregational members and God?

Most CRC and RCA congregations appear to emphasize a "spiritual" mission, with most key informants stating that participation

Table 6.5
Congregational Mission by Denomination
(Percent of accomplishment)

How well does each of the following describe your congregation?

	Very Well	Quite Well	Some what	Slightly	Hardly at all	Total
Helps deepen relationship with God						
CRC	17%	58	22	3	*	100%
RCA	23%	46	28	3	1	101%
Expresses denominational heritage						
CRC	20%	46	25	9	1	101%
RCA	8%	28	34	26	3	99%
Has clear sense of mission and purpose						
CRC	14%	39	34	11	3	101%
RCA	17%	42	31	8	1	99%
Trying to increase its diversity						
CRC	6%	18	25	26	26	101%
RCA	7%	14	29	28	22	100%
Is working for social justice						
CRC	2%	15	39	36	7	99 %
RCA	2%	13	34	41	9	99 %
Trying to preserve ethnic heritage						
CRC	3%	6	17	31	44	101%
RCA	3%	9	13	25	50	100%

* less than 1 percent

in congregational life serves to help those involved to deepen their relationship with God. Fully three-quarters of those in the CRC (75 percent) and more than two-thirds of RCA participants (69 percent) reported that the phrase "helps deepen one's relationship with God" described their congregation life either "very well" or "quite well." Moreover, only a handful (less than 5 percent) in either denomination rated this item as only "slightly" or "hardly at all" descriptive of their church.

Secondly, preserving denominational uniqueness was seen as a central mission for many congregations, although the CRC tended to place a greater emphasis on expressing their denominational heritage than did the RCA. Nearly two-thirds (69 percent) of Christian Reformed congregations are described as expressing their denominational heritage either "very well" or "quite well," while only a little more than a third (36 percent) of Reformed Church respondents are so described: denominational heritage is only "slightly" or "hardly at all" expressed in nearly one-third (29 percent) of RCA congregations.

Thirdly, almost half of the assemblies in both denominations seem to suffer from the lack of a clear sense of mission and purpose. While 59 percent of the RCA and 53 percent of the CRC congregational respondents believed that their church "had a clear sense of mission and purpose" (answering "very well" or "quite well" on this item), many others felt more ambivalent about this crucial component of the life and mission of Reformed congregations.

In contrast, most survey participants within the two denominations do not describe "working for social justice" or "preserving [their] ethnic heritage" as being particularly reflective of their congregational life. In fact, fewer than 20 percent of the respondents in either the CRC or the RCA report that "working for social justice" described their congregational life either "very well" or "quite well"; most report that working for social justice describes the emphasis of their congregation only "somewhat" or "slightly" so. Similarly, only about 10 percent in either group appear to emphasize their Dutch heritage as a significant "mission." In fact, at least twice as many key informants assert that their congregation is making a concerted effort to increase their diversity than that it is seeking to preserve its ethnic heritage. Nearly a quarter (24 percent) of the CRC survey participants rate the phrase "trying to increase its diversity" as describing their congregational life "very well" or "quite well," while more than one-fifth (21 percent) of the key informants in the Reformed Church do so.

Liturgical Life

If many Reformed congregations fail to have a clear sense of mission and purpose, does such confusion become evident in the liturgical life of the congregation? If the Bible serves as the primary basis of authority across congregational life in the two denominations, then what themes typically serve as the focus of sermons or the broader liturgy within the worship life of the congregation? These are questions that are addressed next, as the FACT survey also contained questions that asked respondents to assess the focus of worship in terms of the following characteristics: God's love and care, practical advice for daily living as a Christian, personal spiritual growth, and social justice.

Despite the apparent lack of clarity about congregational mission and purpose, there appears to be little difference in the liturgical life of CRC and RCA congregations. As can be seen in Table 6.6, the most common emphasis within congregational worship life is God's love and care, with 37 percent of CRC and 44 percent of RCA key informants reporting that such an affirmation always occurs within the worship of their congregations; less than 5 percent of key informants in both denominations responded that such an emphasis is only sometimes, seldom, or never expressed within their worship.

Ranking second in terms of focus is personal spiritual growth, as in both denominations nearly a quarter reports it is "always" and an additional three-fifths report that it is "often" emphasized. Advice for daily living receives a relatively similar, though somewhat less frequent,

Table 6.6
Focus of the Liturgy by Denomination
(Percent of occurrence)

How often does the following occur during worship in your congregation?

Focus of the Liturgy	Always	Often	Some times	Seldom	Never	Total
God's love and care						
CRC	37%	58	4	*	0	99%
RCA	44%	52	4	0	0	100%
Personal spiritual growth						
CRC	24%	63	12	*	0	99%
RCA	27%	61	11	1	0	100%
Advice for daily living						
CRC	21%	55	21	3	*	100%
RCA	24%	56	20	1	0	101%
Social justice or social action						
CRC	1%	15	57	25	2	100%
RCA	1%	15	57	27	*	100%

* less than 1 percent

emphasis in Reformed congregational life. Between one-fifth and one-quarter of the congregations, regardless of denomination, report that daily living advice is always stressed within their worship, while a relatively equivalent proportion report it to be only sometimes, seldom, or never emphasized as a liturgical focus in their worship life.

Social justice does not rank as a theme commonly heard within the worship life of either denomination. Relatively identical patterns are reported within both the Christian Reformed and Reformed Church, as only 16 percent report a rather frequent (either "always" or "often") emphasis on social action. Such an emphasis is not totally lacking, as a majority of respondents (57 percent) report having heard this affirmed on occasion ("sometimes"). Still, it is somewhat surprising that, given the historic emphasis on social justice within the Reformed tradition, such a relatively low percentage of congregations report hearing any stress on justice in any regularly occurring pattern.

While the emphasis of the liturgy may be relatively similar across Reformed congregations in the American context, are the styles of worship through which such emphases are made also similar? Over the past several decades, there has been within American Protestantism a growth in worship services characterized by a more informal and intimate format. Some congregations have chosen a more contemporary worship style, in which worship teams have become liturgical leaders in the place of the pastor, guitars and drums have replaced the organ, and praise melodies are sung more frequently than traditional hymns.

To what extent, then, do Reformed congregations differ in their styles of worship? Overall, the liturgical practices of CRC and RCA churches tend to be relatively similar, with some slight differences in focus (data not shown). Various traditional liturgical forms of worship continue to be evident within Reformed congregations at the turn of the millennium. For example, almost all churches use the organ or piano every Sunday during worship, as 84 percent of CRC and 88 percent of RCA congregations report always using it during corporate worship. Expository preaching is also frequently[2] evident within the worship services of both CRC and RCA assemblies, though it occurs somewhat more frequently within Christian Reformed than Reformed Church congregations (76 percent versus 59 percent, respectively). Finally, a majority of congregations in both denominations report that

---

[2]   The word "frequently" is used here to encompass those practices that either "always" or "often" occur.

the readings of creeds or statements of faith frequently occurs within their worship, though its practice is somewhat more common in CRC (68 percent) than RCA congregations (52 percent).

At the same time, there is evidence that a sizable proportion of congregations in both the Christian Reformed Church and the Reformed Church in America are employing more contemporary forms of worship. About one-quarter to one-third of congregations in both denominations report frequent use of such musical instruments as electronic keyboards, electric guitars, and drums in their worship services. Other forms of contemporary worship are somewhat less common; for example, the use of personal testimonies is a more occasional practice, as only 14 percent of CRC and only 9 percent of RCA congregations responded that time for testimonies is frequently provided in their worship services. Similarly, the use of dance or drama occurs only rarely: 7 percent of Christian Reformed and 10 percent of Reformed Church congregations report using such forms of worship with any frequency.

It is also clear that Reformed congregations are experimenting with changes in their liturgical practices (data not shown). Each of the key respondents was asked to compare the style of their congregation's worship five years ago to their current practice. More than one-tenth of the churches within both denominations reported that their worship style had changed a great deal over the specified time period. In fact, when one combines those congregations stating that their worship service had changed "somewhat" over the past five years with those asserting it has changed a "great deal," a majority of the CRC congregations and almost four out of ten RCA congregations have exhibited notable changes in their worship practices over the past decade.

By combining responses to these different worship styles,[3] one can classify Reformed congregations as those that employ more

3   The measure assessing worship style was constructed in the following manner: if the congregation reported (1) that they never employed an electronic keyboard, an electric guitar, and/or drums during their worship service, and (2) that they did not employ the use of visual projection equipment, then it was classified as "conventional" in its worship style. If the congregation did not always use the piano or organ in their worship, or if it was reported that they sometimes use electronic keyboards, guitars, and/or drums in their worship service, the congregation was classified as "mixed" in their worship style. But if it was reported that the congregation used electronic keyboards, guitars, and/or drums in the service with some

conventional, more mixed, and more contemporary forms of worship. The resultant patterns suggest that Reformed Church assemblies are more prone than their CRC counterparts to employ more traditional liturgical practices in their worship services or, conversely, that CRC churches are more willing than RCA groups to use "mixed" or contemporary forms of liturgical practices in their weekly worship (data not shown). More than one-half (52 percent) of all Reformed Church in America congregations at the turn of the millennium could be classified as employing a conventional worship style, while a little more than one-third (38 percent) of the Christian Reformed Church can be so classified. On the other hand, nearly one-third (31 percent) of CRC and almost one-quarter (24 percent) of RCA congregations conduct their services with relatively contemporary modes of worship.

There is a relationship, however, between the congregation's mission emphasis and its style of worship. Those congregations placing a relatively greater emphasis on deepening relationships with God are more likely to employ contemporary forms of worship in their congregational life. This is true for both CRC and RCA congregations, and the strength of the connection is virtually identical across the two denominations (data not shown).

Likewise, those churches seeking to express the denomination's history or preserve their ethnic heritage are more likely to employ traditional forms of worship practice. There is also a clear relationship between those congregations that stress the authority of doctrine and those that attempt to preserve their denominational uniqueness, ethnic heritage, and to further social justice. Not surprisingly, those congregations that place a greater emphasis on the historic creeds and doctrines of the denomination are far more likely to report that the congregation reflects and values its denominational heritage well. Those congregations that emphasize the authority of the historic creeds and doctrines of the church are also more likely to be characterized as trying to preserve the ethnic heritage of the congregation (data not shown). These patterns hold for both denominations.

Congregational Activities

What forms of ministry and outreach do Reformed congregations provide beyond conducting services of worship? This issue is addressed

---

regularity along with the use of visual projection equipment, then it was classified as being "relatively contemporary" in terms of its worship style.

in Table 6.7, which examines the forms of outreach and ministry engaged in by Reformed congregations, including the types of social service programs CRC and RCA congregations report that, alone or in cooperation with others, they have sponsored in the past twelve months. Sixteen possible programs are examined, and they are presented in descending order of importance according to CRC responses.

Nearly all churches (80 percent or more) within both the CRC and RCA report that they provide emergency kinds of social services through

Table 6.7
Social Service Programs Provided
by Reformed Congregations by Denomination

In the past 12 months, did your congregation directly provide, or cooperate in providing, any of the following services for your own members or for people in the community?

		CRC*	RCA
1.	Cash assistance to families or individuals	96%	81%
2.	Food pantry or soup kitchen	88	97
3.	Thrift store or thrift store donations	74	71
4.	Prison or jail ministry	56	35
5.	Senior citizen programs	42	51
6.	Elderly, emergency, or affordable housing	41	45
7.	Counseling services or "hot line"	40	65
8.	Hospital or nursing home care	40	50
9.	Substance abuse programs	33	40
10.	Organized social issue advocacy	31	23
11.	Employment counseling, placement or training	27	10
12.	Day care	25	39
13.	Health programs, clinics, health education	23	27
14.	Tutoring or literacy programs	21	21
15.	Voter registration or voter education	17	9
16.	Programs for migrants or immigrants	16	9

* USA congregations only

the operation of food pantries or soup kitchens. Large majorities of the congregations also supply some form of cash assistance to individuals and families in times of financial crises. In addition, most groups (approximately three-quarters of the congregations in both the CRC and RCA) operate a thrift store or provide donations for the operation of such a facility.

No other social service is sustained by a majority of both denominations' congregations, although there are unique emphases in the CRC and RCA. Nearly two-thirds of Reformed Church groups report operating some kind of counseling or "hot line" service, and approximately one-half offer programs related to nursing home, hospital, and senior citizen care. On the other hand, a majority of CRC congregations offer, or cooperate in providing, some kind of prison or jail ministry.

The least commonly reported forms of social programs within the CRC and RCA are related to health care (with approximately one-quarter of congregations in both denominations reporting that they offer such programs), tutoring or literacy efforts (with a little more than one-fifth of the congregations providing such programs), and programs for migrants and immigrants, as well as those for voter registration and education outreach (with about one-seventh to one-tenth of congregations providing these ministries, depending on denomination). For the most part, little difference exists in the overall patterns between the two denominations. The major variations relate to counseling services (much more prevalent within the RCA) and prison or jail ministry programs (more emphasized in CRC churches).

Congregational Participation

To what extent, then, do different congregations within the CRC and RCA engage their members in the corporate life of the church? Does offering more programs and services enhance congregational participation, or do the same people tend to do all the work regardless of the ministry under consideration? And, do different mission emphases and styles of worship affect the extent to which individuals participate within the congregational life of the two denominations? In order to answer these questions, the level of participation by members is assessed in terms of three dimensions reported by the key informants: (1) estimated average attendance at Sunday morning worship; (2) reported difficulty of getting volunteers to fill the programmatic needs of the congregations; and (3) estimated percentage of congregational members who have been involved in congregational programs over the past twelve months.

As shown in Table 6.8, Sunday morning church attendance in the CRC tends to be somewhat greater than that in RCA congregations—with the mean Sunday attendance in CRC churches being 257, and, in RCA churches, 237. This lower level of attendance in RCA churches can be clearly attributed to the lower levels of attendance found in the Reformed Church in America in the East, where one-third of all RCA churches are located, and where Sunday attendance averages at 112 (data not shown).

Table 6.8
Average Sunday Morning Attendance
by Style of Worship and Pattern of Authority

		(Numbers of members)	
		CRC*	RCA
Mean Sunday Morning Attendance		257	237
Style of Worship			
Conventional		255	156
Mixed		256	229
Relatively Contemporary		259	416
Mission Emphasis			
Social Justice	1	235	192
	2	263	222
	3	259	265
Deepening One's			
Relationship with God	4	297	293

*   USA congregations only

Similar patterns appeared between CRC and RCA congregations when exploring the difficulty of getting members of the congregation to serve within the programs of the church. Approximately one-fifth of the key informants in both the CRC and RCA (23 percent versus 19 percent, respectively) reported no problem with membership participation in programs. But the vast majority of key informants (68 percent in the CRC versus 74 percent in the RCA) reported that their congregation faces a "continual challenge" to fill volunteer positions, though in the end they are able to find enough participants to serve (data not shown). Slightly fewer than one in ten of the groups in both the CRC and RCA (9 percent and 7 percent, respectively) report that they cannot find enough individuals to fill the programmatic needs of their congregations (data not shown).

However, when one examines in Table 6.8 the relationship between the style of worship and attendance at Sunday morning church services, one finds somewhat different patterns within the two denominations. For the CRC, there is no variation in frequency of church attendance due to congregational style of worship. Instead, average attendance hovers around the mean for all three styles of worship (traditional, mixed, and contemporary). The RCA, in sharp contrast, shows a clear progression in the average number of Sunday morning worship attendees as one moves from a more conventional style of worship (a low of 156 attendees) to those employing more contemporary forms (the highest attendance of 416).

There is greater similarity between the CRC and RCA when comparing the mission emphasis of the congregation[4] with average Sunday morning worship attendance. In general, the average attendance at worship services increases as the mission emphasis of the congregation moves away from a relatively greater emphasis on social justice and toward deepening congregants' personal relationship with God. This is true for both denominations, though the magnitude of such differences tends to be greater for the RCA. Overall, Table 6.8 suggests that there may be some relationship between the style of worship employed by a congregation and membership participation (at least for the RCA), as well as between the mission emphasis of the church and the level of congregational participation.

However, Sunday morning church attendance may not necessarily be the best method to assess participation in congregational life, particularly since a large number of RCA churches in the East have rather small congregations. Consequently, rather than examining the absolute number of those at worship services, it may be better to determine the relative portion of congregants who are actively

---

[4]   This measure was constructed in the following manner: the value representing the extent to which "seeking social justice" described congregational life was subtracted from the value representing the extent to which "deepening relationships with God" described that particular congregation.   This procedure created a measure that reflected a net difference between the relative emphasis placed on social justice versus the relative emphasis paced on deepening one's relationship with God.

engaged in the life and programs of the church. Therefore, the relationship between worship style and participation, and between mission emphasis and participation, is reviewed once more, but this time viewing congregational participation through the proportion of members who are actively engaged in church programmatic life.

Using this second approach, it is clear that worship style is more clearly related to greater congregational participation than is the mission emphasis of the group (data not shown). This is true for both the CRC and RCA, though the relationship proves stronger in the Christian Reformed Church than in the Reformed Church in America. For both denominations, a plurality of survey participants report that between 21 and 40 percent of their membership is actively engaged in the programs of the congregation. But, as one moves from conventional to more contemporary forms of worship, the percentage of those who report that more than 40 percent of their church members are actively engaged in congregational life increases (data not shown). In some ways, this may not be surprising, since more contemporary forms of worship tend to be more participatory in nature—with their use of worship teams, bands, and drama.

On the other hand, one might anticipate that congregations emphasizing social justice would also have relatively large proportions of their members engaged in ministry—even when they may be relatively small in total membership. However, in both the CRC and RCA, the relationship between individual participation and the mission emphasis of the church is very weak at best. Hence, worship style, rather than mission emphasis, is more strongly related to congregational involvement in church life.

Congregational Conflict

Congregations not only provide different types of programs and activities, they are also arenas in which conflict can transpire. How much conflict is there within CRC and RCA congregations today? Table 6.9 seeks to address this question by reporting the percentages of churches experiencing "moderate" or "serious" contention over a variety of matters.

Table 6.9 reveals, in the first place, that conflict within Reformed congregations is not rare. Approximately one-quarter of all congregations in both the CRC and RCA have experienced what their informants labeled "serious" problems sometime during the last five years (25 percent for CRC and 23 percent for RCA congregations).

Table 6.9
Level and Sources of Conflict in Reformed Congregations
Over the Past Five Years
(Percent reporting)

Conflict	CRC	RCA
Level of conflict		
Any report of serious congregational conflict regardless of source	25%	23%
Any report of either "moderate" or "serious" conflict regardless of source	58	56
Source of "Moderate" or "Serious" Conflict		
Worship Conduct	28%	21%
Members' Behavior	24	18
Leadership Style	21	24
Decision Making	15	18
Program/Mission	14	12
Theology	14	7
Pastor's Behavior	11	13
Money	11	19
Other	9	7
Minimum "N"	508	399

When "moderate" levels of conflict are added to these figures, nearly three-fifths of all churches in both denominations have experienced congregational conflict (58 percent for CRC and 56 percent for RCA congregations).

Secondly, it is clear that conflict within congregations can arise from many different sources, ranging from "worship conduct" to "money," from "leadership style" to "decision-making." For Christian Reformed churches, the most frequently listed source of congregational disagreement is "worship conduct," with more than one-quarter (28 percent) of all CRC key informants listing it as a "moderate" or "serious" source of conflict within the past five years. Among Reformed Church congregations, "leadership style" was the most commonly cited source of conflict, as almost one-quarter of survey participants (24 percent) noted that it served as a basis of "moderate" or "serious" contention in the congregation over the past five years. RCA churches also frequently experienced disagreements about "worship conduct" and "money," while CRC churches most often listed "members' behavior" and "leadership style" as the next most frequent sources of congregational conflict.

Table 6.9 further reveals that Christian Reformed and Reformed Church congregations do not differ significantly in the sources of congregational conflict they experience. In the nine categories that reflect potential sources of conflict, there is not one category in which the difference between the two denominations achieves a magnitude of a ten-percent difference. The largest gap found between CRC and RCA congregations relates to money as a source of congregational conflict, where there is an eight percent difference between the two denominations (with 11 percent of CRC and 19 percent of RCA informants citing it as a source of "moderate" or "serious" conflict within the congregation). For the remaining areas of contention, the differences between the two denominations is marginal in nature.

What kinds of congregations are less likely to experience conflict within their ranks? Analysis reveals that congregations which are "spiritually vital and alive," which help congregants "deepen relationships with God," and which are characterized by "spiritually uplifting/inspirational" worship tend, overall, to be associated with lower levels of internal conflict (data not shown). So, too, do those churches that report that they feel "like a close knit family," have programs to "strengthen personal relationships," and "easily assimilate new people." Not surprisingly, congregations that are financially healthy also tend to have relatively lower overall levels of internal conflict than do those which are financially stressed.[5] Those churches that "clearly express their denominational heritage," have a "clear sense of mission and purpose," maintain "well-organized" programs and activities to "deal openly with disagreements and conflicts," and which welcome "innovation and change" also tend to experience less internal contention than do those congregations that lack these characteristics.

Within the Christian Reformed Church, there is also a positive and significant relationship between "change in worship style over the past five years" and congregational conflict. The direction of this relationship is the same for congregations of the Reformed Church in America, although it is not statistically significant (data not shown).

---

[5]   It is likely, however, that there is an interactive relationship between the two variables; a lack of funds may be both a cause and a consequence of congregational conflict.

These data indicate that churches that have recently changed their worship styles have also experienced the greatest amount of conflict.[6]

In order to provide a more in-depth analysis of intracongregational conflict, we examined conflict over "worship conduct" more fully. This particular source of contention was selected because it is among the most commonly mentioned reasons for conflict in Reformed churches in North America, ranking first among CRC and second among RCA congregations.

In order to examine possible sources of worship service conflict, two sets of variables are analyzed: worship service content and environmental stress. Table 6.10 permits us to look at relationships between "worship service content" and disagreement over the conduct of services within the CRC and RCA. The data reveal that, for both denominations, there is less likely to be congregational conflict over worship when church services are viewed to be "spiritually uplifting." For example, 36 percent of CRC and 45 percent of RCA congregations with very uplifting services report having no conflict, whereas 21 percent of CRC and 40 percent of RCA congregations that fail to exhibit uplifting services report having no internal conflict (data not shown).

Analysts of American religion sometimes contrast "spiritual matters" with "material matters," as if an emphasis on the "spiritual" stands as some polar opposite of "social justice." However, Table 6.10 also demonstrates that congregations who regularly hear sermons on social justice are no more likely to report conflict over worship services than are those that state their worship services are spiritually uplifting. Within the CRC, an identical 36 percent of key informants report no serious disagreement about worship style within their congregations, regardless of whether their worship service is characterized as spiritually uplifting or whether they regularly hear sermons on social justice. Within the RCA, a similar pattern prevails; those congregations that often hear social justice topics are only marginally more likely to report some level of conflict over worship than those where worship is characterized as "spiritually uplifting" (59 percent versus 55 percent, respectively).

On the other hand, the presence of "spiritually uplifting" worship services is no guarantee that congregational conflict can be avoided. A quarter of those CRC informants (25 percent) and one-fifth

---

[6]   Once again some degree of interpretive caution is in order. It is quite possible that this increased conflict may be a consequence rather than a cause of change in worship style.

Table 6.10
Sources of "High" Worship Conflict in Reformed Congregations
(Percent agreeing)

	CRC Conflict			RCA Conflict		
	No	Some	High	No	Some	High
Worship service content						
Worship services are spiritually uplifting	36%	40	25	45%	37	18
Sermons often focus on on social justice	36%	34	30	41%	32	28
Environmental stress						
Regularly participating members increased since 1995	36%	45	19	47%	35	19
Great change in style of primary worship over past five years	13%	37	49	17%	34	49

of those RCA informants (18 percent) who reported that their worship services were "spiritually uplifting" nevertheless indicated that their congregations were marked by high levels of conflict. The same is true for those congregations who frequently hear sermons that focus on social justice. Approximately one in three such congregations (30 percent in the CRC and 28 percent in the RCA) are marked by high levels of congregational conflict. Viewed from this end of the spectrum, congregations that often hear sermons on social justice are slightly more likely to report "high" levels of internal conflict over worship than for those where worship services are characterized as being spiritually uplifting, regardless of denomination.

When one shifts attention away from the worship service content to factors that might be more "environmental" or "contextual" in nature, congregational conflict can also be evaluated. For example, changes in the "number of regularly participating adults" in the church could potentially shape contention in different directions. On the one hand, increasing participation may indicate vibrant ministry and reflect greater satisfaction with worship as presently practiced. But increasing numbers may also draw new people with different ideas and preferences, creating a context for potential discontent. Likewise, declining membership may also prompt calls for changes in the worship format and emphases in an attempt to draw new, and possibly younger, individuals to attend.

For both the CRC and RCA, negative relationships between such environmental flux and disagreement are evident. First, increasing membership clearly is not a panacea for the absence of conflict over worship styles. For example, among congregations reporting an increase in the number of regular participating members over the past five years (between 1995 and 2000), only about one-third of CRC (36 percent), and fewer than one-half of RCA (47 percent) churches had not experienced contention about worship practices.[7] Thus, congregational growth does not necessarily create high levels of satisfaction among members regarding the way worship is conducted.

It is also apparent from Table 6.10 that alterations in worship format are likely to be associated with high levels of congregational conflict over worship. Of course, the data cannot reveal whether the changes are the cause or the result of such contention. Nevertheless, relatively few churches report having experienced *no* disagreement about worship style when they also state that they have undergone a "great change" in the type of worship over the previous five years (13 percent in the CRC versus 17 percent in the RCA). Conversely, almost half (49 percent) of all CRC and RCA congregations that have experienced a "great change" in their style of worship report high levels of conflict over the conduct of worship.

Conclusion

This chapter has examined congregational life in the CRC and RCA today in terms of sources of authority, mission emphases, and styles of worship, evaluating how those factors may relate to participation in church life. The analysis has revealed considerable similarities between the two denominations. First, nearly all congregations in both the Christian Reformed and the Reformed Church report that the Bible serves as the foundational basis of

---

[7]   Again a word of interpretive caution is in order, since it is possible that congregational harmony may actually help increase the number of participating adults in a congregation. The arrow of causality probably points in both directions as these variables interact with each other.

authority governing their congregational life. Likewise, congregations in both denominations tend to mirror each other in their mission emphases, with most congregations reporting that congregational life helps deepen relationships with God. Similarly, the liturgical emphases and practices within both denominations are generally alike, though CRC congregations were somewhat more prone than their RCA counterparts to report notable changes in their worship style over the past five years.

While congregations in both the CRC and RCA tended to reflect similar patterns in sources of authority, mission emphases, and styles of worship, there was some variation in each of these factors within both denominations. These differences were found to be associated with tendencies within congregational life. First, the relative emphasis placed on creeds as a source of authority is related to preserving ethnic heritage, increasing diversity, and working for social justice. Second, congregations that strive to deepen the relationships of congregants with God were more likely to employ contemporary styles of worship. Finally, differences between the denominations in mission emphases and styles of worship are related to varying levels of congregational participation—whether such participation is measured by attendance at Sunday morning worship, the proportion of members actively involved in church ministries, or the types of social ministries in which congregational members choose to be engaged.

CHAPTER 7

'Come Labor On'?
Current Issues of Ecclesiastical Life within the CRC and RCA

The previous chapter addressed various matters related to congregational life, including painful issues related to congregational conflict. In this chapter, we shift our attention away from congregations to several issues frequently understood to be linked to divisions within both the CRC and the RCA. Specifically, this chapter will examine the views of clergy and laity related to the status of women and homosexuals within the two denominations.

At one time, divisions between the Reformed Church in America and the Christian Reformed Church, as well as those within each denomination, centered primarily on doctrinal matters. However, as was noted in chapter 2, during the last decades of the twentieth century, the centrality of historic religious doctrines within the life of the church appears to have waned. As a result, one of the more important characteristics of the current religious landscape is that issues being debated within the RCA and CRC today tend to reflect theological differences related to social policy debates transpiring within the larger American society. Members of the two denominations once differed over such questions as access to the Lord's Supper or the centrality of Calvinist doctrines like "total depravity" or "limited atonement." Today, however, the fault lines frequently run between those who adopt more "conservative" versus more "liberal" perspectives on such as issues as the rights and roles of women and homosexuals within church and society. These disputes have generated heated commentaries and created serious rifts within both the CRC and RCA, warranting specific attention.

Women in the Church

Following an extended period of debate, considerable political maneuvering, and extensive theological reflection, women were first ordained as ministers in the Reformed Church in 1979 and in the Christian Reformed Church in 1995. When these decisions were made, there was strong resistance from many in both denominations. For several successive years, overtures to affirm women in the ministry were rejected by a sizable number of classes. Within the RCA, efforts to change the constitution to allow inclusion of women failed to muster the requisite two-thirds vote of classes on several occasions, often falling just one or two classes short of approval. When the decision was finally settled (through judicial fiat rather than legislative agreement), there were many disgruntled members, but few left the denomination. Meanwhile, within the CRC, the conflict actually led to the exodus of a number of congregations from the church. The contrasting responses mirror the two denominations' differing emphases on doctrinal purity versus church unity. While there is not yet parity between women and men being called to CRC and RCA pastorates, the number of women in ministry has been growing in both churches.

However, within both denominations, women continue to face obstacles to serving in the church. At the 2005 General Synod of the CRC, delegates voted against a proposal that that would have allowed ordained women to serve as General Synod delegates. They did agree, however, to discuss the issue again when at least one-half of all classes allow for the ordination of female ministers. Indeed, it is in the role of minister of Word and sacrament where women continue to face the greatest hurdle. Not surprisingly, given the nearly two-decade difference between the Reformed and the Christian Reformed Church in permitting the ordination of women, these barriers are much more evident within the CRC today than within the RCA.

Table 7.1 analyzes responses of laity from both denominations at the turn of the millennium, assessing whether women are currently prohibited from holding offices in the congregations of which they are members. Within the RCA, excluding women from holding church office is relatively uncommon, although they are still barred from serving on consistories in some RCA congregations. Slightly less than one in six RCA survey participants reported that women were not allowed to be deacons (13 percent) or elders (14 percent) in their church. A slightly higher percentage of respondents (18 percent) noted that women were prohibited from serving as a minister of Word and sacrament within their congregation.

Table 7.1
Practice of Prohibiting Women's Ordination
in the CRC and RCA: 2000
(Percent agreeing)

Does your congregation prohibit...

	CRC	RCA
the election of women as ordained deacons?	44%	13%
the election of women as ordained elders?	62	14
the calling of women as ordained ministers?	71	18

Restrictions against women holding church offices are much more common in the Christian Reformed Church. Nearly half of the CRC laity (44 percent) reported that their churches prohibited women from serving as deacons, and nearly two-thirds (62 percent) replied that they were barred from being elders. An even higher percentage of CRC survey participants (71 percent) noted that women could not be ordained as ministers within their congregations.

So far, this discussion has focused on actions taken by individual congregations. Table 7.2 addresses the question of whether such congregational patterns reflect the perspectives of individual members. Clearly, members of a congregation may disagree with the policies that have been adopted by their church council. Thus, we shift our focus from the policies evident within one's congregation to the perspectives of congregational members themselves related to the ordination of women.

Despite this shift in analysis, there continue to be significant differences between the Reformed and Christian Reformed survey participants in terms of support for allowing ordination of women as ministers of the gospel. Whereas more than three out of four RCA laity (78 percent) agree that women should be permitted to hold the office of minister of Word and sacrament, only about one in two from the Christian Reformed Church (48 percent) concur. Clearly, CRC respondents are much more reluctant than their RCA counterparts to support female clergy.

Some of this difference in lay support for women's ordination across the two denominations may be a function of the length of time such a practice has been permitted within each group. For example, in the 1991 RCA laity survey, only 61 percent of those surveyed expressed approval to the same item (data not shown), whereas that percentage had grown to 78 percent in the most recent survey (Luidens and Nemeth 2003). Thus, with the lapse of time, there may well be similar increases in support among CRC laity.

What correspondence was found between congregational policies and individual perspectives? When comparing Tables 7.1 and 7.2, it is noteworthy that, while seven out of ten CRC laity (71 percent) report that their congregations prohibit the calling of female ministers, nearly half of these same CRC respondents (48 percent) believe that women should be permitted to serve in such a capacity. While these comparisons may indicate that the supporters of women's ordination are concentrated in the larger congregations (so that their overall numbers would have an impact on fewer congregations), it also suggests a wide-spread disjuncture between a sizable minority of the laity and the official policy of their church bodies. Within the Reformed Church, differences between congregational policy and the opinions of the laity are much less pronounced.

Clergy of both denominations tend to be more supportive of women's ordination than the members of their churches, though the difference between ministers and laity on this issue is rather small in the RCA. More than four out of five Reformed Church clergy (82 percent) support the ordination of women to the ministry, while three of five Christian Reformed pastors (60 percent) do so.[1] RCA ministers tend to be marginally more supportive of women's ordination than their parishioners (82 percent versus 78 percent, respectively). However, in the CRC there is a much more significant gap between the levels of support voiced for women holding the office of minister among clergy (60 percent) than among laity (48 percent).

Table 7.2 also examines the responses of laity in terms of age, gender, and region. For surveyed ministers, comparisons were made among several age categories. Since there are relatively few women clergy serving congregations in either denomination (but particularly the CRC), gender comparisons were not analyzed among responding

---

[1]   This percentage increased to 63 percent among CRC clergy in 2005, while it remained at 82 percent for RCA clergy.

Table 7.2
Level of Approval among CRC and RCA Laity and
Clergy for Women in Church Office: 2000
(Percent agreeing)

Agree that women should be allowed to hold the
office of Minister of Word and sacrament

	CRC	RCA
All Laity	48%	78%
Sex		
Male	49%	75%
Female	47	80
Age		
Under 40	49%	76%
40 thru 59	53	80
60+	42	77
Region		
Canada	61%	*
East	41	94
Midwest	44	71
Remainder	45	76
All Clergy	60%	82%
Age		
25-40	61%	77%
45-54	62	84
55+	58	82

* Canadian laity not surveyed in the RCA.

pastors. Also, clergy responses were not analyzed cross-nationally, since the surveys asking this question were confined to those pastors serving congregations in the United States.[2]

---

[2]   This restriction was based on the fact that the original intent of the survey was to examine how religious factors may have shaped the political attitudes and behavior of CRC and RCA clergy during the course of the previous U.S. presidential election.

Some interesting differences appear in the response patterns across the two denominations. For example, among RCA laity, women are slightly more supportive of female ordination than are men (80 percent versus 75 percent, respectively). In the CRC, the opposite is true, with men somewhat more likely to approve of female ministers than are women (49 percent versus 47 percent, respectively). While the differences are not large, the overall pattern is clear; both men and women in the Reformed Church are more supportive of women's ordination than are their counterparts in the Christian Reformed Church.

Likewise, when one examines support for female ordination among RCA members in terms of respondent's age, one finds fairly equivalent levels of approval across the three age-categories: relatively young, middle-aged, or relatively old. If any pattern emerges, it would be that the middle-aged respondents tend to be slightly more supportive of the practice than either the younger or older respondents, although the data are remarkably consistent across the age groups. Among the CRC laity, however, a greater disparity exists with regard to the age of the respondent; CRC members who fall into the category of sixty years or older are the least supportive of women's ordination.

Finally, there are also some notable regional differences within the United States across the two denominations. In the RCA, nearly all laity who reside in the East voice their approval for women serving as ministers of the Word (94 percent approving), whereas approximately three-quarters of Reformed Church membership in the Midwest or the remaining portions of the country do so (71 percent and 76 percent, respectively). By contrast, members of the CRC in the eastern United States are the least supportive of women's ordination (41 percent), and when examining the Midwest or the rest of the country, the differences deviate very little (44 percent and 45 percent, respectively).

Interestingly, though relatively few CRC congregations permit the calling of women as ordained ministers, a substantial majority of Christian Reformed survey respondents (60 percent) reported having heard a woman preach (data not shown). This number nearly approaches the figure reported by RCA laity, with three-quarters (75 percent) of RCA survey participants reporting having heard a woman preach.

Within the Reformed Church, increased approval of women's ordination among RCA laity has been seen over time—from 79 percent in 1991 to 86 percent in 2000 (Luidens and Nemeth 2003).

While considerable opposition remains to women holding church office within the Christian Reformed Church, it is likely that time will dissipate these negative opinions as it has done in the RCA. Not only do younger members of the CRC support women's ordination more strongly than do older members, but CRC ministers are more supportive of such ordination than are the church's laity as a whole. The clergy's role as leaders and promoters of policy and agenda is likely to bring the membership along in their direction. This evolution in acceptance may be instructive for the changes underway in relation to the status of homosexuals in the church.

Homosexuality

Perhaps no issue divides the Christian church today more than that of homosexuality and the role homosexuals should play in church life. It is the source of considerable theological and doctrinal debate as well as of sociological, psychological, and biomedical investigation. As is true for many denominations, this issue continues to simmer through both the CRC and RCA. Beginning with its 1973 General Synod report, which distinguished between homosexual orientation and homosexual practice, the CRC has engaged in an extended debate (for example, see the Fall 1997 issue of the Calvin Seminary *Forum*).[3] Most recently, the topic of homosexuality was raised at the CRC's 2005 General Synod, where delegates debated what to do in response to a church in Toronto, Ontario, that purportedly allows members living in same-sex unions to hold church office.

Likewise, debate in the RCA has been taking place since the Christian Action Commission proposed a formal statement in 1974. The Reformed Church discussion intensified during 2004 and 2005, rising to a crescendo at its 2005 General Synod, where the Reverend Norman Kansfield, retiring president of the denomination's New

[3]   The distinction between "orientation" and "practice" has become a significant one in much of the church, although defining the two terms has been difficult. The former signifies, for some, a biological or inherent genesis for homosexuality; for others, it implies a matter of choice. The term "practice" has been even more ambiguous, ranging from an understanding of "practice" referring to on-going, monogamous, committed relationships between same sex individuals, to an implied pattern of promiscuity with multiple partners—or perhaps it means a level of tentativeness (practicing to develop full homosexuality?) that infers choice. In the end, while both terms are unsatisfactory, their currency in the literature, policy, and conversation on this topic necessitate their use in this discussion.

Brunswick Theological Seminary in New Jersey, was tried and convicted of presiding over the marriage of a same-sex couple. Numerous measures, representing all sides of the issue, have been generated in both denominations over the past three decades, so it does not come as a great surprise to find a considerable difference of opinion on this topic in our surveys.

In the laity surveys conducted at the turn of the millennium, both Reformed and Christian Reformed respondents were asked whether or not homosexual individuals should be welcomed into the church as members. If they were to be welcomed, what roles, if any, should they be permitted to play in the church? Should they serve as elders or deacons? Should homosexuals be ordained as ministers of the Word? Three possible responses to each question were included in the survey: yes, all homosexuals; yes, but only nonpracticing homosexuals; and no.

Several patterns emerge in Table 7.3, which includes the survey results. First, relatively few members of either denomination would deny homosexuals the opportunity to be members of the church. Only about one in ten members from both groups respond that homosexuals, whether they are practicing or not, should be denied membership in the church (12 percent versus 13 percent in the CRC and RCA, respectively). Yet, the emphasis on inclusion is linked, in part, to whether the individuals are sexually active. Members of the RCA are much more willing to accept practicing homosexuals within the church than their CRC counterparts (51 percent versus 34 percent expressing such willingness, respectively). A majority of Christian Reformed members (55 percent) are willing to accept homosexuals into the church so long as they are nonpracticing sexually.

Not surprisingly, there is greater reluctance to allow homosexuals to hold an office in the church than to accept them as members of the group. In this case, the distinction between orientation and practice does not hold. A majority of the laity in both the CRC and RCA are opposed to having any homosexual serve in any church office (59 percent and 55 percent for the CRC and RCA, respectively). While there is a much greater openness among the Reformed Church respondents than those from the CRC to permit practicing homosexuals to hold the office of elder or deacon, less than one-quarter of RCA laity expressed such support (22 percent in the RCA versus 7 percent of CRC survey participants).

Even more members of both denominations oppose ordaining homosexuals as ministers of Word and sacrament than oppose allowing

Table 7.3
Level of Approval among CRC and RCA Laity
for Homosexuals in Church Office: 2000

Group Question Homosexuals should be allowed to....	CRC	RCA
Laity		
Be members		
Yes, practicing homosexuals	34%	51%
Yes, but only non-practicing homosexuals	55	36
No	12	13
Hold office of elder or deacon		
Yes, practicing homosexuals	7%	22%
Yes, but only non-practicing homosexuals	34	23
No	59	55
Hold office of Minister of Word and sacrament		
Yes, practicing homosexuals	5%	16%
Yes, but only non-practicing homosexuals	25	17
No	70	67
Clergy		
All clergy positions should be open to practicing homosexuals	3%	13%

them to hold the offices of elder or deacon. More than two-thirds of survey participants from both churches expressed clear opposition to having homosexuals serve as clergy (70 percent and 67 percent of CRC and RCA laity, respectively). Only one in twenty Christian Reformed members (5 percent) would permit practicing homosexuals to hold the office, while less than one in six RCA laity (16 percent) would do so.

When examining attitudes toward women as ministers of the Word, clergy in both denominations tended to be more accepting than were their lay colleagues. By contrast, pastors are marginally less open than laity toward homosexuals filling those roles. Only three percent of CRC ministers surveyed in 2001 agreed that all clergy positions should be open to practicing homosexuals; a similar 5 percent of Christian Reformed members felt the same. The Reformed Church showed a similar pattern: 13 percent of pastors expressed agreement with such a policy, and 16 percent of the laity concurred.

Table 7.4 examines responses to these questions among CRC and RCA laity by geographical region. Within the Christian Reformed Church, there is little variation in the responses of the laity regardless of their geographic residence; but as has been noted with some regularity in previous data, important regional differences are found within the Reformed Church. Among the CRC membership, the percentages are virtually equivalent between members in the East and the Midwest. In fact, individuals who live in eastern regions of the country are slightly more conservative than those residing in midwestern states. This is shown both in the percentage of those members saying "no" to each of the three questions and in the greater willingness of CRC survey participants in the Midwest than in the East to permit practicing homosexuals to be members of the church (37 percent of those living in the Midwest versus 26 percent of the laity located in the East).

This pattern is significantly reversed in the RCA. Reformed Church survey respondents who reside in the East are much more likely than their counterparts in the Midwest to say that homosexuals, regardless of their level of sexual activity, should be permitted to hold church office. Only one in twenty (5 percent) of the eastern laity expressed opposition to having any type of homosexual become a member of the church, while about one in six (16 percent) of members in the Midwest did so. These regional differences become even more evident when examining the responses tied to practicing homosexuals becoming members of the church or holding church office. For example, when asked whether practicing homosexuals should be permitted to be church members, nearly four out of five RCA members in the East (79 percent) responded affirmatively, while only about two out of five Midwest participants (42 percent) did so. This same trend holds true when examining the question of election to different offices in the church. While the absolute level of agreement declines as one moves from church membership to holding the offices of elder or deacon—and from holding those offices to being ordained as a minister of Word and sacrament—the regional differences persist. RCA parishioners residing in the East are more much willing to accept homosexuals into church roles than are Midwest RCA members. Based on personal conversations with Reformed Church delegates to the 2005 General Synod trial of Norman Kansfield, this regional variation appeared quite evident in the debate and decision of that assembly.

To this point, we have examined matters related to church membership and church office. It is worthwhile to pursue whether

Table 7.4
Level of Approval among CRC and RCA
Laity for Homosexuals in Church Office: 2000

Agree that homosexuals should be allowed to...	CRC			RCA		
	All	Midwest	East	All	Midwest	East
. . . be members.						
Yes, practicing	34%	37%	26%	51%	42%	79%
Yes, only non-practicing	55	52	61	36	43	16
No	12	11	13	13	16	5
. . . hold office of elder or deacon.						
Yes, practicing	7%	7%	10%	22%	12%	51%
Yes, only non-practicing	34%	32%	27%	23%	24%	22%
No	59%	61%	63%	55%	65%	28%
. . . hold office of Minister of Word and Sacrament.						
Yes, practicing	5%	4%	7%	16%	8%	38%
Yes, only non-practicing	25	24	17	17	17	18
No	70	72	77	67	75	45

concerns about "maintaining the purity of church office" necessarily spill over into roles held in society more generally. To what extent are the patterns found in Tables 7.3 and 7.4 evident when one shifts from the presence and roles of homosexuals in the church to their involvement in other institutions in society?

In the various RCA laity and clergy surveys conducted by Luidens and Nemeth over time, Reformed Church members and ministers have, since 1986, been asked whether homosexuals should be allowed to teach in public schools. Table 7.5 examines the opinions of both RCA clergy and RCA laity regarding homosexuals as public school teachers and analyzes changes in responses to those questions over time.

First, ministers of the Reformed Church are much more willing than RCA members to permit homosexuals to teach in public schools— though there was relatively little difference between clergy and laity in the level of such support in 1986, with more than three-fifths of both RCA laity and clergy opposed to homosexuals serving as public school teachers. Over time, however, there has been considerable change related to this issue. Both pastors and members have become more willing to express agreement that homosexuals should be permitted to teach in public schools. Today, only a minority of both RCA groups opposes the practice. The greatest shifts have been from the "disagree" categories to the "agree" classifications, as the "neutral" and/or "undecided" response percentages have experienced little change in proportion during the period of time under consideration. Remarkably, this growing "liberalization" in the response of RCA ministers has occurred at the same time there has been, as evident in chapter 3, a growing theological "conservatism" within their ranks.

RCA clergy crossed the mid-point on this measure in 1999, with a larger group agreeing that homosexuals should be allowed to teach than those in opposition. While laity continue to be predominantly conservative on this question, their trend line has been steadily liberalizing, with less than one-half of respondents denying homosexuals the right to teach in public schools in the 1999 survey. Data for CRC lay members gathered in 2000 indicate that they exhibit more conservatism on this item than their RCA counterparts, with only one-fifth (20 percent) responding in agreement and well over one-half (58 percent) in disagreement. Interestingly, the responses of CRC

Table 7.5
Level of Approval among RCA Laity and Clergy for Homosexuals
to Teach in Public Schools, over Time

	CRC Laity	RCA Laity	RCA Clergy
1986			
Strongly Agree/Agree	*	13%	19%
Neutral/Undecided	*	24	21
Disagree/Strongly Disagree	*	63	60
1991			
Strongly Agree/Agree	*	20%	30%
Neutral/Undecided	*	24	19
Disagree/Strongly Disagree	*	56	51
2000			
Strongly Agree/Agree	20%	26%	48%
Neutral/Undecided	22	25	18
Disagree/Strongly Disagree	58	49	34

* CRC laity not surveyed in 1986 or 1991. CRC clergy not surveyed on this question in any year.

members in 2000 basically mirror the survey responses of RCA laity expressed a decade earlier.

The issue of homosexuality has garnered increasing discussion across the country over the last fifteen years. However, during 2003 and 2004, considerable national attention was focused on the issue. Among other venues, the national media reported various stories related to gay rights and concerns including Vermont's passage of legislation permitting civil unions between homosexuals and pictures of gay couples exiting the court house in San Francisco following civil marriage ceremonies authorized by the mayor of the city. The media also hosted debates on the topic on a legion of talk radio and cable news network programs. Moreover, during the course of the 2004 election campaign, eleven states had ballot initiatives that would ban gay marriages.

Consequently, one would anticipate that, over time, CRC and RCA clergy would report having addressed the issue of gay rights and homosexuality on a relatively regular basis. The extent to which CRC and RCA ministers of Word and sacrament have provided theological instruction or insight related to the debate can be addressed, in part, by data gathered from the clergy themselves. The Smidt and Penning clergy surveys asked ministers if they have "made their views known publicly in any way," whether inside or outside the church, on a variety of public topics—including the issue of "gay rights or homosexuality."

Responses to this particular question are presented in Table 7.6. It is immediately evident that the controversy over homosexual involvement in the church and society has increasingly captured the attention of clergy in both denominations, as the percentage of clergy who report having spoken either "often" or "very often" about homosexuality has steadily increased over the time period examined.[4] Whereas about one in six CRC clergy (17 percent) reported in 1989 that they had addressed the issue with some regularity, two out of five (40 percent) reported in 2005 that they had done so. And, while one-fifth of RCA ministers (20 percent) had talked about homosexuality relatively often in the 1989 survey, in 2005 nearly one-half (45 percent) had spoken often or very often about the controversy.

---

[4]   Obviously, this item did not ask the manner in which respondents addressed the issue of homosexuality or the content of that message. So while the issue of homosexuality has received increased attention from the pulpit, this does not necessarily mean that attitudes related to homosexuals and gay rights have grown more positive or favorable.

In addition, Table 7.6 reveals that Reformed Church pastors report addressing the question with a somewhat greater frequency than their CRC counterparts—regardless of the year analyzed, though such differences tend to be rather modest in nature. But, regardless of this difference between the two denominations, it is evident that the issue has captured the increasing attention and concern of Reformed clergy over the past two decades.

Table 7.6
CRC and RCA Clergy Addressed
Gay Rights or Homosexuality, over Time

	CRC	RCA
1989		
Very often/often	17%	20%
1993		
Very often/often	21	*
1997		
Very often/often	23	30
2001		
Very often/often	29	34
2005		
Very often/often	40	45

* RCA clergy not surveyed in 1993

As noted earlier, the debate about homosexuality is an example of how issues that come to the fore on the national political agenda become more specialized debates within the church. However, it is unclear how the larger national discussion may color the ways in which Reformed clergy and laity respond to such issues. While there have been no surveys of CRC or RCA members conducted immediately following the 2004 presidential election, surveys of CRC and RCA clergy were conducted during the early months of 2005. The questionnaires of these studies contained an item that addressed the issue of gay rights, though the statement employed is relatively general and therefore ambiguous. Following each presidential election since 1989, CRC and RCA pastors have been asked in the Smidt and Penning surveys to express their level of agreement or disagreement with the statement, "Homosexuals should have all the same rights and privileges as other Americans."[5]

This wording does not specify what the particular "rights and privileges" might be, and, as a result, it is unclear just what framework of interpretation a pastor may have used when responding to the statement. For example, some clergy may answer the query thinking that homosexuals should be able enjoy the same procedural rights (such as voting) or the same economic opportunities (access to employment based on one's skills) as other Americans. Other ministers may make an assessment in terms of homosexuals' "right" to marry or to adopt children. Consequently, responses to this particular item are likely to differ from the opinions expressed about the issue of permitting homosexuals to teach in public schools.

Moreover, given the question's ambiguity as well as the prominence of the issue of gay marriage during the later part of President George W. Bush's first administration, it is likely that an increased percentage of Reformed clergy in 2005 responded to this survey item within the framework of "gay marriage" than may have been the case previously. Consequently, some of the increased "liberalization" on homosexuality evident in Table 7.5 may not be evident in responses to this question on the most recent survey, particularly when comparing responses over the past four years. In this case, it is possible that the larger social and political environment will have resulted in a movement of clergy response away from agreement with the statement.

The responses of CRC and RCA survey participants to the statement following each of the last five presidential elections are presented in Table 7.7. Not surprisingly, given the ambiguity and phrasing of the item,[6] there is a higher level of agreement expressed by ministers from both denominations to this item than to approving of homosexuals teaching in public schools. Still, in many ways the

---

[5] RCA clergy were not surveyed following the 1992 election, and though CRC clergy were surveyed, they were not asked to respond to this particular statement.

[6] One noted American cultural value is that of equality and equal treatment under the law. The phrasing of the item, "enjoy the same rights and privileges," places in tension this generally held American value when it is applied to a particular group generally held in low social esteem.

patterns evident in Table 7.7 are similar to those seen in Table 7.6. First, RCA clergy are somewhat more willing than their CRC counterparts to agree with either statement (that is, "Homosexuals should be permitted to teach in public schools," and, "Homosexuals should have all the same rights and privileges as other Americans") in each of the years the survey question was asked between 1989 and 2001. Furthermore, over the years there was a steady, though slow, growth in the willingness of pastors from both denominations to express agreement with both statements. The rate of increase in the support for "gay rights" associated with the more ambiguous item was much more gradual than for allowing homosexuals to teach in public schools, in part because a significantly higher percentage agreed with the former item initially. There was, however, a considerable jump among CRC ministers from 1989 to 1997, when the percentage of clergy agreeing that homosexuals should have the same rights as other Americans jumped from 43 percent to 52 percent.

However, it is also clear that there was significant erosion in agreement with the statement among ministers from both denominations following the 2004 presidential election. The percentage of Christian Reformed ministers who expressed agreement that "homosexuals should enjoy the same rights and privileges as other Americans" dropped by 10 percent between 2001 and 2005, so that in the most recent survey nearly the same percentage of CRC clergy disagreed with the statement as affirmed it (37 percent and 44 percent, respectively). While the level of change was not as large among RCA respondents, there was nevertheless a decline of 7 percent in the level of expressed agreement with the statement between 2001 and 2005 (dropping from 65 percent down to 58 percent). It is very evident that the current context of social debate on the issue of gay rights has shaped the way clergy from the two Reformed denominations view homosexuals' access to "all the same rights and privileges as other Americans." While support for gay rights had been building during the two decades prior to 2004, the highly politicized national atmosphere reversed the previous patterns dramatically.

Finally, given the attention paid to the issue of gay marriage in the months surrounding the 2004 presidential election, CRC and RCA participants were asked in the 2005 Smidt and Penning survey whether they agreed that "it is appropriate for clergy to perform same-sex marriages." Clergy in both denominations strongly rejected the assertion, though, as usual, RCA ministers were more willing to accept

Table 7.7
Attitudes of CRC and RCA Clergy toward the
"Rights of Homosexuals," over Time

	CRC Clergy	RCA Clergy
1989		
Strongly Agree/Agree	43%	60%
Neutral/Uncertain	20	12
Strongly Disagree/Disagree	38	28
1993		
Strongly Agree/Agree	*	+
Neutral/Uncertain	*	+
Strongly Disagree/Disagree	*	+
1997		
Strongly Agree/Agree	52%	62%
Neutral/Uncertain	13	10
Strongly Disagree/Disagree	36	28
2001		
Strongly Agree/Agree	54%	65%
Neutral/Uncertain	16	11
Strongly Disagree/Disagree	30	25
2005		
Strongly Agree/Agree	44%	58%
Neutral/Uncertain	17	13
Strongly Disagree/Disagree	39	29

 * Question not asked
 + Clergy not surveyed

the statement than were CRC respondents. While almost all Christian Reformed clergy (94 percent) opposed the practice, a smaller percent of RCA clergy (76 percent) did so. Conversely, a mere 1 percent of the CRC pastors indicated they believed it was appropriate to perform same-sex marriages, while 17 percent of RCA clergy believed such ceremonies to be legitimate (data not shown).[7]

7   These percentages do not add up to 100 percent, as the responses of those who expressed uncertainty on the matter are not reported in the text.

Despite the shift among CRC and RCA clergy between 2001 and 2005, there likely has been growth in the recognition that gays should not be discriminated against, at least in certain arenas of social and economic life. Two factors are likely at work in this general "liberalizing" of the Reformed Church of America and, to a smaller extent, the Christian Reformed Church on this highly divisive issue—nationwide trends and personal experiences. Studies from throughout the country suggest that Americans have begun to look more broadly at the issue of homosexuality. The highly visible cases of hate crimes against homosexuals have been central to this growing awareness. In the process, there is an increasing recognition of homosexuals and of homosexuality as a fact of American life. Needless to say, this has not been an unchallenged trend; but there is convincing evidence in public opinion polls and in anecdotal records that the pattern is widespread.

A key component of this broadened view, and one that is undoubtedly at work in the lives of many individuals in both the RCA and CRC, has been personal experience. As more and more homosexuals reveal themselves to their families, friends, and congregations, Reformed members are encountering "the issue" as "persons." Both the Christian Reformed and the Reformed Church have called for a period of discernment, an important step in bringing homosexuality to the forefront of conversation. This period has allowed church members to step back from prior perspectives and to reflect as congregations and as faithful Christians on the lives and status of their friends and fellow believers who happen to be homosexual.

Priorities

A final area of comparison between the Christian Reformed and the Reformed Church concerns priorities for the church. Obviously, there are many pressing needs and many worthwhile endeavors competing for the scarce resources of the church. Should the church be working to overcome social injustice? Should it be seeking to provide counseling for those needing help? Where do charity and evangelism rank as priorities among the many activities expected of churches? Which of these tasks should receive the greatest emphasis today?

Responses to these questions were obtained from a survey conducted in 1989 of CRC and RCA ministers currently serving churches. Pastors were presented with five tasks in which churches might be expected to participate and were asked to rank them on a five-point scale from highest priority (5) to lowest priority (1). These six tasks were charity to individuals in need, work for social change to overcome injustice and oppression, guidance and counseling for individuals needing help, work for Christian moral standards nationally, and evangelism in North America. Clergy's assessments of the importance of the items are presented in Table 7.8.

Table 7.8
Priorities of CRC and RCA Clergy for Churches in North America: 1989
(Ranked on a scale from 5 (highest) to 1 (lowest) in priority)

Tasks	Mean Score		% Choosing Task As Highest Priority	
	CRC	RCA	CRC	RCA
Evangelism	4.2	3.8	60%	53%
Guidance and Counseling	2.5	3.0	10	17
Charity to persons in need	2.4	2.8	9	13
Work for social change to overcome injustice	2.3	2.3	14	15
Work for Christian moral standards	1.3	1.4	4	3

The rankings reveal a remarkable consistency between ministers in the two denominations. Not only do CRC and RCA pastors rank these five church tasks similarly in importance, but they also assign relatively similar levels of importance to each of the priorities. Of the five options listed in Table 7.8, evangelism received the highest mean score by a large margin, with a majority of ministers in both denominations ranking it as the church's top priority (60 percent and 53 percent among CRC and RCA pastors, respectively). The next most important task was guidance and counseling, and it was given the highest emphasis by only one in ten CRC pastors (10 percent) and by less than one of five RCA clergy (17 percent). Following in priority, for pastors in both denominations, was charity to persons in need and working to overcome social injustice. Clergy from both denominations agree that the task of working for Christian moral standards was the least important of the five church tasks listed (with less than one of twenty pastors in either denomination choosing it as the highest priority).

Of particular interest to this study of the Christian Reformed and Reformed Church is the emphasis clergy place on greater cooperation between the two denominations. Table 7.9 includes the responses of CRC and RCA ministers to five questions concerning possible areas in which the two denominations could increase their cooperation as well as the overall priority they place on greater cooperation between the CRC and RCA.

Table 7.9
Priorities of CRC and RCA Clergy
Relating to Greater Cooperation between the Two Denominations: 1989
(Ranked on a scale from 5 (highest) to 1 (lowest))

Areas of Greater Cooperation	Mean Score		% Choosing High or Very High Priority	
	CRC	RCA	CRC	RCA
Projects addressing local social problems	4.3	4.3	95%	93%
Mission work overseas	4.0	4.2	80	89
Projects of local evangelism	4.0	4.1	84	83
Between local congregations	3.9	4.0	80	86
Between the two denominations overall	3.2	3.2	68	67
Possible integration of colleges and seminaries	2.9	3.3	34	47

Similar to the pattern found in Table 7.8, clergy are extremely consistent across the denominational boundaries in assigning priorities for greater cooperation between the two church bodies. There is overwhelming agreement (nearly nineteen out of twenty ministers from each denomination) among CRC and RCA pastors that the two denominations should seek ways to work cooperatively in addressing local social problems. And more than four out of every five CRC and RCA clergy thought the two church bodies should work to promote overseas mission work, undertake local evangelism, and foster greater cooperation between local congregations of the two denominations. Slightly weaker support exists for broader interdenominational cooperation, with about two-thirds of the survey participants (68 percent of CRC and 67 percent of RCA pastors) rating this enterprise as a high or very high priority. The only specific area of interaction that is not ranked as having high importance is integration of the two denominations' colleges and seminaries. Only about one-third of CRC ministers (39 percent) and slightly less than one-half of their RCA counterparts (47 percent) ranked this area of possible cooperation as "high" or "very high." As has been seen before, the issue of education—both for children and for young adults—is one of the strongest dividing lines between members of the CRC and RCA.

Conclusion

In recent years differences over social issues have increasingly supplanted divisions over theology as defining attributes of both the Christian Reformed Church and the Reformed Church in America. On many of the most volatile issues currently debated in the public square, the members and ministers of Reformed churches are decidedly on the conservative side. Indeed, there seems to be an overall trend of growing conservatism. However, on two issues—growing ambivalence about the use of the death penalty and the appropriate place of homosexuality in the church—movement within the CRC and RCA has been in the opposite (more liberal) direction. Although our data concerning acceptance of women in church office is limited, one suspects that there is also a trend toward more liberal attitudes on this issue as well.

The data suggest that, while there may be divisions between the CRC and RCA (and within each denomination itself) over key social questions, the variations may not present insurmountable obstacles to future efforts at denominational cooperation or merger, particularly since the direction in which opinion is changing seems to be following the same pattern for both the CRC and RCA. The current talks about greater integration between the CRC and RCA are enhanced as clergy from both bodies are in general agreement about the need to place greater priority on cooperation between the two denominations, both overall and in several specific areas of church life.

CHAPTER 8

'Where Cross the Crowded Ways of Life'? Concluding Thoughts on the Future of the CRC and RCA

This volume has described, measured, and surveyed the lives of the Reformed Church in America and its offspring, the Christian Reformed Church in North America. From their disparate roots in seventeenth- and nineteenth-century Netherlands to their entwined legacies in the New World, these two denominations have shared much in common and have diverged in many and lasting ways.

Most prominently, the two churches share a common heritage of Reformed confessionalism, an inheritance with a past of irenic agreements punctuated by episodes of bitterness and pain. From the birth of Dutch Calvinism, the stories of saints and heretics have been told and retold and have been distilled into the historic Heidelberg and Belgic Confessions and the Canons of Dort. Rich in their substance and somber in their timbre, each has been the source of interpretations and counter-interpretations almost as convoluted as those attributed to Holy Writ.

Out of this embroiled past, the RCA and CRC have crafted their narratives in North America. As noted in chapter 2, these narratives were often bitterly opposed, yet, at times, they also converged on points of common interest. In many ways, the narrative of each denomination has moved toward greater convergence, as the Christian Reformed Church has become ever more "Americanized" in the motifs of contemporary evangelicalism and the Reformed Church in America has shifted from its more urbane and urban eastern roots toward midwestern successors steeped in the evangelical tradition of the American frontier.

In this chapter, we will review our findings and make suggestions about their implications for the future. This crystal ball gazing, resulting in educated guesses at best, is informed by our extensive experience inside these two denominations with which we have been intimately connected for our entire professional careers. We trust that the implications of our conclusions will have a felicitous impact on the future of these two religious bodies that we have long held close to our hearts.

A Return to Secularization

One of the starkest realities confronting many Protestant denominations today is their nearly four decades of continued membership decline, a trend particularly pronounced in mainline denominations, among which the RCA has long been counted. From an apex of nearly 235,000 "active" members in 1966, the Reformed Church has dropped to around 180,000 today. More than three decades ago, Dean Kelley (1972, 29) contrasted the fortunes of the RCA and CRC and suggested that the continued growth in the CRC was a function of its "conservative" adherence to traditional beliefs and standards—its stalwart capacity to fend off the dire consequences of secularization. In contrast, Kelly argued that the RCA had succumbed to the temptation to make concessions to modernity, and, as a result, the denomination had bled members.

In the intervening years, what has become clear is that membership declines have been more a function of demographic than theological change. It is true that most of the decline in the RCA, and the beginnings of membership decrease within sections of the CRC, are found in those regions which are the most "liberal" in their theological perspectives. Indeed, the Reformed churches in the eastern United States account for almost the entire numerical drop in membership. The denomination reached its high point in 1966. At their peak, membership rolls in the eastern wing of the RCA contained more than ninety thousand active communicants, while their current rosters include barely fifty thousand. However, in the last decade, other sections of the RCA—and many regions of the CRC—have plateaued in their numbers, so the "liberal" East of the Reformed Church is not the only one facing demographic challenges.

Does this loss of members indicate that "secularization" is affecting the RCA (and, increasingly, the CRC)? We would argue that this is a dangerous and facile conclusion to draw, despite the tendency of many critics to argue the contrary. In their analysis of Presbyterian baby boomers (the group most likely to leave the church), Hoge, Johnson, and Luidens (1990) found that, rather than become secular (or irreligious), the vast majority of those who departed from the church did just that—they left the institutional church. However, while they were now outside the organizational structure of church life, they continued to describe themselves as good Christians, whether or not they attended religious services, were members of a religious community, or engaged in personal acts of piety. Indeed, when challenged that these failures to engage in such activities were all indications of their *lack* of faith, they bristle at the charge. They were not irreligious; neither had they lost their faith. Rather, in their eyes, they simply see themselves as religious people who, with very deliberate intention, are no longer affiliated with what they viewed as a religion- and life-stifling institutional context.

As suggested in chapter 1, this highly "individualized" (or "privatized") form of Christianity is very much in evidence around the United States and Canada. Scholars talk about experiencing the "disestablishment" of the church during a "post-Protestant age" in which faith and spirituality are expressed and experienced outside of conventional institutional contexts (Carroll and Roof 1993). Moreover, the form and content of that disestablished faith and spirituality is highly individualistic and very idiosyncratic to the believer.

It would appear, from the evidence presented above and in other analyses of RCA and CRC members, that the vast majority of former members have found a path towards this deinstitutional faith. For them, the traditions and confessions of the Reformed community, so richly embellished and so bitterly wrought, have lost their salience. "Winning them back" to the church is an unlikely objective. Moreover, the church to which they would return would be one that has de-emphasized its seventeenth-century confessions and standards and has become more "open to the Spirit."

For those individuals who have chosen to remain active communicants, survey data from the RCA indicate little or no decline in the transmission of religious practices between them and their children (Nemeth and Luidens 1997). These data indicate that virtually all children born to RCA members are baptized, and that more than eight out of ten of these baptized children eventually make a profession of faith. Moreover, nearly all youngsters have at some time in their lives attended Sunday school on a regular basis, and about two-thirds of children still at home currently do so. When the same religious practices are analyzed by age cohorts among RCA members, the data indicate no significant decline in baptism rates between the baby-boom generation of RCA parishioners and those members who fell within age cohorts that either immediately preceded or followed it. Only slight declines were found when the three generational groups were compared on the basis of whether the respondents' children in each cohort were confirmed, or whether the children of each cohort attended Sunday school and church. Thus, existing survey data would indicate that, if individual-level secularization has made any headway into the RCA, it has been quite limited and is only in its initial stages.

If not Secularization, What other Challenge?

Many RCA and CRC congregations have moved toward a more free-flowing approach to worship and ecclesiology as their institutional salvation. They have, in fact, de-emphasized the creeds and confessions of the Reformed tradition and joined the larger evangelical flow, adopting worship cadences and proclamation techniques that resound throughout contemporary Protestantism. In fact, so powerful has been this pull that one could posit that the adoption of this form of popular evangelicalism is doing more to undermine the rich confessional legacy of Reformed Christianity than all of the so-called "secularization" forces of modernity. Still, within both denominations there has been a driving force to eschew things that are seen as the most encumbering elements of the Reformed legacy in favor of the expediency of contemporary, popular appeal.

As discussed in chapter 3, much of the theological and social agenda around which CRC and RCA members find common ground is reflective of the broad, "general theology," variety. The overwhelming majority of members agree with the divinity of Jesus, the "virgin birth" (a concept which carries important symbolic meaning for some and literal meaning for others), and other basic theological matters. However, considerably more difference in perspective exists in terms of what we have called the tenets of Reformed theology. Notions such as predestination and the determination of salvation by God's unfettered grace have given way to very "Arminian" notions of self-reliance. In resonance with the American theme of "making one's own way in the world," many Reformed Christians have come to believe that one can have a significant hand in determining one's own eternal fortune, making and breaking such salvation with good actions and correct beliefs. Moreover, when asked about the seminal creeds and standards of their church, the overwhelming majority of RCA members and a sizable number of their CRC counterparts are unaware of the tenets and of their content. Among those who do know these distinctive formulations, many label them antiquated and irrelevant to their faith. Distinctions between RCA and CRC parishioners are much stronger here, with the former far more relaxed about this Reformed legacy.

With some former CRC and RCA members departed for more individualistic forms of religious expression and others finding their faith in conventional evangelicalism, the viability of the two denominations becomes very problematic. What holds them together? What is the distinctive glue that brings cohesion and a sense of commonality to each? If tradition falters, if creeds and confessions ring hollow, if each congregation sings its own songs, what can hold these denominations together?

These persistent questions confound much of the church today. Understanding the dimensions of "loyalty" to the denomination is one response. Chapter 4 found tradition to be the nexus around which some RCA members have found common ground. They are loyal to the Reformed Church in America because of its—and their—history and traditions. But this was seen to be a diminishing focal point. In fact, among most clergy and laity, issues of political and social importance may have greater unifying power than theological or creedal tradition. For others, strong patterns of personal piety (regular Bible reading, personal prayer, and family-based devotions) serve as a common bond. In both of these forms, however, contemporary expressions of "Reformed" Christianity are more reflective of the mainstream evangelical flow than of Reformed tradition.

On the surface, the pattern is not surprising and is certainly in keeping with what is transforming much of American cultural Protestantism. However, these theological and ecclesiological trends within the CRC and RCA continue to beg the question, "What is unique to these Reformed denominations that would predict their continued existence and vitality?" As forms of worship and belief structure in the two denominations become more and more reflective of the broader strands of popular Christianity, what remains distinctively Reformed about them?

Congregationalism as One Answer

The distinctive and vital signs may have shifted dramatically from the denominational level to the congregational one. In fact, for the vast majority of the survey respondents, their religious identity—an expression of "loyalty"—is tied to the life of their congregations. They "join" and support their congregations; here they find their faith-identity. Denominations represent a more distant bureaucracy and a fading history that may carry resonance with clergy but have decreasing import for the membership. But can individually constituted and variously composed congregations be uniquely "Reformed"?

Chapter 6 provides an overview of the broad variety of worship styles and theological formulations that cut across the congregational lives of RCA and CRC churches. While more commonality exists within the CRC, even here differences in worship, preaching topics and styles, and liturgy prevail. And, again, the broad characteristics suggest that these congregations as an aggregate reflect patterns found amid broadly evangelical denominations. Little suggests a "Reformed" emphasis or focus to these congregations.

Their growing distance from, perhaps even disillusionment with, denominational bureaucracies and agencies, coupled with their own increased internal fiscal needs, have led congregations increasingly to withhold funding from their parent denominations (Nemeth and Luidens 1999). As a result, denominational leaders have had great difficulty maintaining a broad spectrum of activities and programs, leading some to increase efforts to intrude on the lives of local congregations (Luidens 2005). For denominational CRC and RCA institutions—such as Calvin and Hope colleges, and Western, New Brunswick, and Calvin theological seminaries—the result has been a broadening of their institutional base as they seek students and resources from outside the denominations.

Shifting Social and Political Grounds

While congregational individualism has been one response to the diminishing importance of denominations and the decline of denominational coherence, a second response has been found in social and political issues. One powerful way to bridge gaps between congregations and across individual interests has been to focus on highly visible social and political concerns. Topics such as abortion, homosexuality, and capital punishment in the lives of citizen-believers have been galvanizing. For many Christians today, one's stance on these litmus-like issues determines not what *kind* of a Christian one is, but whether or not one can be considered a Christian *at all*.

As discussed in chapter 7, differences over social issues have increasingly supplanted divisions over theology within both the Christian Reformed Church and the Reformed Church in America, and the laity and clergy of both denominations fall decidedly on the conservative side of such issues. Given the presence of a conservative majority within both denominations, the temptation for the denominations may be to move toward issue-based segmentation by finding bases of commonality and cooperation on political, rather than theological, grounds. To a certain extent, the actions of the 2005 General Synods of both the CRC and RCA can be viewed in such a fashion, with the CRC continuing to refuse women the right to serve as delegates to the General Synod and the RCA engaging in the Kansfield trial related to performing a marriage of homosexuals.

Three Possible Scenarios

Where does all this lead? What is likely to happen in the years ahead as the CRC and RCA continue through the contending tides of contemporary Protestantism? Three possible scenarios present themselves that may be described as: first, staying the (receding) course; second, merging for survival; and third, merging for purity.

Staying the Course

At this juncture, the futures of the RCA and CRC look rather grim as separate and distinctive denominations. The growth or decline of both denominations must be viewed within broader national trends of an aging population, declining birth rates, increasing geographical mobility, and the difficulty both the Christian Reformed and the Reformed Church has in recruiting ethnic/racial minorities as new members. A highly mobile and changing America has meant that the homogeneous, ethnic enclaves that nourished both denominations into maturity have largely disappeared. While pockets of "Dutch" Americans remain in western Michigan, Ontario, and Iowa, they are quickly disappearing. Moreover, the fertility rates of Dutch-Americans, like that of all other established European ethnic groups in North America, have declined.

A consistent trend over the past quarter century has been the aging of the CRC and RCA membership. Although they were not "young" denominations in the 1970s, the median age of CRC and RCA members has risen steadily. As a result, both are now at a point where over one-half of their current membership role is over the age of fifty-five.

This aging of both denominations reflects two long-term trends. The first is simply the general aging of the North American population. Both denominations grew with the baby boom generation following World War II. As that generation now ages, so too do both denominations.

However, this first trend is exacerbated by a second trend—the difficulty of recruiting younger members. The second trend is partially the result of declining fertility in America. From a high of nearly four children per family in the years immediately following World War II, the birth rate for white Americans today has dropped by nearly one-half. This decline and its impact on Protestant church membership in general, and the RCA in particular, is obvious when the two trends are plotted next to each other (Nemeth and Luidens 1994). The very high correlation between birth rates within the RCA and in the general populations provide strong evidence that, at least since 1950 and probably for much longer, the RCA's (and other mainline Protestant denominations') membership roles depended principally upon "natural growth"—the retention of youth born into and raised in the denomination. Undoubtedly, the same has been true for the CRC over this time span.

These facts destroy any idea that there can be "internal growth" from traditional sources. As the eastern Reformed Church has long known, the RCA and CRC today find themselves in a larger, "free-market," religious environment. Newcomers will have to be drawn from the ranks of mainline and evangelical Protestants, erstwhile Catholics and Orthodox, and converts from other faiths. Recruiting new members from growing ethnic and racial minorities has also proven to be a most difficult task for both denominations. While the presence of "non-Europeans" within the two groups has grown over the past three decades, their numbers remain very low and are quite unrepresentative of American society in general. Based upon membership size of congregations with racial/ethnic council affiliation and on survey results, it appears that only about 4 to 6 percent of the current RCA membership consist of people of color (Luidens and Nemeth 2003).

Bold and energetic initiatives (such as the current RCA project to add four hundred congregations by 2013) are long shots at best, and they are more likely than not to end with greater disillusionment and disappointment.

Once seen as a growth area for the RCA, even the western United States has not fulfilled its promise. Reaching a high of just under twenty thousand members in the early 1990s, there are fewer than fifteen thousand in the California classes today, despite the highly visible and successful appeal of the Garden Grove Cathedral under the Reverend Robert Schuller. Moreover, membership in both the RCA and CRC throughout the Midwest has hit a plateau, and, in many local areas, it has seen significant declines. Even the cities of Holland and Grand Rapids, Michigan, have seen a significant "consolidation" of member congregations, so that fewer churches exist today than only a score of years ago. This retrenchment has resulted in larger congregations in many cases, but the number of small, highly personalized churches has declined greatly. In sum, the prognosis for "staying the course" seems a dire one for both denominations.

Merging for Survival

One alternative that has been suggested by many denominational leaders, especially in the Midwest, has been a merger between the RCA and CRC. But what are the prospects of reuniting these Reformed offspring? Who might find it beneficial, and who might find it difficult?

It is apparent that much of the conversation about reconnecting these erstwhile Dutch siblings has had a note of desperation about it. Indeed, the impetus seems to come from a sense that one or both will slip into denominational oblivion and that joining forces might withstand that sorry fate—if even for a short while. In the "merging for survival" model, all efforts would be focused on finding commonalities of spirit and practice which can help bridge existing differences. As this study has suggested, there are a variety of grounds on which to advocate for reunification. Congregations have much in common in their worship style and theological outlook; individual members share a generally activist orientation toward society, as well as a strong tradition of personal piety. In all of this, there are bases on which to build a joint future.

Having said this, the history of mergers has not been an easy one. Recent re-connections of northern and southern branches of both the Methodist and the Presbyterian churches have resulted in a single denomination that is less than the sum of the two parts. Indeed, throughout Presbyterian history, this has been the case (Luidens 1990).

One of the consequences of merging for expediency is the existence of members and congregations who find it difficult to accede to a "forced" association with others, which generally results in an exodus of churches. In the wake of the reunification of southern and northern branches of the Presbyterian Church, for instance, there was a vast out-migration of the more conservative churches (especially in the South) to join the more conservative and evangelical Presbyterian Church of America. Those who value denominational "purity" and tradition generally view mergers that are not based on theological unity of purpose as a threat.

In the case of the Reformed Church in America and the Christian Reformed Church, one might expect that a merger based on the fear of demise would necessitate casting a rather wide net, seeking to include as many congregations as possible. But such an inclusive effort would enhance the differences between the two denominations so that, for some, they would become particularly potent. For instance, the RCA has long supported the public school system, while the CRC prides itself on the strength and scope of its parochial schools, contributing considerable funds to support the private system. In any merger of convenience, there would be considerable tension over this issue, which can be anticipated and, perhaps, defused in advance.

A more volatile issue, however, involves the differing roles accorded to women in the CRC and RCA. The Reformed Church has long ordained women to the ministry of the Word as well as to the offices of elder and deacon. Virtually every classis in the RCA has female elders and deacons, and the vast majority has female pastors as well. In the Christian Reformed Church, a more "localist" model applies, in which a minority (twenty-two out of forty-seven) of the classes permits the ordination of women. Moreover, in its most recent General Synod, the CRC reaffirmed its opposition to the inclusion of women in its ranks. In sharp contrast, for more than two decades women have played central roles as delegates to the RCA's General Synod. In any merger based on the need to survive, the continued full involvement of women would certainly be a non-negotiable point among members of the RCA.

In sum, should the RCA and CRC see merger as desirable, largely in terms of expediency, these nettling issues would likely come to the fore. In such a situation, with the case for reuniting made with the assertion that the initial separation was an unfortunate one and that the greater good for all would be served by reunion, constraints on divergences would have to be minimal. All manner of diversity would have to be welcomed at considerable risk to the full inclusion of both denominations. Such diversity would almost certainly lead the most conservative congregations, especially those from the CRC, to express extensive objections. As a result, a merger for survival would lead many individuals and congregations from the more traditional regions of both the Christian Reformed and the Reformed Church, e.g., those most opposed to the ordination of women to the office of minister of Word and sacrament, to look elsewhere for their affiliation.

Merger for Purity

A third course of action is also possible. What if the leading theologians and pastors from the CRC and RCA hammered out a set of new confessional standards? What if, in effect, "purity" formed the framework on which reunification was to take place? What if the concerns of those who oppose female ordination were included, so that women would no longer serve in such positions (the current stance which prevails in a majority of CRC classes, and one which would reflect their *sine qua non* for membership)? This scenario would leave the conservatives happily mollified, but it would generate a strong reaction from other regions and congregations that would likely "vote with their feet" and depart.

The recent trial of the Reverend Dr. Norman Kansfield, former president of the RCA's New Brunswick Theological Seminary, in New Jersey, is instructive, offering a real life example of the likely consequences of any potential "merger for purity." Among other charges, Kansfield was accused of despoiling the "purity" of the RCA by performing the wedding ceremony for his lesbian daughter and her partner. In the throes of the debate, it became clear that a significant majority (approximately two-thirds) of the RCA found grounds on which to reclaim purity by convicting Kansfield. As might be expected, the conservative regions of the denomination propelled this adjudication most forcefully, while the more liberal members found themselves at a crossroads. While some were reassured that a denomination-wide vendetta would not be launched on the issue of homosexuality, others immediately began preparations to leave the denomination entirely.

A reunification of the two denominations based on a limited set of principles and theological tenets that would be based on a "pure" and distinct set of standards clearly risks alienating parishioners who fall outside such delimitations. While the RCA and CRC certainly share much common ground in the middle, each group includes regions and constituents who fall far from that center. In a merger for purity, a significant number of members would feel too constrained by the new denomination and likely find good reason to depart.

Put more bluntly, should the Christian Reformed and the Reformed Church in America decide to merge out of expediency, they would have to cast a wide net. Under such conditions, many CRC (and RCA) members in Canada, as well as pockets of congregations in the Midwest, would find the grounds for engagement too threatening and would leave the new church, perhaps feeling more comfortable in the Presbyterian Church in America or another evangelical denomination. While it is difficult to estimate the number of members who would effectuate such a withdrawal, let us estimate, for the time being, that perhaps as many as 100,000 of the total 400,000 active communicants in the two denominations would be involved. Examining the other side, should the merger be effected on the basis of "purity" or conformity to theological standards, many in the eastern sections of the RCA would find it impossible to continue their affiliation with the church. Other "liberal" congregations, especially the large number who have included women at the heart of their community lives, would be equally distressed. In the end, let us estimate that perhaps 100,000 members would again depart. Regardless of the extent to which these particular estimates are accurate, the point is simply that either approach is likely to result in a sizable number of defections from any of the two merger scenarios.

Skirmishes in individual communities would also be difficult. Throughout much of the Midwest, in small towns and rural communities, CRC and RCA congregations have lived in gentle tension for more than a century. These churches, used to making subtle distinctions between themselves, would find it very difficult to overcome these differences. In many cases, the small communities are barely capable of sustaining two sanctuaries, and arguments would quickly be made for one to join the other. Under such conditions, experience has shown that, once again, the sum of the two congregations will be less than the individual parts. Some parishioners will look elsewhere rather than worship together. While this is perhaps a sad commentary, it is a reality of small town existence nonetheless.

As discussions of a possible merger between the two denominations continue, many "smaller" differences and distinctions are likely to become magnified. For example, support and expectations about parochial schools, Sunday evening worship services, family devotions, and the loss of denominational identity (an issue that was raised in past merger talks) are likely to become major discussion points, culminating in reasons for many members to leave the merged church.

At the same time, a significant array of agencies and institutions related to the two denominations would demand attention under a newly reunified group. For instance, seminaries and colleges located in close geographical proximity would find themselves in the awkward position of recruiting from the same pool of youth as well as the same set of benefactors. Publishing, missionary, and other agencies would have to be reconsidered, as would the distinctly different bureaucracies (RCA administration is scattered throughout the United States, with "national" offices in a dozen centers, while the CRC is centered in western Michigan). Theological faculty at colleges and seminaries would be subject to considerable scrutiny, examining liberal viewpoints (in the case of a merger for purity) or conservatism (should the merger be for survival of the church). Thus, while there may be a growing sense that the historic split between the CRC and RCA is unfortunate, it is abundantly clear that any route taken to merge the two communions would be extremely difficult.

A Final Word

Gazing into a crystal ball is a seductive enterprise, with signs of challenge and threat always more visible than the springs of hope and creativity that well from the lives of the faithful. Undoubtedly, neither of the discussed idealized scenarios is likely to occur. While each denomination struggles with its own internal challenges, it will be looking over its shoulder at its neighbor. What are you doing? How is it going? And, the plans for denominational growth may be at least partially successful. It is likely that the breadth of commonalities, many of which have been stipulated in the foregoing chapters and discussion, will rise to the surface and provide greater reason for growing cooperation.

Perhaps short of formal merger, individual members seeking like-minded brothers and sisters from across the historical divide will reach out and join together. Specific congregations, the life-blood of the church today, will find common cause. As individual churches find that they can perform their ministries in concert more effectively than if they continued to "go it alone," they will increasingly seek ecumenical partners. In these quiet, unplanned, unintended, unanticipated ways, the chasm will be bridged: person to person; congregation to congregation; community to community—and, perhaps in time, communion to communion.

References

2002 FACT Survey Report. Study completed in collaboration with the Cooperative Congregational Study of Hartford Seminary.

Beardslee III, John W. 1986. "Orthodoxy and Piety: Two Styles of Faith in the Colonial Period." Pp. 1- 14 in *Word and World: Reformed Theology in America*, ed. James Van Hoeven. Grand Rapids: Eerdmans.

Becker, Penny. 1999. *Congregations in Conflict: Cultural Models of Local Religious Life*. New York: Cambridge Univ. Press.

Bellah, Robert, Richard Madsen, William Sullivan, Ann Swidler, and Steven Tipton. 1985. *Habits of the Heart: Individualism and Commitment in American Life*. Berkeley: Univ. of California Press.

Bennison, Charles Jr. 1999. *In Praise of Congregations: Leadership in the Local Church Today*. Cambridge: Cowley Publications.

Berger, Peter. 1967. *The Sacred Canopy*. New York: Doubleday.

Berger, Peter. 1992. *A Far Glory*. New York: Doubleday.

Berger, Peter. 1996/97. "Secularism in Retreat." *The National Interest* 46 (Winter): 3-12.

Beuker, Gerrit Jan. 2000. "German Oldreformed Emigration: Catastrophe or Blessing?" Pp. 101-113 in *Bridges and Breaches: Reformed Subcultures in the Netherlands, Germany, and the United States*, ed. George Harinck and Hans Krabbendam. Amsterdam: VU Uitgeverij.

Bratt, James. 1982. "Dutch Calvinism in America." Pp. 290-306 in *John Calvin: His Influence on the Western World*, ed. W. Stanford Reid. Grand Rapids: Zondervan.

Bratt, James. 1984. *Dutch Calvinism in Modern America: A History of a Conservative Subculture*. Grand Rapids: Eerdmans.

Bratt, James. 1985. "The Reformed Churches and Acculturation." Pp. 191-208 in *The Dutch in America: Immigration, Settlement, and Cultural Change*, ed. Robert Swierenga. New Brunswick: Rutgers Univ. Press.

Brinks, Herbert. 1983. "Ostfrisians in Two Worlds." Pp. 21-34 in *Perspectives on the Christian Reformed Church: Studies in its History, Theology, and Ecumenicity*, ed. Peter De Klerk and Richard De Ridder. Grand Rapids: Baker Book House.

Brinks, Herbert. 1985. "Religious Continuities in Europe and the New World." Pp. 209-223 in *The Dutch in America: Immigration, Settlement, and Cultural Change*, ed. Robert Swierenga. New Brunswick: Rutgers University Press.

Brinks, Herbert. 2000. "Henry Beets (1869-1947): Historian of the Christian Reformed Church." Pp. 125-140 and pp. 49-60 in *Bridges and Breaches: Reformed Subcultures in the Netherlands, Germany, and the United States*, ed. George Harinck and Hans Krabbendam. Amsterdam: VU Uitgeverij.

Brouwer, Arie. 1977. *Reformed Church Roots*. New York: Reformed Church Press.

Brown, Willard Dayton. 1982. *A History of the Reformed Church in America*. New York: Board of Publication and Bible Work.

Bruins, Elton. 1974. "What Happened in 1857?" *Reformed Review* 27 (Winter): 120-126.

Bruins, Elton. 1983. "The Masonic Controversy in Holland, Michigan, 1879-1882." Pp. 53-72 in *Perspectives on the Christian Reformed Church: Studies in its History, Theology, and Ecumenicity*, ed. Peter De Klerk and Richard De Ridder. Grand Rapids: Baker.

Bruins, Elton. 1985. "Americanization in Reformed Religious Life." Pp. 175-190 in *The Dutch in America*, ed. Robert Swierenga. New Brunswick: Rutgers Univ. Press.

Campbell, Angus, Philip F. Converse, Warren E. Miller, and Donald E. Stokes. 1964. *The American Voter*. New York: John Wiley & Sons.

Carroll, Jackson W., and Wade Clark Roof, eds. 1993. *Beyond Establishment: Protestant Identity in a Post-Protestant Age*. Louisville: Westminster/John Knox.

Cooper, John. 1991. *A Cause for Division? Women in Office and the Unity of the Church*. Grand Rapids: Calvin Theological Seminary.

Corbett, Michael. 1991. *American Public Opinion. Trends, Processes, and Patterns*. White Plains: Longman.

Dekker, Gerard. 1993. "Is Religious Change a Form of Secularization? The Case of the Reformed Churches in the Netherlands." Paper presented at the 22nd International Conference for the Sociology of Religion. July 1993, Budapest.

Dekker, Gerard, Donald Luidens, and Rodger Rice. 1997. "Introduction: Setting the Stage." Pp. 1-23 in *Rethinking Secularization: Reformed Reactions to Modernity*, ed. Gerard Dekker, Donald Luidens, and Rodger Rice. Lanham: Univ. Press of America.

Dobbleleare, Karel. 1981. *Secularization: A Multidimensional Concept*. Beverly Hills: Sage Publications.

Dobbleleare, Karel. 1984. "Secularization Theories and Sociological Paradigms: Convergences and Divergences." *Social Compass* 31: 199-219.

Douglas, Mary. 1982. "The Effects of Modernization on Religious Change." *Daedalus* 111 (Winter): 1-19.

Eenigenburg, Elton. n.d. [c.1959]. *A Brief History of the Reformed Church in America*. Grand Rapids: Douma Publications.

Eenigenburg, Elton. M. 1986. "New York and Holland: Reformed Theology and the Second Dutch Immigration." Pp. 31-43 in *Word and World: Reformed Theology in America*, ed. James Van Hoeven. Grand Rapids: Eerdmans.

Faber, Jelle. 2000. "Spiritual Cargo of Secession Theologians in America, 1870-1900." Pp. 115-124 in *Bridges and Breaches: Reformed Subcultures in the Netherlands, Germany, and the United States*, ed. George Harinck and Hans Krabbendam. Amsterdam: VU Uitgeverij.

Finke, Roger. 1992. "An Unsecular America." Pp. 145-169 in *Religion and Modernization: Sociologists and Historians Debate the Secularization Thesis*, ed. Steven Bruce. Oxford: Clarendon Press.

Fowler, Robert Booth, Allen D. Hertzke, and Laura R. Olson. 1999. *Religion and Politics in America*, 2nd ed. Boulder: Westview Press.

Ganzedvoort, Herman. 1985. "The Dutch in Canada: The Disappearing Ethnic." Pp. 224-239 in *The Dutch in America: Immigration, Settlement, and Cultural Change*, ed. Robert Swierenga. New Brunswick: Rutgers Univ. Press.

Guth, James, John Green, Corwin Smidt, Lyman Kellstedt, and Margaret Poloma. *1997. The Bully Pulpit: The Politics of Protestant Clergy*. Lawrence: Univ. Press of Kansas.

Hadaway, C. Kirk, and Penny Long Marler. 1993. "All in the Family: Religious Mobility in America." *Review of Religious Research* 35,2: 97-116.

Hadden, Jeffrey. 1969. *The Gathering Storm in the Churches*. New York: Doubleday.

Hadden, Jeffrey. 1987. "Toward Desacralizing Secularization Theory." *Social Forces* 65, 3: 587-611.

Hadden, Jeffrey. 1989. "Desacralizing Secularization Theory." Pp. 3-26 in *Secularization and Fundamentalism Reconsidered: Religion and the Political Order*, Vol. 3, ed. Jeffrey Hadden and Anson Shupe. New York Paragon House.

Hageman, Howard. 1985. "The Synod of Dort and American Beginnings." *Reformed Review* 38 (Winter): 99-108.

Harms, Richard. 2000. "Forging a Religious Identity: The Christian Reformed Church in the Nineteenth-Century Dutch Immigrant Community." Pp. 189-205 in *Bridges and Breaches: Reformed Subcultures in the Netherlands, Germany, and the United States*, ed. George Harinck and Hans Krabbendam. Amsterdam: VU Uitgeverij.

Heideman, Eugene. 1976. "Theology." Pp. 95-110 in *Piety and Patriotism*, ed. James Van Hoeven. Grand Rapids: Eerdmans.

Heideman, Eugene. 1986. "Heidelberg and Grand Rapids: Reformed Theology and the Mission of the Church." Pp. 107-117 in *Word and World: Reformed Theology in America*, ed. James Van Hoeven. Grand Rapids: Eerdmans.

Henry, Paul B. 1974. *Politics for Evangelicals*. Valley Forge: Judson Press.

Hesselink, John. 1983a. "Christian Schools: Barrier to Reunion?" *Banner* (January 10): 18-19.

Hesselink, John. 1983b. "The Future of a Distinctive Dutch-American Theology in the Reformed Church in America and the Christian Reformed Church." Pp. 273-296 in *Perspectives on the Christian Reformed Church*, ed. Peter DeKlerk and Richard DeRidder. Grand Rapids: Baker.

Hoekema, Anthony. 1983. "The Christian Reformed Church and the Covenant." Pp. 185-201 in *Perspectives on the Christian Reformed Church: Studies in its History, Theology, and Ecumenicity*, ed. Peter DeKlerk and Richard DeRidder. Grand Rapids: Baker.

Hoge, Dean R., Benton Johnson, and Donald A. Luidens.   1994. *Vanishing Boundaries: The Religion of Mainline Protestant Baby Boomers.* Louisville: Westminster/John Knox.

Honey, Charles.   2002.   "CRC Synod OKs talks with RCA Officials." *Grand Rapids Press* (June 13): A19.

Hunter, James Davison.   1983.   *American Evangelicalism: Conservative Religion and the Quandary of Modernity.*   New Brunswick: Rutgers Univ. Press.

Hutchison, William.   1976.   *The Modernist Impulse in American Protestantism.* Cambridge: Harvard Univ. Press.

Janssen, Al.   2000.   "A Perfect Agreement? The Theological Context of the Reformed Protestant Dutch Church in the First Half of the Nineteenth Century. " Pp. 49-60 in *Bridges and Breaches: Reformed Subcultures in the Netherlands, Germany, and the United States*, ed. George Harinck and Hans Krabbendam. Amsterdam: VU Uitgeverij.

Japinga, Lynn.   1992.   "The Glue That Holds Us Together: History, Identity, and the Reformed Church in America." *Reformed Review* 45 (Spring): 181-201.

Japinga, Lynn.   2001.   "Conflict and Change in the Reformed Church in America Since 1945."   Pp. 84-93 in *Reformed Encounters with Modernity: Perspectives from Three Continents*, ed. H. Jurgens Hendriks, Donald Luidens, Roger Nemeth, Corwin Smidt, and Hijme Stoffels. Capetown, South Africa: Print24.com

Jesse, David.   2002.   "CRC Synod Proposal Seeks Merger with RCA." *Holland Sentinel.* Saturday, June 8, 2002.   Web source: http:// www.hollandsentinel.com/stories/060802/rel_060802031.shtml

Kelley, Dean M.   1972.   *Why Conservative Churches are Growing: A Study in Sociology of Religion.*   New York: Harper and Row.

Kennedy, Earl William.   1976.   "From Providence to Civil Religion: Some 'Dutch' Reformed Interpretations of America in the Revolutionary Era." *Reformed Review* 29 (Winter): 111-123.

Kennedy, James C. and Caroline Simon. 2005. *Can Hope Endure? A Historical Case Study in Christian Higher Education.* Grand Rapids: Eerdmans.

Kits, Harry. 1991. "'Verzuiling' and Social Involvement: The Canadian Case." Pp. 338-348 in *The Dutch in North America,* ed. Rob Koes and Henk Otto Neushafer. Amsterdam: VU University Press.

Kloosterman, Nelson and Cornelis Venema. 1991. *A Cause for Division: The Hermeneutic of Women's Ordination.* Orange City, Iowa: Mid-America Reformed Seminary.

Kromminga, John. 1957. "Our First Hundred Years." Pp. 9-66 in *One Hundred Years in the New World; the Story of the Christian Reformed Church from 1857-1957: Its Origin, Growth, and Institutional Activities, Together with an Account of the Celebration of its Anniversary in its Centennial Year.* Grand Rapids: Centennial Committee of the CRC.

Kromminga, John. 1974. "What Happened in 1857?" *Reformed Review* 23 (Winter): 112-118.

Kromminga, John. 1985. "The World Council of Churches and the Reformed Ecumenical Synod: Dutch Influence Within Ecumenism." *Reformed Review* 38 (Winter): 140-47.

Luidens, Donald. 1990. "Numbering the Branches: Membership Trends Since Colonial Times." Pp. 29-65 in *The Mainstream Protestant "Decline": The Presbyterian Pattern,* ed. Milton J Coalter, John M. Mulder and Louis B. Weeks. Louisville: Westminster/John Knox Press.

Luidens, Donald. 1993. "Between Myth and Hard Data: A Denomination Struggles with Identity." Pp. 248-269 in *Beyond Establishment: Protestant Identity in a Post-Protestant Age,* ed. Jackson Caroll and Wade Clark Roof. Louisville: Westminster/John Knox.

Luidens, Donald. 2005. "National Engagement with Localism: The Last Gasp of the Corporate Denomination?" Pp. 410-435 in *Church, Identity, and Change: Theology and Denominational Structures in Troubled Times* ed. David Roozen, Nancy Ammerman, and Adair Loomis. Grand Rapids: Eerdmans.

Luidens, Donald A., and Roger J. Nemeth. 1987. "'Public' and 'Private' Protestantism Reconsidered: Introducing the 'Loyalists.'" *Journal for the Scientific Study of Religion* Vol. 26:4 (December): 450-464.

Luidens, Donald A., and Roger J. Nemeth. 1998. "Refining the Center: Two Parties of Reformed Church Loyalists." Pp. 252-270 in *Reforming the Center: American Protestantism, 1900 to the Present*, ed. William Trollinger and Douglas Jacobsen. Grand Rapids: Eerdmans.

Luidens, Donald, and Roger Nemeth. 2000. "Dutch Immigration and Membership Growth in the Reformed Church in America: 1830-1920." Pp. 169-188 in *Bridges and Breaches: Reformed Subcultures in the Netherlands, Germany, and the United States*, ed. George Harinck and Hans Krabbendam. Amsterdam: VU Uitgeverij.

Luidens, Donald, and Roger Nemeth. 2003. "Then and Now: Our Changing Identity." *Church Herald*, January: 9-15.

Marsden, George. 1980. *Fundamentalism and American Culture: The Shaping of Twentieth-Century Evangelicalism, 1870-1925*. New York: Oxford Univ. Press.

Marshall, Paul. 1984. *Thine is the Kingdom*. Grand Rapids: Eerdmans.

Martin, David. 1965. "Toward Eliminating the Concept of Secularization." Pp. 169-82 in *Penguin Survey of the Social Sciences*, ed. Julius Gould. Baltimore: Penguin.

Marty, Martin E. 1970. *Righteous Empire: The Protestant Experience in America*. New York: Dial Press.

Mayer, William G. 1996. *The Divided Democrats*. Boulder: Westview Press.

Monsma, Stephen V. 2000. *When Sacred and Secular Mix*. Lanham: Rowman & Littlefield.

Mouw, Richard J. 1976. *Politics and the Biblical Drama*. Grand Rapids: Eerdmans.

Nemeth, Roger, and Donald Luidens. 1994. "The Reformed Church in America in the Larger Picture: Facing Structural Realities." *Reformed Review* 47(2): 85-112.

Nemeth, Roger, and Donald Luidens. 1994b.   "Congregational vs. Denominational Giving: An Analysis of Giving Patterns in the Presbyterian Church in the United States and the Reformed Church in America." *Review of Religious Research* Vol. 36:2 (December): 111-122.

Nemeth, Roger, and Donald Luidens, 1997. "Intra- and Intergenerational Transmission of Religious Practices in the Reformed Church in America." Pp. 247-263 in *Rethinking Secularization: Reformed Reactions to Modernity*, ed. Gerard Dekker, Donald A. Luidens, and Rodger Rice. New York: Univ. Press of America.

Nemeth, Roger, and Donald Luidens. 1999. "Show Me the Money! Funding the Reformed Church in America." *Reformed Review* Vol. 53:1 (Autumn), 5-20.

Nemeth, Roger, and Donald Luidens. 2001. "Fragmentation and Dispersion: Postmodernity Hits the RCA." Pp. 125-134 in *Reformed Encounters with Modernity: Perspectives from Three Continents*, ed. H. Jurgens Hendriks, Donald Luidens, Roger Nemeth, Corwin Smidt, and Hijme Stoffels. Capetown, South Africa: Print24.com.

Neuhaus, Richard John. 1984. *The Naked Public Square: Religion and Democracy in America*, 2nd ed. Grand Rapids: Eerdmans.

Nie, Norman H., Sidney Verba, and John R. Petrocic. 1976. *The Changing American Voter*. Cambridge: Harvard Univ. Press.

Oldfield, Duane M. 1996. *The Right and the Righteous: The Christian Right Confronts The Republican Party*. Lanham: Rowman & Littlefield.

Osterhaven, M. Eugene. 1974. "The Experiential Theology of Early Dutch Calvinism." *Reformed Review* 27 (Spring): 180-189.

Osterhaven, M. Eugene. 1986. "Saints and Sinners: Secession and the Christian Reformed Church." Pp. 45-74 in *Word and World:*

Reformed Theology in America, ed. James Van Hoeven. Grand Rapids: Eerdmans.

Penning, James M., and Corwin Smidt. 1996. "The Christian Reformed Church: Religious Commitment and Denominational Distinctiveness in a Changing Environment." Paper presented at the Annual Meeting of the Society for the Scientific Study of Religion and Religious Research Association, Nashville, Tennessee, November 8-10.

Penning, James M., and Corwin E. Smidt. 1997. "The Influence of Secularization on the Church: Christian Reformed Ministers' Perceptions." Pp. 219-245 in *Rethinking Secularization: Reformed Reactions to Modernity*, ed. Gerard Dekker, Donald Luidens, and Rodger Rice. Lanham: Univ. Press of America.

Penning, James M., and Corwin Smidt. 2001. "Reformed Preachers in Politics." Pp. 157-176 in *Christian Clergy in American Politics*, ed. Sue E.S. Crawford and Laura R. Olson. Baltimore: Johns Hopkins Univ. Press.

Penning, James. M., and Corwin E. Smidt. 2002. *Evangelicalism: The Next Generation*. Grand Rapids: Baker.

Penning, James M., Corwin Smidt, and Donald Brown. 2001. "The Political Activities of Reformed Clergy in the 2000 Election." Paper presented at the annual meeting of the Southern Political Science Association, Atlanta, Georgia, November 7-10.

Potts, Wesley. 1992. "Foreword." Pg. 4 in *Women in the Service of Christ*, by Norman Shephard. South Holland, Ill.: Cottage Grove CRC.

Reformed Church in America (RCA). 1981 and 2001. *Acts and Proceedings of the General Synod*. Vols. LXI and LXXXI. New York: Reformed Church in America.

Roof, Wade Clark, and William McKinney. 1987. *American Mainline Religion: Its Changing Shape and Future*. New Brunswick: Rutgers Univ. Press.

Roosen, David, William McKinney, and Jackson Carroll. 1984. *Varieties of Religious Presence: Mission in Public Life*. New York: Pilgrim Press.

Runia, Klaas. 1983. "The Christian Reformed Church and the World Council of Churches." Pp. 325-343 in *Perspectives on the Christian Reformed Church: Studies in its History, Theology, and Ecumenicity*, ed. Peter DeKlerk and Richard DeRidder. Grand Rapids: Baker.

Schaap, James. 1998. *Our Family Album: The Unfinished Story of the Christian Reformed Church*. Grand Rapids: CRC Publications.

Shephard, Norman. 1992. *Women in the Service of Christ*. South Holland, Ill.: Cottage Grove CRC.

Sherratt, Timothy. 1999. "Rehabilitating the State in America: Abraham Kuyper's Overlooked Contribution." *Christian Scholar's Review* 29 (2): 323-346.

Skillen, James W. 1990. *The Scattered Voice: Christians at Odds in the Public Square*. Grand Rapids: Zondervan.

Smidt, Corwin E., ed. 2004. *Pulpit and Politics: Clergy in American Politics at the Advent of the Millennium*. Waco: Baylor Univ. Press.

Smidt, Corwin E., James M. Penning, and Christianne Van Arragon. 2000. "Subcultural Identity and Religious Vitality." Paper presented at the annual meeting of the Society for the Scientific Study of Religion, Houston, Texas, October 19-22.

Smidt, Corwin E., Lyman Kellstedt, James Guth, and John Green. 2006. "Religion in The 2004 American Presidential Election." Pp. 422-450 in *American Politics, Media, and Elections: Contemporary International Perspectives on the U.S. Presidency, Foreign Policy, and Political Communication*, ed. Thomas Pludowski. Turin and Warsaw: Adam Marszalek and Collegium Cicitas Press.

Smith, Eric R.A.N. 1989. *The Unchanging American Voter*. Berkeley: Univ. of California Press.

Spykman, Gordon. 1976. "Sphere Sovereignty in Calvin and the Calvinist Tradition." Pp. 163-208 in *Exploring the Heritage of John Calvin*, ed. David Holwerda. Grand Rapids: Baker.

Stark, Rodney, and William Sims Bainbridge. 1986. *The Future of Religion: Secularization, Revival, and Cult Formation*. Berkeley: Univ. of California Press.

Stokvis, Pieter. 2000. "The Secession of 1834 and Dutch Emigration to the United States: Religious Aspects of Emigration in Comparative Perspective." Pp. 21-32 in *Bridges and Breaches: Reformed Subcultures in the Netherlands, Germany, and the United States*, ed. George Harinck and Hans Krabbendam. Amsterdam: VU Uitgeverij.

Swierenga, Robert. 1996. "'Pioneers for Jesus Christ': Dutch Protestant Colonization in North America as an Act of Faith."   Pp. 35-55 in *Sharing the Reformed Tradition*, ed. George Harinck and Hans Krabbendam. Amsterdam: VU Uitgeverij.

Swierenga, Robert. 2000. "True Brothers: The Netherlandic Origins of the Christian Reformed Church in North America, 1857-1880." Pp. 61-83 in *Bridges and Breaches: Reformed Subcultures in the Netherlands, Germany, and the United States*, ed. George Harinck and Hans Krabbendam. Amsterdam: VU Uitgeverij.

Swierenga, Robert. 2001. "'Burn the Wooden Shoes': Modernity and Division in the Christian Reformed Church in North America." Pp. 94-102 in *Reformed Encounters with Modernity: Perspectives from Three Continents*, ed. H. Jurgens Hendriks, Donald Luidens, Roger Nemeth, Corwin Smidt, and Hijme Stoffels.   Capetown, South Africa: Print24.com.

Swierenga, Robert, and Elton Bruins, eds. 1999. *Family Quarrels in the Dutch Reformed Churches in the Nineteenth Century*. Grand Rapids: Eerdmans.

Tanis, James. 1985. "Frelinghuysen, the Dutch Clergy, and the Great Awakening in the Middle Colonies." *Reformed Review* 23 (Winter): 109-118.

Te Velde, Melis.   2000. "The Dutch Background of the American Secession from the RCA in 1857." Pp. 85-100 in *Bridges and Breaches: Reformed Subcultures in the Netherlands, Germany, and the United States*, ed. George Harink and Hans Krabbendam. Amsterdam: VU Uitgeverij.

Van Belle, Harry.   1991.   "From Religious Pluralism to Cultural Pluralism: Continuity and Change among the Reformed Dutch in Canada." Pp. 308-337 in *The Dutch in North America*, ed. Rob Koes and Henk Otto Neushafer. Amsterdam: VU University Press.

Vander Zicht, Sandra L. 1983. "The CRC and RCA: Divorced but Still Dating." *Banner* (January 10): 5-6.

Van Engen, Abram. 2002. "Sketch of the General History of the RCA and CRC." Unpublished manuscript, Calvin College, Summer.

Van Ginkel, Aileen. 1996. "The Place of the Church in Society: Views of Dutch and American Ministers in Canada in the 1950s." Pp. 139-158 in *Sharing the Reformed Tradition: The Dutch North American Exchange, 1846-1996*, ed. George Harrink and Hans Krabbendam. Amsterdam: VU Uitgeverij.

Van Hoeven, James. 1986. "Dort and Albany: Reformed Theology Engages a New Culture." Pp. 15-30 in *Word and World: Reformed Theology in America*, ed. by James Van Hoeven. Grand Rapids: Eerdmans.

Voskuil, Dennis. 1986. "Piety and Patriotism: Reformed Theology and Civil Religion." Pp. 119-139 in *Word and World: Reformed Theology in America*, ed. James Van Hoeven. Grand Rapids: Eerdmans.

Wald, Kenneth D. 2003. *Religion and Politics in the United States*, 4th ed. Washington D.C.: Congressional Quarterly Press.

Warner, R. Stephen.   1993a.   "The Place of the Congregation in the American Religious Configuration." Pp. 54-99 in *American Congregations, Volume 2*, ed. James Lewis and James Wind. Chicago Univ. of Chicago Press.

Warner, R. Stephen. 1993b. "Work in Progress toward a New Paradigm for the Sociological Study of Religion in the United States." *American Journal of Sociology* 98 (March): 1044-1093.

Wentz, Richard. 1999. *The Culture of Religious Pluralism.* Boulder: Westview Press.

Wolterstorff, Nicholas. 1974. "Contemporary Christian Views of the State: Some Major Issues." *Christian Scholars Review* 3 (4): 311-332.

Wuthnow, Robert. 1992. *Rediscovering the Sacred: Perspectives on Religion in Contemporary Society.* Grand Rapids: Eerdmans.

Zwaanstra, Henry. 1973. *Reformed Thought and Experience in a New World.* Kampen: J. H. Kok.

Zwaanstra, Henry. 1991. *Catholicity and Secession: A Study of Ecumenicity in the Christian Reformed Church.* Grand Rapids: Eerdmans.

Appendix

The following surveys are the source of most of the data employed in this volume.

Survey of CRC and RCA Clergy, 2001. Two datasets collected as part of the "Cooperative Clergy Project," a national study of clergy from more than fifteen denominations.

Survey of Members of the Christian Reformed Church, Spring 2000. Survey conducted by the Calvin College Center for Social Research.

Survey of RCA Clergy and RCA Members, 2000. Survey conducted by Professors Donald Luidens and Roger Nemeth, Hope College.

CRC and RCA Pastors Survey, 1997. Survey conducted by the Calvin College Center for Social Research.

Survey of CRC Clergy, 1993. Survey conducted by Professors James Penning and Corwin Smidt, Calvin College, in conjunction with the Calvin College Center for Social Research.

Survey of RCA Clergy and RCA Members, 1991. Survey conducted by Professors Donald Luidens and Roger Nemeth, Hope College.

Survey of CRC and RCA Clergy, 1989. Survey conducted by Professors James Penning and Corwin Smidt, Calvin College, in conjunction with the Calvin College Center for Social Research.

Survey of RCA Clergy and RCA Laity, 1986. Survey conducted by Professors Donald Luidens and Roger Nemeth, Hope College.

Survey of RCA Laity, 1976. Survey conducted by Professors Donald Luidens and Roger Nemeth, Hope College.

Index

Abolitionists, 27

Abortion, 120-21, 123-24, 126, 130, 186

Accommodation, 5, 7, 109

Adam and Eve, 56-58, 63-64

Adaptation, 6, 7, 31, 35

Affirmative action, 121-22

Afscheiding, 29, 31, 32, 35, 44

Age, 11, 49, 50-52, 72, 75-76, 88-89, 103, 105, 111, 117, 156, 162-164, 184, 187-88

Agrarian, 4, 20, 33, 50-52, 135, 192

Aid for disadvantaged, 115, 121

American Bible Society, 41

Americanization, 22, 24-25, 29, 31-32, 35, 38-39, 41, 45-46

American Revolution, 23, 26, 51

Anabaptist, 22, 40

Antithetical model/Antitheticals, 36-37, 40

Apostles Creed, 16, 77-82

Arminian, 21, 25, 184

Arminius, Jacobus, 21

Assimilation, 32, 52

Athanasian Creed, 77

Baptism, 37, 95, 183-184

Belgic Confession, 16, 19, 26, 45, 77-81, 83, 181

Bible reading, 16, 86-97, 103, 185

Biblical authority, 57, 59

Birth rate, 10, 11, 52, 104, 187-88

Bultema, Harry, 40

Calvin, John, 22, 77

Calvin College, 3, 43, 186

Calvinism, 43, 59-60, 97, 159, 181

Calvin Seminary, 44, 46, 77, 165, 186

Canons of Dort, 16, 19, 21, 24-26, 28, 32, 77-81, 83, 181

Capital punishment, 123-24, 179, 186

Catholic, 9, 15, 38, 188

Charities/Charitable giving, 93-94, 97, 176-177

The Historical Series of the Reformed Church in America
Books in Print

Cornelia Dalenberg with David DeGroot
Sharifa
The biography of a missionary nurse, born to farm parents in South Holland, Illinois. Dalenberg served in Bahrain with the famous Dr. Paul Harrison, beginning in 1921. Her other fields of service included a leper colony in Amarah, visits to Basrah, WWII, continued service in Bahrain, medical "touring" in Arabia, and visits to Qatar. Pp. xviii, 233, illustrations. 1983. Out of print.

Marvin D. Hoff
Structures for Mission
Describes the gradual development within the polity of the Reformed Church in America of structures that enabled the church to become a leader in international and national mission. The account moves from 1628 to 1980 and includes charts of mission boards and agencies, as well as a chronology. The role of fundraising is included as well as organization. Pp. xxvii, 243, bibliography. 1985. $15.

James I. Cook, editor
The Church Speaks, Papers of the Commission on Theology, Reformed Church in America, 1959-1984
The papers include "The Historical Character of the Book of Genesis"; "Revised Declaration on Holy Scripture"; "A Confession of Faith"; "Notes on the Doctrinal Standards as they Relate to the Scriptures"; "The Place of the Standards in the Life of the Church"; "The Baptism of the Holy Spirit"; "The Fullness of the Spirit"; "Authority and Conscience in the Church"; "A Statement on Infant Baptism"; "Infant Dedication an Alternative to Infant Baptism? "; "Baptized Non-Communicants and the Celebration of the Lord's Supper (1977 and again in 1984) "; "Concerning Rebaptism"; "The

217

Nature of the Ministry"; The Nature of Ecclesiastical Office and Ministry"; "The Evangelistic and Social Task of the Church"; "A Reformed Theology of Nature in a Crowded World"; "Christian Observance of the Lord's Day"; "A Critique of the Thought of Sun Myung Moon"; "Christian Faith and the Nuclear Arms Race"; "A Biblical Perspective on the Conversion of the Jews . . . "; "The Holocaust and Christian Witness"; "Some Guidelines for Officiating at Marriages"; "Biblical Perspectives on Marriage, Divorce and Remarriage"; "Abortion"; "Moral and Spiritual Values Raised by the Practice of Abortion"; "Maleness and Femaleness"; "Homosexuality: A Biblical and Theological Appraisal"; "Christian Pastoral Care for the Homosexual." Each section bears an introduction by the editor placing the study in its context. Pp. xviii, 268. 1985. $20.
James W. Van Hoeven, editor

Word and World: Reformed Theology in America
The contributions include "Orthodoxy and Piety: _Two Styles of Faith in the Colonial Period," by John W. Beardslee III; "Dort and Albany: _Reformed Theology Engages a New Culture," by James W. Van Hoeven; "New York and Holland: Reformed Theology and the Second Dutch Immigration," by Elton M. Eenigenburg; "Saints and Sinners: Secession and the Christian Reformed Church," by M. Eugene Osterhaven; "Immigration and Authority: the Reformed Church Engages Modernity," by Paul R. Fries; "Prose and Poetry: Reformed Scholarship and Confessional Renewal," by I. John Hesselink; "Heidelberg and Grand Rapids: Reformed Theology and the Mission of the Church," by Eugene P. Heideman; "Piety and Patriotism: Reformed Theology and Civil Religion," by Dennis N. Voskuil. Pp. xxiii, 166, index. 1986. $15.

Gerrit J. tenZythoff
Sources of Secession: The Netherlands Hervormde Kerk on the Eve of the Dutch Immigration to the Midwest
The origin of this volume was a doctoral thesis done under Martin E. Marty at the University of Chicago. Accordingly, the study is detailed and objective in analyzing the social, political, and religious contexts leading to the secession from the Netherlands Hervormde Kerk and emigration to America. Pp. xxii, 189, index. 1987. $15.

Jack D. Klunder and Russell L. Gasero, editors
Servant Gladly: Essays in Honor of John W. Beardslee III
"Recollections of the Beardslee Family," by Marion de Velder; "Advocacy for Social Justice in the Reformed Church in America," by Arie R. Brouwer; "Reformed Perspectives on War and Peace," by John Hubers; "A History of Synodical Opposition to the Heresy of Apartheid: 1952-1982," by Jack D. Klunder; "The Origins of the Theological Library at New Brunswick," by Russell L. Gasero; "From Calvin to Van Raalte: The Rise and Development of the Reformed Tradition in the Netherlands, 1560-1900," by Elton J. Bruins; "From Pessimism to Optimism: _Francis Turretin and Charles Hodge on 'The Last Things,'" by Earl Wm. Kennedy; and a bibliography of works by John W. Beardslee III. Pp. xviii, 134, index. 1989. $12.

Jeanette Boersma with David DeGroot
Grace in the Gulf, the Autobiography of Jeanette Boersma, Missionary Nurse in Iraq and the Sultanate of Oman.
Beginning her ministry before the end of WWII, Boersma passed through Baghdad to Basrah, where after two years she was sent to Amarah and later to Oman until her retirement in 1986. The index enables one to find her interaction with other personnel of the Arabian mission. 1991. Pp. xix, 296, illustrations, index. $20.

Arie R. Brouwer
Ecumenical Testimony
Divided into three sections. "For the Healing of the Nations" recounts Brouwer's involvement in social action and justice issues, from working with the Russian Orthodox in the nuclear days of the Cold War to addressing apartheid in South Africa and racial and justice issues in the States._ "For the Unity of the Church" deals with ecumenical issues on the local, national (NCCC), and international levels (WCC), in all of which Brouwer was intimately involved. "For the Renewal of the Tradition" reveals his commitment specifically to the Reformed Church in matters of worship, education, and relations with the Christian Reformed Church. Pp. xx, 329, illustrations, index. 1991. $20.

Daniel J. Meeter
Meeting Each Other in Doctrine, Liturgy, & Government
An account of the history of the Constitution of the Reformed Church in America, which comprises its doctrinal commitments as expressed in the creeds and the Reformed confessions, together with its liturgy and *Book of Church Order*. This solid historical study speaks to immediate concerns of our identity as a church, and as such is essential reading for all who are in positions of authority and leadership within the church. Pp. xi, 212, indices. 1993. $15.

Gerald F. De Jong
The Reformed Church in China, 1842-1951
Beginning with an overview of the political context in which mission took place within the period, De Jong traces the efforts of the Reformed Church in America from its first missionary, David Abeel, to the expulsion of American missionaries as the United States entered the Korean War. Sensitive to the cultural context, the missionaries hastened to train indigenous leadership. They also offered a Romanized script so that common people could become literate. In their determination to create one indigenous church in common with Presbyterians and the London Mission they offered to resign rather than organize a separate denomination. By the fourth decade of the twentieth century women were included in ordained church offices. Pp. xiii, 385, illustrations, index. 1992. $28.

Allan J. Janssen
Gathered at Albany, A History of a Classis
Set thoroughly within its historical context, the book traces the development

of this unit of church governance (roughly equivalent to a Presbytery) from 1771 and its beginnings with a new nation, through its reaching into Canada, its response to the revivalist movement from 1820-50, its growth and outreach, the development of its rights and responsibilities, its mid-twentieth-century activism, and a case study on the ordination of women. Pp. xi, 163. 1995. $12.

Elton J. Bruins
The Americanization of a Congregation, second edition
The volume (see above) has been brought forward in time and furnished with twenty-two appendices, including the names of church members in church vocations, elders, and deacons and their dates of service. Appendices are also devoted to superintendents of Sunday schools, presidents of Ladies' Aid, Women's Missionary Society, Women's Missionary Auxiliary, Reformed Church Women's Ministries, church organists and choir directors, members serving the board of Holland's public schools, charter members, and ordained and installed ministers and their years of service. The index includes the names of everyone included in the book. Few churches have been graced with such a scholarly and comprehensive history. 1995. Pp. xxiii, 235, illustrations, index. $15.

Gregg A. Mast
In Remembrance and Hope, the Ministry and Vision of Howard G. Hageman
This scholarly tribute to one of the great leaders of the Reformed Church in the twentieth century is divided into thematic sections: "Our Worship," in pulpit, at table, in prayer and praise; "Our Work" in ministry; "Our Witness" in South Africa and in our cities; and Howard's stellar lectures, "A History of the Liturgy of the RCA." Included is a chronology of the life and work of Hageman, including sermons, lectures, and publications. Pp. xxiii, 229, illustrations, appendix, index. 1998. $18.

Janny Venema, translator & editor
Deacons' Accounts, 1652-1674, First Dutch Reformed Church of Beverwijck/Albany
The deacons of the First Church of what is now Albany kept meticulous records of both income and distributions of their funds. These resources, sometimes in beaver pelts, sewant, or currency, were collected both in church and in alms boxes in taverns. Expenditures were for food for the poor, rental of a pall for funerals, repairs to homes of the indigent, for nails, and "for one half barrel and one anker of small beer used by Clas Ullenspegelt when his wife was in childbed" (p. 39). An invaluable insight into seventeenth-century Dutch colonial life. Pp. xxi, 293, glossary, bibliography, index, 6 x 9". 1998. $30.

Morrell F. Swart
The Call of Africa, The Reformed Church in America Mission in the Sub-Sahara, 1948-1998
Missionary biography and autobiography of Robert and Morrell Swart beginning with their service in the last days of the Anglo-Egyptian Sudan, then in the independent Sudan; their removal to Ethiopia when civil war broke out; and yet a third period of mission in Kenya. The mission in the Sudan took place primarily in Akobo and Pibor, in Ethiopia in Omo, and later in Alale,

Zambia, Nairobi, and Malawi. Told with vivacity and intimate personal insight into mission life. Pp. xvi, 536, illustrations, maps, glossary, index. 1998. $35.

Lewis R. Scudder III
The Arabian Mission's Story: In Search of Abraham's Other Son
A scholarly history of the Arabian mission of the Reformed Church in America by a missionary to the Mideast, born of missionary parents who served that mission. Scudder presents a background of Middle Eastern mission, a history of the development of the Arab nations, and a history of the missions of the Reformed Church. The main areas of mission in education, evangelism, and medical work are chronicled, together with the areas of mission in Basrah, Bahrain, Kuwait, and Oman. Also included is a history and analysis of the varying relationship of the mission to the denomination and home churches. A magisterial history. Appendices include a timeline of the Arabian mission and missionary appointments and distribution by station. Pp. xxvii, 578, bibliography, index, 6 x 9". 1998. $39.

Renée S. House and John W. Coakley, editors
Patterns and Portraits, Women in the History of the Reformed Church in America
Joyce D. Goodfriend writes of women in the Colonial Dutch Reformed Church; Johan van de Bank exams the piety of Dina van den Bergh; John W. Beardslee III describes Dutch women in Two Cultures; Firth Haring Fabend describes the evangelical mother in Reformed Dutch households in nineteenth century New York and New Jersey; Elton J. Bruins and Karsten T. Ruhmohr-Voskiul tell the Christina de Moen Van Raalte story; Russell Gaseio describes the rise of the Woman's Board of Foreign Missions; while Renée S. House analyses the work of the *Mission Gleaner*. The preparation of women for foreign missionary service is described by Jennifer Mary Reece, while Joyce Borgman de Velder shares her memories of the struggle for the ordination of women. Carol W. Hageman describes the decline, fall and rise of women in the Reformed Church, 1947-1997; and Mary L. Kansfield writes of New Brunswick Theological Seminary women past and present. Pp. xiii, 182, index. 1999. $15.

Elton J. Bruins and Robert P. Swierenga
Family Quarrels in the Dutch Reformed Churches of the Nineteenth Century
The account begins where the tenZythoff (cf. above) volume ends. From the *Afscheiding* of 1834 through immigration, union with the Reformed Church in America, the secession of 1857, and a mass secession in 1882, the story is briefly but objectively told. Pp. xviii, 158, illustrations, bibliographic essay, index. 1999. $18.

Allan J. Janssen
Constitutional Theology: Notes on the Book of Church Order *of the Reformed Church in America*
An absolutely indispensable aid to anyone responsible for the governance of the church, whether deacon, elder, minister, or denomination executive. Personnel and churches could be prevented from floundering, time in classes and synods

could be saved, if only these guides for living together were followed, rather than approaching issues on an ad hoc basis. The wisdom of centuries has gone into this guide for governance. Janssen reaches beyond the pragmatic to show the underlying theology that governs our living in consistories, classes, and synods. Pp. xii, 321, index. 2000. $25.

Gregg A. Mast, editor
Raising the Dead, Sermons of Howard G. Hageman
Perhaps one of the most erudite and eloquent preachers of the latter half of the twentieth century, from his pulpit in the North Reformed Church in Newark Hageman was in demand as preacher and lecturer, as well as a professor of preaching, and later president, at New Brunswick Theological Seminary. Two series of sermons on Christ's seven last words open the book, followed by seven Christmas sermons, six for Easter, and four each for Ascension and Pentecost. While Hageman's eloquence was a gift improbable to teach or imitate, nonetheless these sermons will stimulate and excite all who care about great preaching. Pp. xxix, 241. 2000. $20.

James Hart Brumm, editor
Equipping the Saints, the Synod of New York, 1800-2000
The editor describes the convening of the Synod of New York, while Christopher Moore moves us from the early days in the mill to the present millennium. Betty L King describes the historic St. Thomas Reformed Church in the Virgin Islands, while Anna Melissa James describes the experience of black people in the Reformed Church in America. Scott Conrad and Stephen Hanson describe the different perspective of the northern reaches of the synod in the Classis of Mid-Hudson. Herman D. De Jong describes the changes in the Classis of Queens, while Michael Edwards offers practical perspectives on urban ministries. John E. Hiemstra describes the remarkable growth of the Asian church in the synod, while Russell L. Gasero offers a pictorial view. There is also a chronological list of congregations (which at one time ranged through New Jersey to Illinois to Oklahoma). Pp. xii, 185, illustrations, index. 2000. $16.

Joel R. Beeke, editor
Forerunner of the Great Awakening, sermons by Theodorus Jacobus Frelinghuysen, 1691-1747
The virile pietism of Frelinghuysen and his preaching seeking an experientially defined conversion is acknowledged as the beginning of the Great Awakening. An excellent introduction to Frelinghuysen is offered by Joel R. Beeke. Twenty-two sermons are included, intended to bring the hearer to an intimate awareness of sin and peril, through God's grace in conversion. The sermons offer an original source understanding of the Awakening. Pp. xliii, 339, 6 x 9". 2000. $28.

Russell L. Gasero
Historical Directory of the Reformed Church in America, 1628-2000
This newest edition of the historical directory contains the six thousand ordained ministers serving in over tweny thousand individual areas of service in more than seventeen hundred congregations. The listings of ministers, missionaries, and churches follows that of the directory of 1628-1992 (above). Pp. xvi, 720, 6 x 9". 2001. $70.

Eugene P. Heideman
From Mission to Church, The Reformed Church in America Mission to India
The story chronicles the period from the beginning of the mission under John Scudder in 1819 to 1987. Beginning with a focus on evangelism with the initiative in the hands of missionaries and mission societies, the organization of the Classis of Arcot puts the churches into relationship with the church in America. At the same time there is a growth of institutions in education and medicine. With the independence of India and the formation of the Church of South India in 1947, mission is seen as partnership, with the mission playing a supporting role to a self-determining church. The history is an honest portrayal of both failure and success. Pp. xix, 748, illustrations, maps, bibliography, index. 2001. $50.

James I. Cook, ed.
The Church Speaks, Vol. 2, Papers of the Commission on Theology Reformed Church in America, 1985-2000
Includes "The Use of Scripture in Making Moral Decisions." Under "Church and Faith" are papers on liberation theology, the Nicene Creed, confirmation, conscience clauses, and the uniqueness of Christ. Under "Church and Sacraments" are considered children at the Lord's Table, while "Church and Ministry" treats the role and authority of women in ministry, the laying on of hands in ordination, the commissioning of preaching elders, moral standards for church offices, and constitutional inquiries. Under "Church and Witness" are the relationship to Muslims and the farm crisis. "Church and Sexuality" considers homosexuality. Pp. xix, 315, appendix, scripture index, name index, subject index. 2002. $28.

John W. Coakley, editor
Concord Makes Strength, Essays in Reformed Ecumenism
Herman Harmelink III revisits the first volume in this series; Lynn Japinga describes our hesitant ecumenical history; Paul R. Fries discusses the theological roots of our ecumenical disposition; while Karl Blei gives a broader view of Reformed ecumenism. Areas of encounter concern full communion, Roman Catholic dialogue, the Joint Declaration on Justification, a Reformed-Catholic future, Reformed and evangelical and Eastern Orthodox, plus an attempt to see the future by Dale T. Irvin and Wesley Grandberg-Michaelson. Pp. xvii, 194, index. 2002. $19.

Robert P. Swierenga
Dutch Chicago, A History of Hollanders in the Windy City
From the very beginnings of Dutch immigration to Chicago, Swierenga traces the development primarily of Dutch Calvinists, but also of the smaller numbers of Jews and Roman Catholics. Of the former, their enclaves in the Groninger Hoek and Roseland, with further flight to the suburbs. The role of the church and Christian schools, as well as mutual aid societies, social clubs, truck farming, garbage and cartage, stores, services, and ethnic politics are covered in detail. Five appendices include garbage and cartage companies, churches, schools, missions, societies, clubs, and church membership. Pp. xx, 908, illustrations, maps, tables, bibliography, index, 6 x 9", hardcover, dust jacket. 2002. $49.

Paul L. Armerding
Doctors for the Kingdom, the work of the American Mission Hospital in the Kingdom of Saudi Arabia
Drawing upon original source materials from the missionary doctors and nurses involved, Armerding creates a compelling narrative of these men and women who witnessed to the love of Christ through the words and deeds of their medical mission. The book has been translated into Arabic and published by the King Abdulaziz Foundation in Riyadh, Saudi Arabia. The principal doctors cited in the book were featured in *Saudi Aramco World*, May/June 2004. Lavishly produced. Pp. 182, illustrations, glossary, gazetteer, maps, bibliography, 8 1/2 x 10 1/4, hardcover, dust jacket. 2003. $39.

Donald J. Bruggink & Kim N. Baker
By Grace Alone, Stories of the Reformed Church in America
Intended for the whole church. After a consideration of its European background in an introductory chapter "Reformed from What?," the story of the Dutch and their church in the New World from the early seventeenth century to the present is told with attention paid to relationships to Native and African Americans at home and missions abroad. The movement of the church across the continent and immigration to Canada, as well as its ecumenical involvement, leads to a challenge for the future. Additional personal interest stories in sidebars, as well as time lines and resources; accompany each chapter. Pp. ix, 222, illustrations, index, 8 1/2 x 11". 2004. $29.

June Potter Durkee
Travels of an American Girl
Prior to WWII, June accompanied her parents on a trip through Europe to the Middle East and India. Her father, F. M. "Duke" Potter, was for thirty years a major force in mission policy and administration. The world and the missionaries, as seen through the eyes of a precocious ten year old who polished her account at age twelve, makes delightful and insightful reading. Pp. xv, 95, sketches, illustrations. 2004. $14.

Mary L. Kansfield

Letters to Hazel, Ministry within the Woman's Board of Foreign Missions of the Reformed Church in America

A collection of letters, written by overseas missionaries in appreciation of Hazel Gnade, who shepherded them through New York on their departures and returns, inspired this history of the Woman's Board. Kansfield chronicles how a concern for women abroad precipitated a nineteenth century "feminism" that in the cause of missions, took women out of their homes, gave them experience in organizational skills, fundraising and administration. Pp. xiii, 257, illustrations, appendices, bibliography, name index, subject index, 8 1/2 x 11". 2004. $29.

Johan Stellingwerff and Robert P. Swierenga, editors

Iowa Letters, Dutch Immigrants on the American Frontier

A collection of two hundred fifteen letters between settlers in Iowa and their family and friends in the Netherlands. Remarkable is the fact that the collection contains reciprocal letters covering a period of years. While few have heard of the Buddes and Wormsers, there are also letters between Hendrik Hospers, mayor of Pella and founder of Hospers, Iowa, and his father. Also unusual is that in contrast to the optimism of Hospers, there are the pessimistic letters of Andries N. Wormser, who complained that to succeed in American you had to "work like a German." Pp. xxvii, 701, illustrations, list of letters, bibliography, index, 6 x 9", hardcover, dust jacket. 2005. $49.

James C. Kennedy & Caroline J. Simon

Can Hope Endure: A Historical Case Study in Christian Higher Education

Hope was founded as a Christian college. How it has endured to the present without slipping either into secularism or a radical fundamentalism is the account of this book. The course has not always been steady, with factions within the school at times leaning either to the left or right. The account can perhaps be instructive in maintaining Hope's traditional centrist position. Pp. xvi, 249, bibliography, index, 6 x 9". 2005. $28.

LeRoy Koopman

Taking the Jesus Road, The Ministry of the Reformed Church in America among Native Americans

The ministry began in the seventeenth century, carried on by pastors who ministered to their Dutch congregants and native Americans. After the Revolutionary War, ministry moved from pastors to missionaries, increasing in activity following the Civil War. Koopman does not shy away from multiple failed government policies in which the church was often complicit, but he also records the steadfast devotion of both missionaries and lay workers who sought to bring assistance, love, and the gospel to native Americans. Pp. xiv, 512, illustrations, appendices including pastors, administrators, other personnel, and native American pastors, index, 6 x 9", hardcover, dust jacket. 2005. $49.

Karel Blei
The Netherlands Reformed Church, 1571-2005
translated by Allan J. Janssen
Beginning with the church's formation in 1571 during the upheavals of the
Reformation, Karel Blei's *Netherlands Reformed Church* follows a dynamic path
through over 400 years of history, culminating in the landmark ecumenical
union of 2004. Blei explores the many dimensions of the Netherlands
Reformed Church's story including the famous splits of 1834 and 1886,
the colorful and divisive theological camps, and the hopeful renewal of the
church in the mid-twentieth century. Also included are incisive explorations
of new confessions, church order, and liturgical renewal. Pp. xvi, 176, index,
6x9, 2006. $25.00

Janel Sjaarda Sheeres
Son of Secession: Douwe J. Vander Werp
Janet Sjaarda Sheers has written a moving, sympathetic, and exciting
biography of Douwe Vander Werp, one of the key figures in the Netherlands
Afscheiding of 1834 and a principal minister in the early development
of the Christian Reformed Church. Credited with having founded ten
congregations, Vander Werp was a man zealously committed to his
understanding of God's Word and its implications for his life, even when
it required the painful sacrifice of three secessions. Sheeres's sociological
observations add interesting insights into Vander Werp's fascinating and
fractious times. *Son of Secession* is a challenge to our understanding of the
historical origins of the Christian Reformed Church as well as that church
today. Pp. xxii, 210, Appendices, bibliography, index, 6 x9 ", 2006. $25.00.

Allan J. Janssen
*Kingdom, Office, and Church. A Study of A. A. van Ruler's Doctrine of Ecclesiastical
Office.*
A. A. van Ruler is one of the most influential twentieth-century theologians
from the Netherlands. One of the many challenging aspects of his work is
his theology of the kingdom of God and its relationship to the church and its
ecclesiastical offices. Allan J. Janssen draws on extensive pastoral and ecclesial
experience as well as closely reasoned analysis to set forth the implications of
van Ruler's theology for the church today. Christo Lombard of the University
of the Western Cape writes: "when theologians grappling with the realities
of the new millennium are re-discovering the exciting and challenging work
of one of the most original theologians of our time. . . .anyone interested in
the way forward for the church in an age of post-modernity and globalization,
should read Dr. Janssen's book, based on meticiulous scholarship and a
passion for God's work in and through us as God's partners." Pp. xvi, 319,
bibliography, index, 6x9", 2006. $35.00.